539.E5
C8

The Consolation of Otherness

*The Male Love Elegy in
Milton, Gray and Tennyson*

M<small>ATTHEW</small> C<small>URR</small>

McFarland & Company, Inc., Publishers
Jefferson, North Carolina, and London

010382045

Library of Congress Cataloguing-in-Publication Data

Curr, Matthew.
    The consolation of otherness : the male love elegy in Milton, Gray
and Tennyson / Matthew Curr.
      p.   cm.
    Includes bibliographical references and index.
    ISBN 0-7864-1239-9 (softcover : 50# alkaline paper) ∞
    1. Elegiac poetry, English — History and criticism. 2. Elegiac
poetry, Latin (Medieval and modern) — History and criticism.
3. Gray, Thomas, 1716–1771. Elegy written in a country churchyard.
4. Tennyson, Alfred Tennyson, Baron, 1809–1892. In memoriam.
5. English poetry — Male authors — History and criticism.
6. Milton,   John, 1608–1674. Epitaphium Damonis. 7. Difference
(Psychology) in literature. 8. Male friendship in literature. 9. Love
in literature. 10. Men in literature. I. Title.
PR509.E4 C87 2002
821.009'353 — dc21   2002004809

British Library cataloguing data are available

©2002 Matthew Curr. All rights reserved

*No part of this book may be reproduced or transmitted in any form
or by any means, electronic or mechanical, including photocopying
or recording, or by any information storage and retrieval system,
without permission in writing from the publisher.*

Manufactured in the United States of America

Cover images © 2002 Art Today

McFarland & Company, Inc., Publishers
  Box 611, Jefferson, North Carolina 28640
    www.mcfarlandpub.com

To Johan

These poets write of love
that weaves connections to each others' loves
and reading them weaves recollections
that in turn collate the syllables
and make up language
more coherent
than the breathless gasp or silenced note we know too well and too long

Contents

Introduction

> Be near me when my faith is dry
> And men the flies of latter spring,
> That lay their eggs, and sting and sing,
> And weave their petty cells and die.
> Be near me when I fade away,
> To point the term of human strife,
> And on the low dark verge of life
> The twilight of eternal day.[1]

John Milton, I believe, loved Charles Diodati much as Gray loved Richard West and Tennyson loved Arthur Hallam. The temper of the times or religious conviction may have prevented these poets, especially the earlier two of them, from conscious expression or even unconscious recognition of the real extent of their devotion, but the love felt for their youthful friends is at the heart of their emotional lives and at the center of their poetic output. The extraordinary coincidence that each of their loved ones died young binds Milton, Gray and Tennyson in communal sorrow just as their writings are linked forever by the commemorative poems that sprang from each one's memory of loss and grief. The genesis of this form of lamentation, what may be termed the male love elegy in English, owes much to the social constraints set upon public articulation of one man's love for another. The stylized and ritualized techniques of distancing observable in Tennyson's *In Memoriam* are valuable means of channeling grief as well as the end development of a mode of personal love safely contained within general applications. The first steps in the development of this socially conditioned and superbly ambivalent mode can be traced from Milton's *Epitaphium Damonis* through Gray's *Elegy*. By the time Tennyson wrote *In Memoriam,* the tradition of such mourning had been so well crafted that Tennyson could employ the vernacular with complete security to speak out and yet still hold back about his loss of the one human being he loved more than almost any other in his life.

Originally, the task of yoking classical sources to English, largely Spenserian sources fell to Milton. it was his genius in *Lycidas* to construct a baroque amalgam of forms that provided the foundations for so much of the apparently easy phrasing upon which Tennyson draws in answering the need to speak out while respecting the requirement to remain partially unheard. Although *Lycidas* does set the pattern of vernacular lament in many aspects of its form, it cannot be cited as the result of passionate bereavement. Milton did not love King. Rather the anxiety behind this poem, that informs it in many ways, is Milton's terror at seeing the tenuity of life which threatened his sole raison d'être. The intensity of his anxiety may itself be accounted for by his social isolation, his obvious otherness as the effeminate undergraduate, the lady of Christ's. To Milton, set aside from more robust male undergraduates indulging in drink and women, the one area of excellence, the world of the mind, becomes his entire universe. To find, by analogy from King's death, that this hope of a safe personal identity in literary fame is threatened closely by the random stroke of mortality is to confront the withering terror of otherness, vacuity and futility. By what must have seemed to Milton an exquisitely cruel stroke of fate, this terror takes on a real form when his beloved companion, Diodati, dies. This time Milton turns to Latin, in *Epitaphium Damonis*, to mourn his lost friend and to screen the most plangent expressions of his love and sense of utter desolation. The sense of despair that permeates this neglected poem is explicable in terms of Milton's genuine devastation but also as a part of the *Lycidas* meditation: the social outsider in search of a justifying meaning for existence or work.

This was the painful predicament with which he wrestled throughout his life. Surely he never thought, gripped as he was within the confines of his religious orthodoxy, that his otherness could be of a more fundamental nature. The beautiful lament for Diodati, one of the gems of English Neo-Latin, his *Epitaphium Damonis*, is shielded by the language of learning from base conjecture and ignoble, prying eyes. Latin keeps at bay the *vulgus profanum* not ready to understand difference, otherness. It has done so for three and a half centuries. In reading this work as the largely unconscious love song of one young man for another, a truth with which the poet himself had probably never consciously come to terms, there is the real excitement of archaeological discovery. Possibly now, however, the world is more accepting of the passions that stormed this English genius's unwitting heart.

At the next stage, Gray's English lament for West is far more confidently poised in the duality of a vernacular that can now both hint at the tremulously personal and explicate, in solemn public measure, the verities of large social concerns. The far less known and much shorter Latin lament that shadows the *Elegy* is deftly submerged under the title of his unfinished didactic poem *De Principiis Cogitandi*. As the English tradition establishes itself and finds a voice for this particularly sensitive love and its compellingly double register, so the Latin shrinks from *Epitaphium Damonis* of 219 lines to the book 4 dedication to West from De Principiis (known from here on as *Ad Favonium*) of 29 lines to no Latin, except the title itself, in *In Memoriam*. It is testimony to the poetic achievement and ingenuity of Milton, Gray and Tennyson that their search for an artistic and intellectual consolation of otherness is enshrined within poems which could be said to have been more anthologized, more read, more drilled into generations of schoolchildren than any others in English. By an extraordinary complicity, of writing by indirection and almost credulous readership, proscribed outsider becomes prescribed text. The means by which otherness is engrafted onto conformist regulation, by which difference is put into the mouth of sameness, seems to demand examination no less than admiration. Ironically, the agony of alienation compels a sensitive poetic consciousness to reach outwards by a remarkable imaginative leap towards a defense of life so wide and convincing in its conception that the very society that alienated that consciousness is brought to admire the privately conceived defense so that is passes back into the culture of that society.

A. L. Rowse, in his somewhat controversial *Milton the Puritan*[2], makes statements on Milton's sexuality which sound too close to accusation to be precise and understanding descriptions of a nature at odds with the majority experience. Rowse makes it appear, if perhaps he does not always mean it to, that Shakespeare is heterosexual, natural, "good," while Milton is repressed, "bad."

> He [Shakespeare] knew all about women — irresistible as he found them. He loved women, appreciated them, was chivalrous and compassionate about them, was their victim, sympathized when they were the victims of life and men, and therefore understood them through and through — no man more so. Thus the other half of human nature was an open book to him, largely closed to Milton[3]

Yet Rowse's findings are perhaps necessary in the gradual process of understanding a side of Milton which readers have repressed. This repression itself and idolization of the public poet-hero is telling of the priorities of readership. Milton is no more to be stigmatized by one part of society for his love of Diodati than he is to be cheered for it by another. Rather his private passion is to be read on Milton's own terms and in the context of his writing life. When Rowse talks of the particular text, his comments are far more enlightening and durable. At the end of chapter 1 he writes:

Milton commemorated him [Diodati] in the most moving of all his poems, the *Epitaphium Damonis*. It is only the fact that it is in Latin that has prevented this poem from being as well known as *Lycidas*. It is significant that it has more personal feeling, is a more poignant expression of grief: Milton felt freer to let himself go in the language in which they had often written to each other.

> Ah! certe extremum licuisset tangere dextram,
> Et bene compositos placide morientis ocellos,
> Et dixisse 'Vale! nostri memor ibis ad astra.

He was now alone. Youth was over.[4]

Christopher Hill is even more tender and fair yet more distinct about his thoughts on Milton's friendship with Diodati:

We can only speculate on Charles Diodati's influence over Milton before his premature death in 1638. Milton clearly adored him more than he ever adored any human being except possibly his second wife. Diodati was slightly younger than the poet, but he went up to the university earlier and started a career earlier. He had all the ebullient charm of Alexander Gil and much more sense. Clearly he took the lead and Milton followed: the latter developed slowly as long as Diodati lived. His death during Milton's absence in Italy was a terrible blow. The *Epitaphium Damonis* was the first poem Milton took the trouble to get separately printed. In Latin because of the continental connections of the Diodatis, it marks some sort of a turning-point and re-dedication of Milton. One of the most extraordinary passages which Milton ever wrote is the conclusion of *Epitaphium Damonis* in which he envisaged the dead Charles enjoying Bacchic orgies in heaven. Earlier lines suggest that he may have seen himself as married to Diodati (65 — "innube"). Psychologists may speculate on the significance for Milton of what looks like a platonic homosexual passion (cf. Milton's sexual confidences to Diodati in Elegy I). What is its relation to the ideal of chastity in *Comus*? Is there any connection between Diodati's death and Milton's decision to marry at the age of thirty-three? What is the relation between Milton's high standards of matrimonial compatibility and this earlier quasi-sexual relationship? Does the first Mrs. Milton suffer for her inability to fill Diodati's place? We can neither answer these questions nor refrain from asking them. What we do know is that, unlike Young and Gil, Diodati did not live to get left behind as Milton grew more and more radical in the sixteen-forties: his memory remained sweet and pure.[5]

So far no one has examined *Epitaphium Damonis* in sufficient detail to decide how far internal evidence may substantiate a sense of the intimacy between the young poet and Diodati. I think this ought to be done now.

CHAPTER ONE

The Phoenix

Charles Diodati and John Milton

τρὶς μὲν "Ὕλαν ἄυσεν ὅσον βαθὺς ἤρυγε λαιμός,
τρὶς δ' ἄρ' ὁ παῖς ὑπάκουσεν, ἀραιὰ δ' ἵκετο φωνά
ἐξ ὕδατος, παρεὼν δὲ μάλα σχεδὸν εἴδετο πόρρω.
νεβροῦ φθεγξαμένας τις ἐν οὔρεσιν ὠμοφάγος λίς
ἐξ εὐνᾶς ἔσπευσεν ἐτοιμοτάταν ἐπὶ δαῖτα·
Ἡρακλέης τοιοῦτος ἐν ἀτρίπτοισιν ἀκάνθαις
παῖδα ποθῶν δεδόνητο, πολὺν δ' ἐπελάμβανε χῶρον.[1]

Theocritus, Idyll XIII, 58–65

Thrice he shouted "Hylas!" as loud as his deep throat could call, and thrice again the boy heard him, and thin came his voice from the water, and, hard by though he was, he seemed very far away. And as when a bearded lion, a ravening lion on the hills, hears the bleating of a fawn afar off, and rushes forth from his lair to seize it, his readiest meal, even so the mighty Heracles, in longing for the lad, sped through trackless briars, and ranged over much country.[2]

Milton, ever the faithful artist, makes it clear in the Latin argument to *Epitaphium Damonis* that the friend he mourns is far closer to him than King in *Lycidas*:

Thyrsis & Damon ejusdem viciniae Pastores, eadem studia sequuti a pueritia amici erant, ut qui plurimum. Thyrsis animi causa profectus peregre de obitu Damonis nuncium accepit. Domum postea reversus, & rem ita esse comperto, se, suamque solitudinem hoc carmine deplorat. Damonis autem sub persona hic intelligitur Carolus Deodatus ex urbe Hetruriae Luca paterno genere oriundus, caetera Anglus; ingenio, doctrina, clarissimisque caeteris virtutibus, dum viveret, juvenis egregius.[3]

> Thyrsis and Damon, shepherds of the same neighbourhood, devoted to the same pursuits, were friends from boyhood up, friends as close as e'er men were. Thyrsis, while on a journey for pleasure's sake, received, in foreign lands, a message telling of his friend's death. Later, after his return home, when he found this message was true, he bemoaned himself and his loneliness.

> In this poem, by "Damon" is meant Charles Diodati, descended on his father's side from the Etruscan city of Lucca. In all things he was an Englishman, a youth, the while he lived, pre-eminent in intellect, in learning, and in all the other brightest and fairest virtues.[4]

Boyhood friends in "a pueritia amici" is extended in the perfectly idiomatic and expressive phrase "ut qui plurimum." This is beyond the formal diction and curt information of *Lycidas*'s introductory paragraph: "the author bewails a learned friend unfortunately drown'd." The adverb "unfortunately" seems to betray little sense of pity, rather of accident alone. In contrast "suam solitudinem … deplorat" spells out at once the intense grief and sense of abandonment felt for Diodati. The list of praise words that conclude the argument ring with the truth of wondering admiration and devoted love. There is a plangent stop to the flow of this laudatory catalogue in the parenthetical clause "dum viveret." This admixture of remembered union suddenly disrupted sets a pattern that runs through the poem as a whole. The cruel intrusion of unaccountable evil clouds the prospects of optimistic youth; the difficulty of transforming "solitudinem" and the sustaining force of passionate respect for another's character are all encased with typical Miltonic precision in the argument.

Similarly, Milton as we know him, is ever the reliable classicist, using references with extraordinary erudition and brevity to punctuate and deepen his meaning. Taking advantage of Latin syntax, in line one of the epitaph he throws up "Himerides" as instant signal to the world of allusion which will inform the lament for Diodati. The island of Sicily, the fens between Etna and the pale sandhills at the shore, the indistinguishable blues of sea and watery sky are the backdrop to this threnody. The highly wrought idylls of Theocritus and Moschus form the immediate literary referent. As a conductor picks out certain members of the orchestra, so Milton now draws us to recall three idylls in particular. "Daphnin" refers to Theocritus's first idyll, "Hylan" to his thirteenth and "Bionis" to Moschus's third idyll. Because few of the Sicilian songs are remarkable for a general concern with death, it could be that Milton merely focuses on those idylls in which mortality and loss are dealt with. This is as far as most critics bother to take the allusions. But we all know how perilous it is to underestimate the recondite quality of this young poet's mind, as exemplified in the phrase "blind mouths" in *Lycidas*, superbly explicated by Ruskin in *Sesame and Lilies*.

Milton uses allusion in many cases as the submerged main clause of his lighter surface elaboration. The first idyll describes Daphnis's fate. Daphnis had married the fairest of nymphs and boasted that nothing could break his passion and fidelity. Aphrodite punishes him by drawing his heart to another. But he fights off this attraction, choosing to die in the struggle rather than forfeit his constancy. In Milton's first Latin elegy he tells Diodati how he watches pretty girls. In his seventh he describes how one in particular smites him:

> Unam forte aliis supereminuisse notabam,
> Principium nostri lux erat illa mali.
>
> (ll. 61–2)

> One by chance I marked, towering [in beauty] over others:
> that radiance was the beginning of all my woe.[5]

Yet in both cases the pangs of this claimed love are rather too easily allayed. In the first elegy he announces his abrupt return to Cambridge and in the seventh he more tellingly explains how the cold stream of learning will keep away the mischievous errors of such love:

> Donec Socraticos umbrosa Academia rivos
> Praebuit, admissum dedocuitque jugum.
> Protinus extinctis ex illo tempore flammis,
> Cincta rigent multo pectora nostra gelu.
> Unde suis frigus metuit puer ipse Sagittis,
> Et Diomedeam vim timet ipsa Venus.
>
> (Conclusion, 5–10)

> Until the shades of Academe proffered to me the Socratic streams,
> and untaught me [and loosed] the yoke I had let fall [upon my neck].
> Straightway, from that moment, the fires were quenched,
> my heart has been unyielding, belted with deep ice.
> Hence the lad fears the cold for his beloved shafts,
> and Venus herself dreads might that matches the might of Diomedes.[6]

Virginity is revered by the poet as a virtuous state, free from the muddling tides of emotional entrapment. (Or is this his rationalization of a coldness for women?) Love is seen to be, in either case, a negative and dangerous state from which one is protected by studious learning. Love is below intellectual life; it is a giving in, a weakness. It is telling that Milton protests too much of his smitten heart and the beauty of this one woman. He relinquishes her attraction with an unconvincing ease and by unlikely cure if the wounds of passion were ever as deeply cut as he claims. Perhaps most telling is the fact that, at the start, Cupid is described hovering at his bedside and is compared to Ganymede (Jove's catamite) and the beautiful youth Hylas whom the nymphs drew down. Hylas is a major referent in the male love elegy. The whole of the seventh elegy may in some way be taken as an elaboration of this figure: Milton, the handsome youth, is drawn down into the dangerous well of female allure just as Hercules's love companion, Hylas of the braided locks, was dragged down into the well by naiads. Milton, ever the complete artist, specifically details this action: "Naiade raptus Hylas" (l. 24). This kind of formulaic qualification is a key to the particular characteristic of Hylas that the poet wishes to employ. Hylas, the romantic partner of the heroic male, on a great expedition with the Argonauts, is drowned by the insatiable and suffocating desire of women. Milton views himself, the male, as pure and purposeful of mind, yet imperiled by the wiles of feminine charm. He, unlike Hylas, is rescued from a watery fate by the cold precision of male learning, the cold stream of the Socratic school, defense against any weakness of the flesh. This attitude toward woman as temptress to virtuous man is familiar from *Paradise Lost* and *Samson Agonistes*; early suspicion and alienation are adumbrated in the later epic portraits. If the poem, at its formal rhetorical level, is an Ovidian explication of Cupid's revenge upon the virginal male, then there is, below its surface, a good deal of unstated and unconscious complication. Cupid is sent to wound the obdurate young man, yet is, in his likeness to Hylas, too much like the young poet himself. It is dangerous, of course, to assume Milton did not mean the real impact of his poem to be that deeper notion which would then be a witty subversion, or conditioning at least, of the formal argument. In that case it may not be complication so much as baroque ingenuity, which option I would choose. The seventh elegy then becomes an important intimation of Milton's identification with the Hylas myth.

To his conscious mind, Milton prizes his romantic friendship with Charles because it is above the apparently cloying condition of other romances. Is he, in *Epitaphium Damonis*, by reference to the absolute fidelity of Daphnis, suggesting his complete dedication to Diodati? Certainly many critics take it for granted that Diodati was in fact the best, if not the only, real companion of the mind, heart and soul Milton ever had. With him Milton enjoyed that remarkably completing identity of the self which suggests unconsciously a security of understanding in the original Platonic sense.

The accusative "Hylan" (*E.D.*, l. 1) somewhat takes up this suggestion and augments it. Idyll XIII is the moving tale of Hercules's love for Hylas of the braided locks. Theocritus does not take Hercules/Hylas to be merely adult protector/young steward but quite definitely casts Hercules as the lover of the beautiful boy. So distinctly, in fact, that one nineteenth-century commentator, wholly out of sympathy for this cultural, if not genetic, phenomenon, writes: "Meineke observes 'tota haec carminis pars luxata et foedissime depravata est.' This whole part of the poem is debauched and disgustingly depraved."[7]

In this tale, the nymphs, the women, steal Hylas from the other male: female love, as at the end of Milton's seventh elegy, is regarded as lustful and unlawful. Homophile devotion is portrayed poignantly in the images of Hercules scouring the countryside for his beloved and Hylas's voice too weak to reach him from the water. Psychologically this myth is replete with significant readings for the state of each poet under consideration here: Milton, Gray and Tennyson. The nymphs' seduction of Hylas could celebrate mythically the rapture of the boy into full manhood; the boy is taken into full adulthood. Hercules's dirge, however, records the hero's inability or unpreparedness to lose himself at this stage. This would suggest, however, that homophile equals immature/wrong while heterosexual equals fully developed/normal. Because Theocritus does not show Hercules as merely protector/teacher for Hylas, this reading must fail. In terms of normative social matrices, by which heroic poets such as Milton, Gray and Tennyson are to be venerated within codified establishment categories, the most generous reading of any Hylas reference would be that it is the model of homophile love as a stage towards better things. Theocritus's Idyll XIII disallows this too, however, just as Milton's *Epitaphium Damonis* does, especially when regarded against his biography or attitude toward women in *Paradise Lost*. Moreover, the internal evidence of incontestable correspondence between Hercules, stricken with grief, searching for lost Hylas, and Milton's persona, Thyrsis, wandering through woods and fields in search of Damon, fixes Theocritus XIII as a primary intertext for the funeral song to Damon. Once more, this agrees with our knowledge of Milton's precision in supplying classical allusions. The inconsolable bereavement of Thyrsis owes more to the tone of XIII than that of I or Moschus's lament for Bion.

Moschus's famous memorial song is invoked in line two of *Epitaphium Damonis*, mainly to enforce the aspect of singer/poet. Damon, after all, was a well-known fifth-century musician, referred to in Plato's *Republic*, and the Diodatis were an accomplished musical family. In Moschus's idyll, nature is called upon to collaborate in the rightful mourning for a poet who formed a part of the natural order of things. This is not the case in Theocritus XIII in which the sufferer, Hercules, is set against nature. The leaves do not fall in sympathy, nor do the flowers wilt in oneness. In fact nature in XIII is remarkably careless, even inimical, of Hercules's plight. This oppositional sense is important to Milton's assumption of a stance *contra mundum* in so many areas. He is against the heady swoops of so-called natural, normal heterosexual passion against so many social dictates of his day, from divorce laws to censorship. He is against royalty, the kingly state, and against the postlapsarian world of intoxicating subtle temptations. Milton is the outsider; he is contrary, I think, as the result of his radical otherness. This may account to a greater extent for his growing "more and more radical in the sixteen-forties" than Hill recognizes. Unconsciously the outsider desires to overturn entirely the society with which he feels subliminally at odds. In this respect the opposition to nature's easy course in Theocritus's XIII emerges as central to *Epitaphium Damonis*, a text of otherness.

The choice of the name, Damon, itself evidences Milton's extraordinary precision and dynamic employment of classical references. Damon was a Pythagorean philosopher of Syracuse bound in closest friendship of the mind to Phintias, who had been condemned to death by the tyrant Dionysius. Phintias begged leave to arrange matters with his relatives in a distant town and offered to leave Damon in his place for execution should he not return on the appointed day. Dionysius accepted the hostage yet did not believe in the promised return. Shortly before the execution of Damon, to the amazement of all, Phintias did return to face his death. Dionysius, astonished by this proof of human fidelity, forgave Phintias and asked to share their friendship (Val. Max. IV.7, Plut. *De Amic. Mult.*).

We know too the debt Milton owed to Spenser. Sir Scudamour, in *The Faerie Queen*, tells of legendary romantic friendships. Milton's commemoration and finally celebration of his love for Diodati is framed in the same terms as that ideal union of the soul that prompts Spenser's knight to speak of "lives although decay'd, yet loves decayed never."[8] Sir Scudamour describes the couples restored in spiritual togetherness:

> Such were great Hercules and Hylas deare;
> Trew Jonathan, and David trustie tryde;
> Stout Theseus, and Pirithous his feare;
> Pylades and Orestes by his syde;
> Myld Titus and Gesippus without pryde;
> Damon and Pythias whom death could not sever:
> All these and all that ever had been tyde
> In bands of friendship, there did live for ever,

Whose lives although decay'd, yet loves decayed never.
Which when as I, that never tasted blis,
Nor happie howre, beheld with gazefull eye,
I thought there never was none other heaven then this;
And gan their endlesse happinesse enuye,
That being free from fear and gealosye,
Meet frankly there their loves desire possesse:
Whilest I through paines and perlous ieopardie,
Was forst to seek my lifes dear patronesse:
Much dearer be the things, which come through hard distresse.

(Bk. IV, Canto X, 27–8)

The names of John Milton and Charles Diodati, we hope, and those of Thomas Gray and Richard West, or Alfred Tennyson and Arthur Hallam would be added to Spenser's list of happy pairs who certainly did gain their friendships' reward "through hard distresse."

To confirm completely the alliance of Theocritus as palimpsest to his own love elegy, Milton, in line three, juxtaposes "Sicilicum" and "Thamesim." At the same time he places "oppida" beside "carmen" to show how the English landscape will echo the sad call of a Sicilian song.

Lines 4 to 9 are the real start of the epitaph itself; its framework has been drawn and now the actual poem begins. The nearest *Lycidas* comes to the tone of immediately uttered grief in 4–9 is at lines 36–7. Even here though the sense of abandonment and vacuity is not evident. There is mournfulness but not desolation:

> Thrice he [Heracles] shouted "Hylas!" as loud as his deep throat could call, and thrice again the boy heard him, and thin came his voice from the water, and, hard by though he was, he seemed very far away. And as when a bearded lion, a ravening lion on the hills, hears the bleating of a fawn afar off, and rushes forth from his lair to seize it, his readiest meal, even so the mighty Heracles, in longing for the lad, sped through trackless briars, and ranged over much country.
>
> Reckless are lovers: great toils did Heracles bear, in hills and thickets wandering, and Iason's quest was all postponed to this. Now the ship abode with her tackling aloft, and the company gathered there, but at midnight the young men were lowering the sails again, awaiting Heracles. But he, wheresoever his feet might lead him went wandering in his fury, for the cruel Goddess of love was rending his heart within him.[9]

"Trackless" comes to gather up the lover's loss of emotional and sexual purpose and meaning. He is now bereft of that very sustaining identity which affords him personhood. Hercules is trackless without Hylas's "centerd passion," as Milton would be lost and rudderless without the assurance of Diodati's love both at the time of Charles's death and throughout his life.

Interrogative pronouns accumulate throughout the poem to suggest the sense of emptiness. The balanced symmetry of "quas" and "quas" in line 4 emphasizes the exhaustive searching of the bereft lover. It is alternated to "quibus" in line 5, which in turn is heavily accentuated by the double ablatives in "assiduis" and "querelis." Thyrsis wearies the countryside as he wearies himself with these assiduous complaints. "Assiduis" suggests the search for a mate. "Exercuit" emphasizes the unflagging attention of a parent for her young or, as here, a lover for his beloved. The sense of a natural and enduring bond shattered is mirrored by the catalogue of nouns, the list of places, everywhere in nature that the poet searches for his partner. The suffixed "que" entrenches the aspect of a comfortless world. "Praeraptum" in line 7 answers this tone of outrage. Thyrsis, like Hercules, is stunned and helpless in the face of this wrong. Milton extends the picture in XIII by showing Thyrsis wandering "pererrans" through the deep night, "altam ... noctem." Much as "trackless" functions inversely in XIII, so "noctem" works to signify the night experienced inwardly by the grieving shepherd/Milton. The places to which he wanders are "sola" as much as his spirit is desolate. Milton's use of the persona and concurrent third-person narrative is remarkably powerful in heightening the pain expressed. Theocritus's analogy of the lion is reworked so that the very removal to third person seems to attribute a pang of impersonality, loneliness and otherness. The poet seems unable to trust his feelings to the first person or the accessibility of the vernacular. The arresting first cry, modified by a five-line section, directs us from the anguished mourner to the silent, indifferent cycle of nature. Time and the countryside proceed unconcerned by the loss that so shatters this lonely shepherd. As opposed to "green things that mourn" in Moschus's lament, the roses called to redden in sorrow, here it is almost unseemly the way the wheat rises up in fresh green. "Totidem" and "numerabant" sound the remorseless pace of time. "Flavas" qualifies "messes" and completes the insult of nature's indifference. Green wheat maturing to golden harvest underscores the deprivation of a youthful friendship that will never reach this maturity; nor will the promise of Diodati's talents ever attain any earthly fame. Instead the menacing phrase "sub umbras" suggests death obscenely swallowing its victim. Thyrsis's sense of guilt at being absent "nec dum viderat" and his anger at the insidious privations worked by Pluto are complicated now by the reason for his absence: "amor Musae."

This very devotion to letters is what bound the friends and what must prove a means of preserving their love. The ironical dart is perhaps sharpened further by Milton's literary pilgrimage to Italy, keeping him from the real presence of the Italian he loved. The relation art/life is a golden thread drawn through this poem.

The poet returns to his major key in lines 14–17. "At" often marks large breaks in Latin verse, famously so in the Aeneid IV.296. Here too the adversative particle sounds a return to the poet's distress. The mind is full, "expleta" and the call of Christian duty to employ the given talents faithfully is heard. But the poet's heart has been pillaged. As soon as Thyrsis returns to the accustomed elm, no amount of learning seems enough to balance the loss of his friend. The repeated blows of "tum ... tum," with the second "tum" occurring immediately after the caesura, imitate not only the strokes of realized loss but the disjunction of the two worlds, the mind and the heart, that were once ideally united in a fructifying friendship. Rowse remarks, about *Paradise Lost*, that "Milton put the whole of his life's experience — except, perhaps significantly, the ardour of his feelings for Diodati — into his great poem.".[10] It may be true for this reason that *Paradise Lost* is in some ways, as Johnson says, written through spectacles. It lacks the warmth of the heart. But then, if in fact the one real emotionally ardent encounter of Milton's life, with Diodati, was cut short, then it follows that not only would he not be able to write about it, but that description of other emotional encounters in the epic would be charged with a persistently deferred emotional force. It could be that the sense of loss felt by Milton at the death of Diodati takes up Rowse's words quoted earlier: he was alone, youth was ended. In that case the idea of paradise lost, a perfect place of youthful beauty and emotional harmony ruined, is very much the reflection of Milton's lost love for his young friend Diodati. The two romantic friends are "sub umbras" (1. 11) and "sub ulmo" (1. 15) to denote that protected innocence of the Horton world, that Arcadia of unsuspecting youthfulness. The sylvan harmony of this intellectual pairing, together away from the world, may well find its echo in the scenes of innocent, prelapsarian love of book IV. But there the subjection of woman's mind to man's betrays a flawed relation even in its perfection, compared to the unanimity and mutual respect of Milton and Diodati. It is this rare marriage of true minds that is present, hauntingly, in Gray's *Elegy* and in *In Memoriam*. The portrayal of lustful Eve, the destroyer of paradise, might also match well: woman as the destroyer of that place of all-male happiness and strong virtue. If a pastoral idyll to Milton is a metaphor for the joy of a perfect youthful world, then the death of Charles could well be represented as the extinction of that pastoral world. The themes of sweet innocence and bitter experience that are woven into *Paradise Lost* through the pastoral motif are then taken up to the mighty concerns of loss and redemption via the painful memory of youth truncated by grief and ushering in a harsh adulthood. In terms of *Epitaphium Damonis* the problem is how the world of mind/art will be able to redeem the loss of heart/life.

One of the most authoritative Neo-Latinists, F. J. Nichols, writes:

> But now the song begins to work only when the poet abandons the pastoral mode. After exhausting all the possibilities of consolation the pastoral mode offers, the deification of his friend, for instance, which here comes towards the beginning of the poem, and ranging widely in time and space; and after the bitter dismissal of the empty work of the imagination already mentioned; then, when the poet begins to conceive of a new and greater kind of song, and when his pipes, the instrument of pastoral, fall apart under the burden of this greater song, only then does the possibility of a consolation for the poet's loneliness become possible. Here too we have an optimistic future, a literary one: the poet will write an epic, but it must be in English, not only in its language but in its subject. A tradition — as well as the language which to Milton apparently now seemed inextricably bound up with the tradition — is being rejected here as no longer viable as a personal means of poetic expression.[11]

There are many difficulties here. The pastoral "works" as a lamentary form, as a means of grieving, from the very first words of the poem. Its success, or resolution, is oversimplified by Nichols into a formulaic and decisive completion of a puzzle of death. Bereavement does not call for a single, mathematically conclusive finality — rather it needs the process of mourning that is so evident in *In Memoriam*. The ritual of grieving is significantly part of the shape of the pastoral in *Epitaphium Damonis*, evident in the refrain and the opiate rhythm of the central verse paragraphs. This pattern of mourning, or process in the writing, is absent from the more lucidly argued sections of *Lycidas*. *Epitaphium Damonis* records the heartrending grief of a loved one left without direction in life while *Lycidas* in no way approximates the depth or intimacy of feeling in the Latin poem. It is odd then to say that Latin is being rejected as a means of poetically expressing personal feeling when so many would agree that Milton seldom overtly expresses personal feeling except perhaps here in the Latin epitaph and, by projection of that experience, in the English poems. The paragraph seems to contradict itself slightly. Considering the significant part played by the pastoral motif in the structure of such central books of the epic as IV, VII and IX, it seems strange to suggest that Milton broke with this tradition at all.

Elsewhere too Nichols argues that the pastoral in *Epitaphium Damonis* is a failed song. In this he follows Condee: "the lines say in substance what the whole poem has been saying through its structure, that the tradition of Theocritean-Vergilian pastoralism, which the early part of the poem embodies, has worn too thin, that the ritual of nymphs and shepherds is threadbare."[12] But perhaps we could adapt this questionable observation to indicate that Milton imbued the pastoral with a grave sense of loss— far more intense than is ever evident in the idylls of Theocritus, for instance, taken as a whole, or Virgil's Eclogues. Particularly in *Epitaphium Damonis* the pastoral bears the freight of his greatest private sadness: it has to show something of that extraordinary accord that existed between himself and Diodati and so represent the loss of youth and the beauty of an innocent, unsullied marriage of the minds (perhaps what Milton's Adam would have preferred?). It is not surprising then, to find Milton speaking of disburdening his "immensum dolorem" (l. 17). This great adaptation of classical pastoral, this revival and massive elaboration of the intensity of the Hylas motif, may well be said not to end, but to continue, even to find its fullest expression, in the loss of youthful innocence, of that completeness of Horton, under generous paternal care, which is in so many ways expressed in *Paradise Lost*. Condee identifies this depth of personal feeling several times in his excellent article, something which Nichols, following too literally on the theme of a failed song, misses. Even the Hylas piece, which is nearest this searing pain of loss, one must remember, is not impelled by the anguish of real bereavement: Theocritus writes of a myth. Milton takes up this suffering, and the process of a complex consolation of the othered self as well as consolation for all of the bereaved, in an entirely new way. This needs to be stressed. Condee aptly notices the flashes of agony even if he does not relate the phenomenon to its tradition. He writes: "the poem glides gently among the flocks, and Thyrsis 'simul assueta seditque sub ulmo' in sibilant calm, only to burst out passionately "Tum vero amissum, tum denique, sentit amicum" with a depth of feeling that startles us in this landscape of stereotypes."[13] Later he adds:

> the poem wrenches itself around to face the dilemma of love and death:
>
> > quis mihi fidus
> > Haerebit lateri comes, ut tu saepe solebas
> > Frigoribus duris ...?

> For an instant we glimpse a depth of personal emotion (as so often in
> his Latin poems and so rarely in the English poems) that is almost too
> painful.[14]

In this regard, Condee sees what Rowse sees in the poem and I believe
he is completely correct. In Latin, Milton was able to speak of his private
feeling as he did nowhere else. It is a pity, though, that Condee speaks of
a lot of stereotypes. This is a trap into which commentators on Gray's *Elegy*
or *In Memoriam* easily fall. The use and development of a tradition, the
rich investment of received material, is important. It is a means of containing the deep grief, powerfully matching emotions to images of equivalent strength and tried dignity. By this means forms are revivified and
given new impetus. Traditional material provides the resonant intertext
that carries the new poem back and forth in time: it creates "the well-connected page," as that great humanist scholar Politian called it. More precisely, such allusions and recollections provide intertexts for the text but
also a context of acceptance for individuals like Milton who felt so acutely
the pangs of otherness and alienation from society. The one regime under
which they could unapologetically claim citizenship was that of letters
and the familial interconnection, the welcome intimacy with like minds,
memorable and recoverable through writing though living in other coun-
tries and ages. The practice of such densely allusive and erudite poetry
becomes in itself a substantial consolation of otherness. In this way the
pastoral conventions cannot be seen as threadbare or defunct. They serve
several crucial functions in the poet's gradual rediscovery of himself, his
new identity as poet. This transference of grief to public role occurs in
Gray and Tennyson as well. The dedication of the beloved, the belief in
the genius of each poet, is held sacred after loss and invested in a dedication of the self to art, thus memorializing the dedication of love from Diodati, West and Hallam.

When Milton speaks of "pecoris relicti/cura vocat" in lines 14–15 he
is continuing a metaphor of Christian pastoral across the pagan ground-
works of a Sicilian scene. One's flock, and the "cura" of it, is the use of,
and duty to use, God-given talents properly for the benefit of others. In
the case of Milton, who always felt outside and suffered the slights of
difference, this need to be attached to society is dramatically heightened.
It accounts for his extraordinary sense of duty. "Cura" provides a useful
directive for belonging. Serving society according to the promptings of his
conscience is a means of belonging. If, in the frequent fulminations of his
prose works especially, he is far too strident, the reason could be sought
in his acute need to belong, and difficulty in accommodating difference.

Duty to use his God-given talents rightly for others is, in a way, convenient, as the notion of election allows him to determine what that duty is, while at the same time involving him in the needed collaboration. The old *Cambridge History of English Literature* describes well his isolation long before the word "difference" became a critical term:

> The upshot of the whole [his spell at Cambridge] seems to be that he was studious, reserved and not quite like other people — once, at least, and, probably, more than once, becoming definitely "refractory." He was always to be studious, reserved and not like other people; and, in his nearly seventy years, the times of truce were not very common and the times of war frequent.[15]

It is important to understand the personal significance of the pastoral metaphor in Milton's work. For without this explanation of the link among the loss of Charles Diodati, the loss of youth and the lost harmony of a Sicilian idyll, it is easy to join a line of critics who find the insistent refrain of *Epitaphium Damonis* gratuitous. But the dismissal of the sheep, sending them home unfed with the harsh imperative "Ite," is tantamount to a rejection of his talents. Milton cannot work, Milton cannot then live, without the sealing friendship of Diodati. The refrain is poetically intrusive to represent the existential obstacle of despair created by Diodati's death. Again and again the line recurs to show the poet struggling to overcome his sense of hopelessness. How can he work without Diodati? It puzzles the will. The final resolution is made appropriately by an alteration of the refrain at line 203. The harsh tone of the refrain in "dominus iam non vocat" is deliberately set to create a mood of disruption and dissonance. It is important at this stage to see how Milton relates work to life right at the very start of his elegy: this relation is essential to the successful resolution of the poem.

The cry of "hei mihi" in line 19 amplifies Thyrsis's desolation. Like Hercules, he is lost without that centering love that granted life purpose and assurance. Strange that neither Dorian,[16] nor Condee in replying to Dorian, take Milton at his word about the Hylas reference. Dorian argues that Milton breaks with tradition: that in all other pastorals nature joins the mourner in regret for the lost one. So the harvest is lost or rivers are dry. He forgets about Theocritus's Hylas idyll: there nature is indifferent to Hercules's sufferings. This is precisely the reference that Milton meticulously foregrounds at the start of his Latin elegy. Condee makes it worse:

> But we must see that the significance of the disagreement [between Hanford and Dorian about the pastoral] lies further along in the argument:

> the poem stresses the inadequacies of pastoral in assuaging sorrow;
> therefore to have the nymphs and shepherds join sympathetically in
> mourning Damon would be to disrupt a major structural element in
> the poem; it would have the effect of softening the essential clash
> between grief and threadbare pastoralism.[17]

By channeling his intensely personal grief into a particular part of
the pastoral tradition, Milton begins the tradition of male love elegy in
English. Here old, mythic songs of characters apart from the poet (in Theocritus, Idyll XIII) are changed for real ones and the way is cleared for
many mourners to speak of a private loss, and for other readers to win
consolation from the graduated process of reconciliation portrayed and
felt through the poem's carefully constructed stages. *In Memoriam* is the
fulfillment in English of this sudden and bold innovation. Far from the
pastoral form being threadbare, it is radically charged by this impulse, and
the reparation of identity and purpose after a death is significantly
enriched by the sustaining strength of this ancient form. There is not a
clash between "profound grief" and "threadbare pastoralism"; rather, there
is a superb congruence. Many of the central verse paragraphs, written
between the recitative of the "Ite procul " motif, attain an anesthetizing
rhythm that, in itself, by the sheer repetition of the sealing words, absorbs
something of the pain and closes something of the wounded soul. As Tennyson puts it:

> But, for the unquiet heart and brain,
>   A use in measured language lies;
>   The sad mechanic exercise,
> Like dull narcotics, numbing pain.
>
> (5.5–9)

The source of this healing rhythm is in the Latin epitaph, for there
Milton links private anguish to the repetitive, mechanical pattern of the
earlier forms. The slow, somnolent structure of Gray's full-dress *Elegy*
owes a great deal to the Latin epitaph and forms a bridge to Tennyson's
plaintive poetic memorial.

Probably the most worrying of Condee's comments, however, and an
indication of at least some difficulty in comprehending the metaphorical
force of the pastoral mode, is in the following lines, where he comments
on the allusion to fending off lions and wolves from the sheepfold:

> Sive opus in magnos fuit eminus ire leones,
> Aut avidos terrere lupos, praesepibus altis?

It is unlikely that Diodati and Milton ever encountered any lions or wolves, and surely it was passages such as this that led Dr Johnson to dismiss the whole poem with the remark that it was "written in the common but childish imitation of pastoral life."[18]

It is useless to hide behind Johnson. He would have realized that lions and wolves are representative of dangers and anxieties in life that threaten protection of one's God-given duty. No one, except perhaps Condee, thought that Milton was advertising his combat with a lion "eminus" or wolves "avidos." It may be no more than a slip, but it causes one to worry about Condee's general grasp of the classical pastoral as an essential means of articulating in lyric form the felt grief of one human being for another, particularly when the development of that lyric and personal form in the vernacular was crude. Its full assimilation into the vernacular only took place among the Romantic poets centuries later.

In XIII, Hylas is mourned only by Hercules and it is this plaintive loneliness that is the keynote of *Epitaphium Damonis* and the two great vernacular laments that are born from it in the eighteenth and nineteenth centuries. It is most significant that in XIII, nature does not join other human or divine mourners: Hercules is entirely alone in his grief. Placing homophile love outside conventional matrices of consolation prompts, or requires, the poet to provide, or imaginatively create, a society or a vision of one that could accommodate such grief. The poet is radically inconsolable by the nature of his rare love. Part of the great challenge facing Milton is the creation of a poetic memorial that suits and dignifies this rare love, despite an English society and his own conscious mind that outlaws completely the Hylas/Hercules relationship. The achievement of *Epitaphium Damonis* is a magical synthesis of the Theocritean form which allows the grieving romantic friend both to speak and yet not speak, or at least be heard selectively. To those that will understand, such as his intellectual beneficiaries, Gray and Tennyson, the form is most eloquent at all levels. To bellowing conformists and skillful gossipers, the poem is cross-barred by *recherché* learning. One cannot but smile at the clumsy efforts of critics out of sympathy with this poet and his grief. Suddenly worshipers of the public-made Milton, the insiders of conformist practice, are outsiders, trying in vain to pick the locks of the text.

The section in lines 19–25 reintroduces the searching interrogative pronouns of line 4. This habit of ritualizing grief, working through the same tormenting sense of loss, almost blindly over and over, is one of the great structural formulations of Milton's lament; one that both Gray and Tennyson take over and expand. As if the sheer repetition becomes a solace, so the slow rhythm of Gray's quatrains and the hypnotic melody of Tennyson's stanzas function too in dulling the pain. Thyrsis calls wildly, "what powers divine shall I name on earth, what in heaven": "quae ... quae?" The shift from bystander poet observing and narrating the "voces quas miser effudit Thyrsis" and the direct speech of the second verse paragraph is stylistically effective. As in much of Milton's epic poetry, the effect is highly visual: we *see* Thyrsis complaining; and now we even *hear* him crying. The appearance of the intimate "te" is sudden and alarming by its carefully contrasted third-person setting. The incongruity empowers the cruelty held in "immiti." Such loss now seems more unnatural than the outlawed intimacy: in a way Milton has turned the first corner. The repetitious "siccine ... sic" reworks the echoing of lamentation begun at line five with "antra," caverns booming sadly in empty reply. Thus Milton employs the highly wrought verbal structures of the Alexandrian tradition to considerable effect. Like "te," the final direct appeal to "Damon" in line 20 is finely anticipated. The name is uttered softly and with great tenderness. In holding over the name by such gentle inquiry, Milton has already invested it with literary permanence/immortality, so that "sine nomine" of 21 is undercut. Similarly "obscuris" is countermanded by the very memorial of the poem itself. Will Damon and Milton's love for Diodati be forgotten among many shades? The effectual bulwark is the poet's construct. The words are the means to hand for the grieving lover. This, his one area of power, will be used to shore up such a sense of emptiness. So the adversative "at" confirms this strong reply to anonymity and the magisterial potency of the divine "virga ... aurea" authenticates a rebuke to nature. The deity that divides the illiterate and uncomprehending herd from those few chosen for virtue uses the significant terms of both the underworld and the puritan saints. The ordered world of the chosen elect is given in the military "agmen" endorsed by the sense of worthiness in "dignum": working double time to deflate the "nefas" of Hylas's love.

The animal herd instinct is perfectly placed in the central "pecus" flanked at each end of the line by the telling forms "ignavum" and "silentum." The few saints will be kept as God's gift (Dio-dati), far from the mass, the madding crowd, which cannot but misunderstand the beauty of Hylas's love. Condee struggles to place pecus." The language of learning and subtle allusion is in many ways the "golden wand" that keeps away the prying eyes of the common herd. (Some sense of phallic sublimation is possible as "virga" in Latin has strongly sexual associations.) Once again the choice of "pecus" says much about Milton's sense of not belonging to the herd and his belief in Diodati's special election and separate virtus (vir-tue), manly worth. This reverence for male goodness is important in reading Adam's temptation or Samson's seduction. Milton turns his estrangement from the majority impulse into a private virtue, however, in at least two ways that are fundamental to his search for consolation: religiously, by which Damon and he are part of a small group of the Protestant elect, and intellectually, through membership in the exclusive world of learning. In considering Milton's deliberate recourse to erudition (what Johnson might call his bookishness) and his conviction of saintly purpose in a fallen world, it is essential to appreciate Milton's feeling of difference from the herd. He looks to the best ground he can in defending his right to autonomy and self-expression. If the bellowing herd uses brutal instruments of prejudice and abuse in dubbing Milton the "lady of Christ's," they must not be surprised if the poet retaliates with much sharper and more enduring instruments of exclusionary language.

Condee does not recognize the intensity of this identification of singularity and thus sees the "pecus" reference in fairly vague ways. He writes:

> As Keightley has pointed out, "*Pecus* is a strange term to use for the dead," and he notes that Milton's line reflects Virgil's "Ignavum fucos, pecus a praesepibus arcent," where "pecus" has its normal meaning.
> Of course Keightley is right; "pecus" is indeed a strange term, with its strangeness in Milton's poem being underlined by the resemblance to the line in Virgil. And it is of course the kind of word that Milton wants at this point. As the "Argumentum" to the poem states, Thyrsis "suamque solitudinem hoc carmine deplorat." Thyrsis is searching for love and companionship. The difference between the instinct of the herd and the love of true friends is the very conflict which the poem explores more fully in lines 94–111,
>
> > Hei mihi! quam similes ludunt per prata iuvenci,
> > Omnes unanimi secum sibi lege sodales
>
> and only resolves at the very end of the poem, in the beatific vision and the "caelicolae" joined in harmonious and eternal ecstasy. This theme of friendship as opposed to gregariousness pervades the whole section (19–25), and when the refrain occurs for the second time, at line 26, it is no mere mechanical repetition: Thyrsis, deprived by death of true companionship, brushes away the insensitive herd that distracts him.[19]

The reading just falls short of saying that Milton's difference, the rarity of his love for Diodati, is what keeps him away from the herd. This radical otherness creates an acute pathos against the easy pattern of observed nature in the fine cameo of the twittering swallow, alone without its mate yet soon replied to and reunited with a female bird. The fullness of nature for some and its leanness for others, the injustice of nature's indifference to a different love underscores the remnant sadness in this passage. It would have helped Condee too had he noticed the deliberate echo of the "common herd" idea at the very end of the poem: "Nec tenues animas, pectusque ignobile vulgi / Hinc ferit" ("not trivial souls and the ignoble hearts of the rabble does he smite hence"). Just as the "aurea virga" will keep Diodati's soul apart, so the darts of Love will strike only men of that purer mind and spirit, such as Diodati. This is no hubristic exclusivity; rather it is the careful refutation of society's own exclusion of the difference of men such as Milton. Thus exclusion is repaid with exclusion.

Although Condee's work on *Epitaphium Damonis* is probably the finest to date, it is a pity that he entitles this 1965 article "The Structure of Milton's Epitaphium Damonis" while not really discussing the overall structure of the verse paragraphs; including the way in which Milton opens with a section of seventeen lines, then contracts them to parts never over ten lines until line 92. This marks a dramatic change in the poem and the change is signaled by an immediate lengthening of the paragraphs. From 93 to the end the sections are never below ten lines and are usually far more than that. This means that from 18 to 92 the sobs of the refrain are far more frequent as the poet can see no hope of comfort. From 93 onwards, however, the iterative lament is half as frequent to echo the argument working itself to a resolution. Given that the introductory part of the poem is seventeen lines long and the work as a whole is 219, the break at 92–3 is a fairly symmetrical center line. In reading the more fragmented, tearful first half therefore, it should be seen that this is part of what is, in admirably Miltonic style, a superbly controlled work of art.

There are eleven of these shorter, initial paragraphs. The start of the second, at line 27, the superstition about being seen by a wolf, recalls Vergil's ninth eclogue. Of course here "wolf" means evil according to the code of the pastoral metaphor as a whole. Here is that "grim Wolf / [which] with privy paw / daily devours apace" (*Lycidas*, 128–9). It is that renegade Satan compared to a wolf in *Paradise Lost* (IV 183–7). Milton, as wayfaring Christian, prays that the evil wolf will not better him. So long as he does not, Milton will ensure that Damon will not go unmourned and that his true honor will be set, just as his place among the true and few will be secured. The dative of advantage in 29–30 is repeated centrally to indicate the honor to Diodati. More important though, this setting of stylized structural units is a vital part of the formalizing, the ritualizing of such blinding grief. Milton's deft adaptation of this highly wrought Alexandrian figure thus sets a pattern for Gray and Tennyson to follow.

The carefully paced, almost anesthetizing regularity of such short balanced sections containing meticulously turned phrases seems in some way to numb the unbearable pain, to soothe the chaotic grief with disciplined art. Painstakingly crafted phrasing becomes therefore in itself a gentle tribute of care for the beloved. Particularly when the open expression of such loss is muzzled by social law or conscious recognition, the need to speak of such emotions within the longed-for areas of acceptance, within allowed forms, invites the poet to pay extreme attention to a description of grief which is in itself a funerary inscription and an appeal for the blessing of the frowning establishment. So the lapidary formality of a graven epitaph is visible in the precise symmetry of lines 31–3. The apparently superfluous, repetitious "post ... post," "dum ... dum" lull the anxious mind, not by the promise that Damon will be second only to Daphnis, nor that he will be remembered as long as Pales loves the country or as long as Faunus does. The mind is eased by the grace of art. The artistry of the bereaved lover is both consolation for the intense otherness of the poet as well as a memorial to the dead. The artistic concern itself provides the mourning poet some useful material occupation. What more fitting gravestone for a "sociumque ... canorum" than exercise of the "Palladisque artes"?

In the third short paragraph, this formality is condensed to a formulaic intertwining of the highly crafted verbal remembrances ("haec praemia") and the dative of advantage twice. The tone of "Damon" again held, as in line 20, to the end has shifted from almost shy tenderness to more assured address. The tension, however, between heartfelt loneliness and the reassurance of art's compensatory immortality returns suddenly with another "at" in 37. The voracious forces of loathed melancholy return to gnaw the self: "mihi" is placed directly beneath "tibi" to point the remorseless jump back to private pain; which is exacerbated perhaps by the half-formed subconscious sense that this love, now gone, was far more significant than ever realized. When the poet sits underneath the old elm (l. 15), he does not merely remember a valuable friend but realizes at once a loss of identity, of the self. Condee is right[20], I think, to point out the almost unbearably personal quality of "quis mihi fidus / haerebit lateri comes." The interrogative has now gathered to it the almost compulsive tone of a charm. Again the repetition of this charm helps to soothe the grief into a familiar form of mourning. The sense of binding in "haerebit" takes this friendship to the congruence of true minds married in learning, trust and a thousand moments of inexplicable unanimity. "Haereo" has strong sexual connotations in classical Latin (see Adams, *The Latin Sexual Vocabulary*, pp. 181–2). The habit of dependence and frequent companionship, the unthinking reliance on another, is beautifully sketched in the pastoral metaphor of Thyrsis and Damon constantly together through forest, heat, or dangers of lion or wolves. As much, however, as the rarity of this relationship was heightened in quality by the harsh world about them and nature pitched against them, so much more bitter is the sense of deprivation later. "Quis" recurs to sound the long mournful note of true elegy in 43. In the word "sopire" is contained a terrible reminder of the pain of living and the need to at least palliate time's insistence with the easy good faith of "fando." The warm pastoral air of this phrase turns in upon itself in that the words of the poem must now keep at bay the hard experience of things, doubly hard without Damon. When considering the matchless sensitivity of this verse paragraph, the exquisite cadences of the poetry that fall from remembered bliss to aching fears, it is a little disappointing to find that Condee takes the appearance of lions and wolves quite literally, and quite obtusely. Why is it so hard to understand the force of a finely modulated metaphor that enforces and vivifies the poetry in so many powerful ways? Why is it so difficult to read the pain of living, of enduring the pangs of otherness, in the presence of the loss of that one companion soul who understood the loneliness of difference, and whose friendship could provide a haven of identity amid a wilderness, as the deprivations of the roaming lion or the hungry wolf? It seems the "aurea virga" of Milton's recondite defenses really does keep out the unsympathetic, the uninitiated.

If the reader needed any clarity about the metaphoric application, Milton, ever the faithful craftsman, establishes it in the very next paragraph. The searching, the quest of the Hylas idyll, is intensified in the disconsolate questionings. "Quis solebit" is echoed in "pectora cui credam." Anxiety about the future is at odds with the mellow enjoyment of the present. "Mordaces curas" is the explicit application of the lion/wolf image. A grieving urgency is taken up by the double "quis" at lines 45–6. In searching to "lenire curas" the poetry itself, by its incantatory repetitions, is growing all the time into a substantial bulwark. One of the most graphic scenes in the poem, as many point out, is of a piece with *L'Allegro*, 80–85. Here, however, the whole scene is charged with larger significance. The security of a love so complete that its perfection was not even fully recognized is captured by the picture of a fire, that warm hearth of oneness beside which Milton and Diodati once sat, little counting their happiness. The cracking of nuts is exactly sounded in "strepitat." The merry ring reinforces Damon's "dulcibus alloquiis." The *L'Allegro* world is cast in the generosity, perhaps fallacious certainty, of a gentle fire that coddles the "molle pyrum." Line 48 is completely dactylic except for the final spondee.

The regularity of rhythm and the rare elision create a smooth flow of sound which tells of the intimate consonance between these two young men. The warning of this beguiling harmony, this *L'Allegro* idyll of youthful content, is signaled by the "at" that tails line 48. The harshness of gnawing cares in the world emerges chillingly in the "malus auster" that confounds things "outside" this cozy nest of warmth and oneness. Above the cottage of friendship's great content storms the mighty south wind amid the high branches of the elms.

In his attempt to substantiate the notion of the pastoral conventions as failed or inadequate, Nichols looks at other Neo-Latin writers. He takes the lines:

> Quis mihi blanditiasque tuas, quis tum mihi risus
> Cecropiosque sales referet, cultosque lepores?
>
> (55–6)

> What Milton did in English by mentioning names, he is here able to do by his choice of words, for the "blanditiae," the "Cecropii sales," as well as the "culti lepores" are expressions that would immediately remind his reader of the tradition of Neo-Latin amatory poetry that culminated in Johannes Secundus, in whose Basia all of these words are found, although the specific phrases used here are derived from the poems George Buchanan wrote in close imitation of Secundus. Interesting too is the fact that here in the later Neo-Latin poem Milton is not rejecting the Neo-Latin amatory mode: it has become impossible for him now that his friend is dead and he is alone.[21]

Nichols is here, as elsewhere, a little too decisive and final in his conclusion. Milton could be using the amatory mode in the allusive subtext as a way of telling others that he bore great love towards Diodati, as much perhaps as some men feel for women — certainly something beyond friendship or even romantic friendship. There is a flaw in the logic that dictates that because Diodati is dead, the amatory significance of the references ceases to function. To compound matters, Nichols goes on to conclude that there is a:

> "central problem for the poet-singer in a Renaissance pastoral eclogue: the failure of love — an obvious consequence of the disappearance of the beloved — may imply the failure of poetry itself."[22]

Once again there are various assumptions here. It does not follow that love has gone with the death of the beloved. Many who have lost loved ones gain in their appreciation and recognition of that love after the beloved has died. Sudden realization of how deep and central that love was becomes one of the major impediments to consolation. The problem for the bereaved is how to carry on living in a way that does justice to the present and abiding memory of someone greatly admired. If the beloved was, like Diodati, West or Hallam, a true believer in the poet's talents, then poetry will not fail but instead will be the very means of living out that love of the sustaining friend. The challenge will be to craft a major work, and so fashion it, that no one will willingly let it pass into obscurity. The art becomes exactly the means of fulfilling a life worthy of the beloved's memory and self. Again, the song is anything but a failed one.

The image of remembered satisfaction is in itself a trap, however, and the temptation of nostalgic unreality billows out in the early part of this paragraph (ll. 51–4). Now a summer scene recreates in full the soporific haze of the balmy Sicilian brush with the cicadas bleating in the heat. The desire to sleep, to forget the anxiety of life, is portrayed in the drowsy Pan replete in the shade of the oak taking his nap ("somnum capit"). Pan is "abditus"; the nymphs seeking "sedilia sub aquis" and the shepherds sheltering from the heat combine to suggest a hiding from reality. The Sicilian landscape is used here to indicate a world of escape to which Thyrsis's memory quickly takes him. The laborer snoring is a return to the light, comic tone of that *L'Allegro* world once familiar from his friendship with Diodati. But the dark shadow of the "quis ... mihi" pattern claims the mourner's mind again. The poet cannot shake himself loose from the feelings of unfairness, wrongness and pain.

Line 55 is an example of deliberate repetition, the mournful tolling of the curfew bell of remembered loss used to intensify the hungry melancholy that preys on the mind again and again. The phrases "blanditias" and "risus," "cecropios sales" and "cultos lepores" indicate but the pale remnants of a lively love now clutched at, but fled in its old form. Line 58 opens with another "at" to continue the reversals that mark lines 14, 23 and 37. To entrench the sense of a reluctant confrontation of the present infelicitous state, "iam" is doubled: "now" ... "now" to match "solus" twice: "alone ... alone." There is a reworking of lines 5–8 taken in turn for the frightening account of Hercules raging at the loss of his beautiful boy, scouring the countryside for him. But from the Theocritean source and Milton's initial lines to the recurrent motif here, there is a perceptible development. The wildness and passion have passed: the precipitate rush of line 6 has weakened and the current force of the participle "pererrans" has submitted to the simple, aimless wandering of "oberro" in line 58 and the lonely vigil of "expecto" in 60.

This is one of the blackest paragraphs in the poem, marking a nadir of misery and wan hope. Section 7 of *In Memoriam* echoes much of it:

> Dark house, by which once more I stand
> Here in the long unlovely street,
> Doors where my heart was used to beat
> So quickly, waiting for a hand,
> A hand that can be clasped no more —
> Behold me, for I cannot sleep,
> And like a guilty thing I creep
> At earliest morning to the door.
> He is not here; but far away
> The noise of life begins again,
> And ghastly through the drizzling rain
> On the bald street breaks the blank day.

Here too in Milton's epitaph for Diodati, it raineth every day, as the dejected lover tries to lose himself in the darkest recesses of the forest, waiting for night's sympathetic cloak. Lines 61–2 echo more fully the grim blast in lines 48–9. "Triste" recalls the savage regrets of Ovid's banishment: to Thyrsis this once-happy world is now just such a place of cruel exile. And of course to the sensitive undergraduate poet who felt so keenly the sneering alienation of his peers, exile has a double force: not merely the loss of a particular friend but the return of an alien world. The cold winds roar and tear the crepuscular stillness; boughs sway grotesquely, throwing shadows across the darkening earth. The deepening gloom of Gray's twilight landscape is charged with the same sense of a failing world, in which the one light of a recognizing and validating companion consciousness glimmers and fades into the night of adult isolation. The ugly sound of line 61 works much as the cacophony of line 124 of *Lycidas*: it catches up the misery and disruption felt by the poet. How suddenly the beauty and harmony have fled and deformity taken its place. Once again there are decisive parallels in the lost garden state of Eden:

> On th'other side, Adam, soon as he heard
> The fatal trespass don by Eve, amaz'd,
> Astonied stood and Blank, while horror chill
> Ran through his veins, and all his joints relaxd;
> From his slack hand the Garland wreath'd for Eve
> Down dropd, and all the faded roses shed.
>
> (P.L., IX.888–93)

The loss of Arcadia, the loss of once-possessed youthful joy and innocence, the loss of Diodati, is the emotional mainspring of the epic. The later work echoes this central, perhaps the only, major romantic crisis of Milton's life. The truncation of his happy years in Horton, under his father's protection, the cruel shadow upon his tour of Europe, the intrusion of death on the unsuspecting youths, the suddenness of that complete ruination, and the bold, obscene prominence of alienating, grimacing evil — all of these are worked out on a huge scale in his epic. Milton's choice of topic, the loss of an early paradise, is a clear indication of his own experience resurfacing in the retrospective of old age.

In differing ways, all of these great elegies by Milton, Gray and Tennyson range outwards from individual deaths to confront the enduring problem of evil: that horrible change in estate which disturbs the carefree innocence of youth, all the youthful perfection of old Elsinore, once known, now ruined.

All about him Thyrsis sees the unweeded garden; his once "culta arva." His world so well ordered and complete is now destroyed by neglect. How can we blindly continue to trench our allotted ground in the face of such injustice? The "seges," the crop of his labors that should be on this earth, is run to seed; the vine has no support, and is "innuba" like himself, widowed, without the support of a mate. Everywhere the external signs of abandonment mirror the problems that cluster about his forlorn state. The green court around him does not mourn in sympathy as that of Moschus in his lament for Bion:

> And in sorrow for thy fall the trees cast down their fruit, and all the flowers have faded. From the ewes hath flowed no fair milk, nor honey from the hives, nay, it hath perished for mere sorrow in the wax, for now hath thy honey perished, and no more it behoves men to gather honey. (fifth stanza) [23]

In *Epitaphium Damonis* the garden is an image of the good Christian's earthly care. The rank weeds in it, the untended crop, upbraid the earthly laborer for his wasted time and talents. But the will to work, the reason of it, has been killed, so that the poet is aimless and left searching, not only for the lost one but for the meaning and purpose that his love gave to things, the ordering force of his friendship. The fruit of the vine is "neglected" and the poor dumb sheep, which should be his first concern in this world, turn their hungry eyes upon a master who is too deeply drowned in sorrow to notice their piteous looks: "inque suum convertunt ora magistrum" (l. 67).

The insistence of the refrain is no weakness in the poetry. It reflects the fundamental problem of immobility in the face of grief: why bother with duty, work or life when the intrusion of death, injustice and evil is so rampant and random? From this paralysis of the will the poet has to recover some justifying impulse to overcome the seemingly absurd course of things.

Thyrsis is blind to the flourishing nature about him that was once so harmonious, now so cruel. One shepherd calls to the hazels, the other to the mountain ashes, all quite oblivious to the disruption of Damon's death. The intricate patterning of 69–72 is some of the most highly wrought in the poem: two couplets each containing four precisely ordered phrases marked first by "ad" four times then "hic" four times:

> Tityrus ad corylos vocat, Alphesiboeus ad ornos,
> Ad salices Aegon, ad flumina pulcher Amyntas,
> Hic gelidi fontes, hic illita gramina musco,
> Hic Zephyri, hic placidas interstrepit arbutus undas,
>
> (*E.D.*, 69–72)

This complex figure of echoing calls draws attention to the here and now of a nature venerated about him but to which Thyrsis is lost. He is "surdo": deaf to its blandishments, scared to trust that growing, changing life that bloomed only to poison his one happiness. He retires to a dark melancholy grotto, away from life.

Lines 75–80 capture exactly the light gossipy quality of the shepherds' world. The speech rhythms are caught by various means, such as the parenthetic afterthought of 76 and the quick alteration of "aut" in 78. The superstition revealed in 79–80 caricatures the dangerous naiveté of the pastoral world: childlike innocence turned to childish ignorance of the real state of a harsh, seemingly unjust and uncaring universe.

The effect of these short paragraphs is subtly to condition the despair of Thyrsis's opening cries; the black melancholy of 60 may now be seen as sullenness beside the immediate and lively energy of the other shepherds. Thyrsis refuses to "turn to life." Who is he to be so singular in his grief? Is this grief for Damon, or self-pity? The lighthearted inquiry of the well-meaning friends, their wonder, now seems to criticize the too obdurate misery of Thyrsis. There are no fellow mourners, no bands of grief-stricken shepherds intoning a funeral dirge, just as there was no wilting nature or outraged gods. Nature, friends, divinities are indifferent. This love furthermore is apart and Thyrsis must bear his loss in double part. The words "quid … futurum est" (l. 82) sound the call to negotiation of this misery. The repeated "veruit" of 88 and 90 tells of the visitors who come more in curiosity than to share his heartsore. Word has got around. But "oculi truces" and "vultu severi" have no place in the palmy world of bucolic song, that youthful domain of "iuventae" which Milton, now scorched by experience, has to quit. From now on the pastoral song he sings will ever be burdened with recollected joy and never recall the clear descant of unreflective, spontaneous delight. When Thyrsis weeps that nothing, nothing, nothing, "nil, nil, nil," can ever move him again, there is enough stubbornness in the determined cry to mark that point in the process of grieving where the subject has worked out the first passions and shocks sufficiently to prefer that state of sightless melancholy to the next even more palpably painful stage of thinking and adjusting to a lonely future: "nil me, si quid adest, movet, aut spes ulla futuri" (l. 92). Echoing 82, the word "futuri" recurs to conclude line 92, the last of the short paragraph sections to reinforce the need to turn from loud complaint to integration of past love into present life. The "blanditiae" and sweet "solacia" of the simple shepherd folk reveal the perspective of common life, an adjusting light to a sadness which now borders too closely on self-indulgence in willful grief. The end of the second movement of this song sees the end of the anxiously searching interrogatives— no more will Thyrsis cry out for "quis mihi." Bereavement has been masterfully and tenderly modulated by the flowing and interwoven poetry of this searing threnody on life.

At line 93 begins the third movement of the poem. To mark this new section clearly "hei mihi" is used at the head of line 94, after the refrain line, to echo the starting point of the short paragraph section at line 19. Here the plaintive words have quite a different ring. From lamentation, the poem has moved to contemplation. The speaker now reflects in meditative and poised verse. The period for sobbing protestation is past. Now Milton looks over things as a whole. This remarkable verse paragraph is at the heart of the poem's consolatory argument. Here, most distinctly, the poet goes beyond the source texts and argues most lucidly about the obstacles and peculiarities of human pairing. If anywhere in the poem there is evidence of the poet's acute awareness of difference, it is to be found here. The paragraph as a whole takes up the word "pecus" in line 25. The poet considers how easy it is for the herd and, we suspect, for the ordinary herd of humans. The young bullocks, single males, are all equally attached to each other: they exist in a herd. No particular soulmate is selected as the lifelong friend of a single animal. Wolves or shaggy-haired asses do much the same; they move in herds, a shared fate. But human beings need one particular mate — a rare, answering identity, a fulfillment. The poet lays his finger on the real source of pain. His love for Charles is no ordinary attachment, no bovine yoking, rather it is a profound empathy that draws mind and soul together, nearer than brothers, or man and wife. Wolves form a pack for food, hairy asses seek their proper mates and, even in the sea, seals are counted in groups. It is telling that he selects images of animal groups while he himself falls outside and is left without any immediate consolation for his otherness. Even the ordinary sparrow always has its mate. If death should strike, not long an answering call will meet the lonely bird's pining song and "protinus ille alium socio petit inde volatu" (105). Crucial lines of the poem follow: 106–11. With human beings there is no such easy partnering, particularly when the candidate is someone like Milton who is unlikely to find even one true love, one utterly responsive companion, an intellectual consort, to assuage the roughness of life (108). This would be as true of Gray or Tennyson. Finding this one true life companion proved hard for Milton. Earlier, line 86 tells us that he who loves late is doubly wretched; the line could actually have meant that he who finds but too late that he has been in love all the time is doubly wretched at the sudden death of the beloved. The full impact of his feelings for the young Diodati only struck Milton later and quite gradually as he discovered the difficulties of finding anything like that same accord. I do not believe he ever again got near it, so that part of his life with Diodati closed over together with his youth. The pastoral world of unsuspecting and innocent joy is the perfect metaphor for such a closure.

The significance of this death cannot be underestimated, for it is both the deeply scored emotional death of the poet's youth and the physical demise of Diodati. The poet who wrote brightly and wittily to Diodati in *Elegies* I and VII is gone. Where is that sprightly quality, that eclogue spontaneity now? The artist of *L'Allegro* is saddened and graver and is moving perceptibly on to the great artist of *Samson Agonistes*. This lost love lacerated him and the pain, the sense of surprised agony, is observable in the vocabulary and tone of the lines that close this pivotal verse paragraph:

> Aut si sors dederit tandem non aspera votis,
> Illum inopina dies qua non speraveris hora
> Surripit, aeternum linquens in saecula damnum.
>
> (109–11)

"Aspera" "aeternum damnum" are the terms of disillusionment and experience. What is of interest to the reader is to see how this poet built up his own characteristic world view; from the ashes of desolation, he constructed enough of a sense of faith and value to console his burning pain of otherness, enough to allow him to return to meet his duty to others. No wonder that the phoenix is the triumphant concluding symbol of the poem (187). For it is in the challenge and achievement of overcoming such a particularly painful private misery that his poetic vision claims our attention. By an extraordinary irony, the outsider poet, stripped of the customary consolation of social belonging, the self in naked isolation, is peculiarly representative of the radical solitude of much general human existence. Exclusion has somehow forced the poet to envisage and record a radical state of loneliness, which for many others is happily disguised by the provisional organization of conformist society. What the poet quite rightly observes as the singularly harsh lot cast to him is, in terms of the challenge to his art, a particularly testing crucible of the imagination. The depth of such isolation prompts the poet to consider fundamentally the reason for being. The responses made by Milton, Gray and Tennyson are so profound and encapsulating of the individual thought and that of their times that the texts came to be revered by society as a whole and thus enshrined.

If the critic should cry out that it is *Lycidas*, not *Epitaphium Damonis*, that is revered by generations of English scholars, of course I should answer that *Lycidas* may not be about King so much as Milton. The poem centers on the predicament of death and existence, the questions of Why carry on? Why bother? What's the point? These questions are actuated and accentuated by the poet's own social isolation, his otherness. *Lycidas*, the epics, and most of the rest of the huge Miltonic corpus, his writings against the system, against the king, against divorce laws or censorship laws—all have a direct relation to his raw sense of otherness, the pain of exclusion, of being mocked for his difference, of his refusal to be silenced and his need to be heard. The elegiac form in English is justly famous, for there the poet apprehends the very issues of death and consolatory art/Christian duty as typical of his best thought and in beautiful language. But there is a deep, personal, felt agony that binds the Latin version to the Hylas idyll (Theocritus XIII), and in turn links Gray's *Elegy* and *In Memoriam*. *Lycidas* and *Epitaphium Damonis* are mirror pieces: one is in a more accessible language but is a lesser grief; the other is in a more distant language but is a greater grief. The two poems are twins and often have been read that way most profitably. It is a mark of the literary development of the day that *Epitaphium Damonis* is more attached and passionate yet submerged in the language of learning while its more detached brother is in English. By the eighteenth century the vernacular emerges as the dominant if carefully guarded text, leaving the passionate lines of *Ad Favonium* still quite hidden in Neo-Latin. Much of the manner of Gray's *Elegy* has been assimilated from *Epitaphium Damonis*: the precisely turned short paragraphs, the imperceptibly graduated process of grief and the meticulously well-connected page. Gray's Latin lament is short, but a vital link in the lyric voice, the immediate and pained intimacy of grief. Here is the linchpin that brings the infinite tenderness of *Epitaphium Damonis* to the *Elegy*. In *In Memoriam* the stylized movement, the apparently effortless elegiac of highly wrought sections, the ritual of mourning, the process of grief — all have been brought to perfection in a perfected vernacular.

The next of the now much longer paragraphs begins "heu quis" (113) but after the crucially contemplative, bravely self-exploratory previous paragraph "heu quis" here has, for the first time, a sound of resignation. The rage of deprivation has passed over into wistful regret. No longer are there anxious calls for who will comfort one now. "Quis" in line 113 qualifies "error" to point the way to a separating of the two lives. Milton blames himself for traveling so far away. This self-reproach is a transition stage in accepting what has happened. The neglect of his flock, of his duty here, is turned about as not a result but a cause of his grief. Had he not left England and his responsibilities, there would not have been so many mountains, streams and rocks between them. The poet's fixed concern with the paralyzing pain of loss alone has shifted. In some ways the recognition of finality now cuts most deeply into the conscious mind. The paragraph works towards the concluding three lines which must surely be some of the most beautiful and exquisitely phrased sentences of pathos written by the poet. These were the lines that attracted Rowse's attention and caused him to write that nowhere else does Milton write with greater personal feeling. I believe that this is true, as it is of Tennyson in *In Memoriam*. Here are the lines that superbly conclude this transitional, valedictory paragraph:

> Ah certe extremum licuisset tangere dextram
> Et bene compositos placide morientis ocellos,
> Et dixisse vale, nostri memor ibis ad astra.

> Ah! surely I could have been allowed one last touch of your hand, and your eyes well composed in peaceful death. And to have said farewell mindful of us as you mount up to the stars.

The sense of infinite longing, the desire merely to have touched the beloved's hand yet once more, and finally, is introduced by the long sigh at the front of line 121 and undercut harshly by the legalistic constraint in "licuisset." The tension between that wished-for love and youth so irreverently, freely enjoyed and the young poet's first bitter experience is perfectly conveyed by the plea in "certe" and the heartless determination of "licuisset." But that desire is still spun out into the next lines: these tenderest lines are pure love song and written with that plaintive cadence which is Milton at the height of his powers. There could be no finer testimony to the rarity and depth of his love for Diodati than is contained here. The wish for his final touch outlives the fact of his cruel separation. What end of gentleness is there in the softly echoing "bene" and "placide?" So much of the agony rung from the earlier sections accumulates and is resolved in this elegiac valediction. Now at last to say it: farewell. The words of the poet, the worthy tribute of his song, are what must softly compose his loved one's eyes. The fingers that long for his touch, touch him now in words. This finality, this moment of reaching out artistically, is articulated in the next line: "et dixisse vale." The torment is modulated through art into an apotheosis of the loved one "nostri memor ibit ad astra." Truly blended, the poetry indeed takes up to immortality the love he felt for Diodati. This is the epitaph, this the offering of his skills, the reworking of the Sicilian sources and the heritage of a funerary form and tone for that rare love which Gray and Tennyson were to draw on so fully. Where else but here does the Victorian poet laureate take some of his most famous lines:

> Doors where my heart was used to beat
> So quickly, not one that weeps
> I come once more; the city sleeps;
> I smell the meadow in the street;
> I hear a chirp of birds; I see
> Betwixt the black fronts long-withdrawn
> A light-blue lane of early dawn,
> And think of early days and thee,
> And bless thee, for thy lips are bland
> And bright the friendship of thine eye;
> And in my thoughts with scarce a sigh
> I take the pressure of thine hand.

(119.1–12)

From this point on Milton begins the resolution of his debilitating melancholy. He realizes that not fame, nor glittering achievement, nor storied urn, nor animated bust, is the monument and end of life's purpose but to have been loved and loved deeply: better indeed to have loved and lost that love than never to have loved at all. He is the monument, his life and art are the living incorporation of Diodati.

In the next paragraph he turns around his self-reproach for going to Italy. In doing so, he pulls the poem about as a consequent argument for living. "Numquam meminisse pigebit," never will he regret his tribute to the pastoral muses. (I wish Nichols had read this again before he spoke of the failed song.) Never will he regret Italy for, as he deftly points out,

Damon himself was Tuscan. The beloved and the country of his muses are one. Now there is the first suggestion of a renewed attention to his flock, his care of letters. He recalls singing with other poets in Italy. The ephemeral heedlessness of youth, complete in its own brief world, is drawn differently now. The poet is not torn by its loss and distraught at its unjust ending. He looks back with a certain distance and considers himself: this self-reflexivity is an important mark in the winning of consolation. He considers his own state past "o ego quantus eram." When he regards this unfearing youth, there is some slight criticism in the description of himself picking now violets, now the tips of myrtles. The line is too neatly symmetrical not to betray the preciousness of carefree (careless) youth.

The following paragraph takes up the criticism and throws the poet forward into his work. The dream section, 140–52, is rebutted by the second half, 153–60. The tension so frequently remarked upon through the poem as a whole, between the idyllic world and the real world, is dramatically presented by the clash between these two sections. Even while "te cinis ater habebat," the reckless Thyrsis is imagining what Damon now is doing. While Thyrsis is pining, he freely imagines the future with Damon. Now they will be together in the shade or should they travel to the waters of Colne (near his father's estate at Horton)? The blithe young shepherd falls into that uncertain zone of self-delusion, in which the mourner refuses to accept final loss but prefers to meander through imagined scenes of happiness, together with the beloved, as if living. This state, a trap to many bereaved souls, is fatal and the poet has to discover some way to escape its vortex of deceptions. He fails to see how dangerously and narrowly the territories of light and darkness exist beside each other. Thyrsis thinks he sees Damon gathering herbs, "tua gramina, succos." The brief flower catalogue so reminiscent of *Lycidas*, 132–151, is a last tribute to the Horton period of the poet's own life. Suddenly the lilt of 152 is overturned with the repeated "pereant, pereant" and answering construction of 153 "damn the wretched weeds." The playthings of youth are no guard against the sea of troubles that engulfs adulthood. If he is to take his commitment to the love of Diodati seriously, then his music must be of a deeper tone, such that people will not willingly let die. He moves his lips to the epic mode and the poor pastoral pipes burst asunder. This is not, however, the failure of the pastoral but the coming of age of the poet. Rather, the pastoral threnody is the surety for its later dedicatory masterpiece, exactly as it was in Virgil. By promising a greater work, by dedicating himself to poetry in remembrance of Diodati, Milton makes the pastoral the very center of his projected epic and of course we know from the finished work just how true this is.

In the next stanza he announces this intention. He will write a great poem. He must think in realistic terms of a suitable and realizable measure of his talents and of Charles's expectations of him. His consolation must be the memorial of his work and, at that, such a theme as befits his "ingenio, doctrina." This was once a plan that he was treasuring to share with Damon. But now it will be a tribute to that love to marshal his powers and produce one strong enduring masterpiece. The clear announcement and determination in "dicam" in 163 is the substantial promise of a work that was previously an idea only toyed with "lenta sub cortice." The indeterminate quality of the imperfect verb "servabam" catches up the mood of youthful fancy and is contrasted by the clarity of adult responsibility in "dicam." The death of Diodati, the loss of that one person with whom he could identify, that "parem de milibus ... unum," the sudden realization of the rarity of that love, strikes a shattering but also formative blow to the young person. From now on his life and work must be a memorial to the high qualities of that love; his time must be a working out of those principles. The airy ideas of youth must, *gratia Damonis*, be encased in art. So from the grave of a dead friend arises the deathless achievement of art, the dedication of a life, the emblem of the phoenix. The loss of those very values and temper that were so peculiarly suited to his own must be redeemed by the skills given him.

Fittingly, in the penultimate paragraph, Milton holds up a two-handled cup, a gift from the Italian subject of another Latin poem, Manso. The work is well wrought, an image of art, the crafted prize of artistic endeavor. On one side is painted a phoenix rising from the ashes, the good sign of Milton's own life dedicated in love rising from the ashes of melancholy grief. On the other side is Amor, but not the ribald Eros, the lust that drove Hercules to despair and causes so many of the eclogues to be threaded with lewd allusions. This Amor is apparently Eros transformed into a desire for godly Love.

This cup of Mansus, of course, recalls that other two-handled cup given as a prize to Thyrsis in Idyll 1. There is no consolation for Hercules's passion in XIII and Milton deftly merges the consolation of art into the lament. From 125 onwards the poem depends on a resolution of grief, a transformation of Diodati's friendship and the assimilation of the Daphnis idyll. This assimilation is remarkable, taking the poem out of the torturing flux of life into the teasing stasis of art. The meticulously formed cup of ivy wood presented to Thyrsis has long been recognized as an image of this redemptive quality of art. Similarly it is a token of the poet's power to grant immortality to his subject. Theocritus was fully conscious of this, and who would know of Odysseus without Homer's poetic celebration of him? Theocritus calls upon the epic tradition of highly decorated artifacts such as the shield of Achilles. Theocritus's heroes, those admonitory and valuable figures he considers as worthy of literary preservation, those bucolic characters cut from humble orders are heroes of a new type, not conquering heroes but exquisitely human. (They, and their ethos, are what Gray reveres in his *Elegy*.) In continuing this reference, Milton also holds up for consideration a range of characters and a rare love as worthy of immortality in verse. At the same time the epic allusion behind Milton's Theocritean source has a powerful application in terms of the English poet's own promise to build an epic song in the vernacular. Thus, with typical Miltonic fidelity, Manso's cup works in three ways: as redemptive art, immortalizing Damon's love, and pointing forward to the epic work. The wonderment of this cup "mirum artis opus" (183) is a record of the joy felt at living through grief and growing stronger by it: Tennyson's white funeral. The song of happiness that follows is a recovery of that identity once secured in his relationship with Charles. That loss has been thought through too, and the poet has regained his own voice and autonomy, understanding the purpose of his art more clearly than ever — that of crafting the epitaph with infinite care has itself been a consolatory process but the experience of feeling and thinking through the seriousness of his devotion to Diodati has chiefly returned to him that gift of confident song.

Critics struggle with this complex passage. It helps I think to trace the poem to its passionate wellspring and thus integrate the allusive background and appreciate the triumphant quality of the last section. This poem records a crucial point in the making of a poet and Milton celebrates his sense of triumphing over debilitating melancholy through a dedication to his discipline and his faith.

Milton is acutely sensitive about his otherness, his awareness that he does not fit in and is not part of the *pecus*. He therefore delights in the erudition of that one domain, of the mind, in which he is a free citizen. (In this way he returns the favor of exclusion as well.) Because of his delight in erudition (in bookishness from the *pecus* point of view) it is dangerous not to follow up minutely his allusions, which are never haphazard or thin. So critics touch on the phoenix image but do not relate it to the force of art over life or Milton's own winning back of his love for Damon. The phoenix is a fitting image for anyone who knows the agony of bereavement and the hard-won conquest of living through it. The magical bird is also an icon: of immortality (it is "vivax" in Ovid's terms) and of poetry comprising the quintessence of life. *Epitaphium Damonis* is the permanent essence of refining love. Milton is the right poet, the poet-maker, who, like Gray and Tennyson to follow, makes something beautiful and lasting from the pain of an unforgettable yet deeply humanizing love in otherness. This is the general and primary application of the phoenix image, which is perfectly crafted in its references and complexity as a suitable climactic moment in the poem's argument. Yet we must follow Milton even more closely to recover the precious nuggets of gold. The phoenix is a mysterious bird and is representative of life eternal. It is a symbol of resurgent life and a refashioned self.

The bird is described as "unica." "Phoenix unica" is a phrase from Ovid's *Amores*. In a lighthearted passage about the death of his mistress's parrot, Naso catalogues the birds that will attend the funeral of such an important companion. Against the ironic/erotic background there are the following verses, tongue in cheek, but in highly competent funerary mode:

> colle sub Elysio nigra nemus ilice frondet,
>   udaque perpetuo gramine terra viret.
> siqua fides dubiis, volucrum locus ille piarum
>   dicitur, obscenae quo prohibentur aves.
> illic innocui late pascuntur olores
>   et vivax phoenix, unica semper avis.
> explicat ipsa suas ales Junonia pinnas;
>   oscula dat cupido blanda columba mari.
> psittacus, has inter nemorali sede receptus,
>   convertit volucres in sua verba pias.
>
>   (*Amores* II.vi 49–58)

Under a hill in Elysium, a grove of black ilex grows, and the ground is ever moist and green. There, to the bird of faith, is the good birds' heaven, barred to all birds of prey. Harmless swans feed there at large with the long-lived solitary phoenix. Peacocks give spontaneous displays, and amorous doves kiss and coo. They have welcomed Parrot to a perch of honour and applaud his pious ejaculations.[24]

The swan is a noble bird of beauty and rarity known for its extraordinary fidelity to a single mate. By contrast the phoenix is "unica." So Milton, once wandering lost and searching for his other half, has now incorporated the love of Diodati through a process of suffering and resolution of pain. He has regained a new and potent autonomy in his dedication to art. He too is "unicus," unpaired, not needing to be paired now; he is alone, more consciously different, but himself and Diodati together. Picking up this reference from *Amores* allows Milton to bid farewell to the lighthearted, chatty tone of his own early *Sylvarum liber* which he wrote in the Ovidian tradition as well as the erotic in general; he and his work will now be like the long-lived, solitary phoenix. (This is no idle claim for he *has* been read and reread ever since.) This marks finally the transition from the love cry of the wild flames of Hercules's love for Hylas to the incandescent, constant light of a disciplined poetic self. Together with this sense of poetic election, which Milton had long felt but now realized intensely through his dedication to Damon, there is the sense of religious election. His virginity, the source of jibes at the university and a sign of his nonheterosexual self to the bigots of his society, is thus, in typical Miltonian fashion, taken as a virtue. The precedent and role of "Virgilianus vates" is adopted and sex is something unclean. So at lines 212–14 Damon is particularly celebrated for his unsullied, virgin state. The accord between pure men is infinitely higher to him than the troubled marriage bed. His love for Diodati will always preserve his mind and soul within the precincts of his art and faith as "unica": unique, alone, other. His work will be "vivax" enduring.

Camerarius,[25] in his book of emblems, makes this aspect of the phoenix's signification clear. The first volume of this compendious work was printed in 1590 and would thus almost certainly have been available to Milton. The phoenix is the last emblem of the book and therefore it is granted a conclusive prominence exactly as in Milton's poem. The magical bird betokens the resurrection and particularly the merited immortality in faith of a person dedicated to righteousness, one whose whole life and useful talents testify to the zeal of this virtuous pursuit. The phoenix is the resolution of the main concerns of the poem. With extraordinary virtuosity the poet allows one association after another to connect and conclude themes in the poem until this symbol resonates with that peculiarly satisfying conclusiveness that marks great art.

As soon as this point is reached and the argument fulfilled however, as soon as there is sublimity in the great lines of "Parte alia polus omnipatens, & magnus Olympus" (190), the poet turns to rejoicing over his achievement with a sense of robust certainty. This allows him in the next line of the penultimate paragraph, 191–7, to speak in jollity of the rosy-cheeked Cupid. There is a witty undertone to the quick parenthetic question "Quis putet?" as if to say, "now who would have expected the venturous intrusion of Love into the company of such profound matters as the sublimity of art over life?" Here is the other side of the Manso vase as well as the other side of Milton's love. If the phoenix is a grave emblem of his love turned to Love, then the figure of Amor is bright with that vivacity now regained in a fully comprehended poetics of life. Once more the ignoble and gossipy, the prying eyes of an insensitive and prurient "vulgus" are warded off. This perfectly links the early separation of the "pecus" by the "aurea virga" ("Not trivial souls and the ignoble hearts of the rabble does he smite thence," 193). Here that exquisite love between men of true minds, their marriage within the private bounds of the intellectual and religious elect, is celebrated. Amor is that love refined that strikes his sacred arrows into the hearts of his chosen few and thus inspires them to regain that "erected wit" of which Sidney speaks.[26] I am not sure that there is not some erotic ripple in this glassy surface however. The tone of quis putet," the arrows which "in erectum spargit sua tela" may just take up the double entendre in "virga," thus brilliantly enclosing the poem in the themes of eros and philia. But primarily the drawing of Amor is set to illumine the poem in its celebration of triumphantly achieved consolation in the final paragraph.

The integration of Diodati's love within the living memorial of his dedicated companion's affection, the coalescence of art and love is pointed to by the repetition of "quoque" in his "sancta simplicitas" and "candida virtus." Diodati will be enshrined in the now-fixed aspiration of the young man as an artist. For this reason tears for that less-understood youthful attachment of earlier days are out of place when something greater and more worthy has arisen from the "cinis ater" of the lifeless flesh. "Nec te," nec tibi" replicate the guarantee of Diodati's transcendent apotheosis; he will always be a part of Milton. With the artist's regained vision and rededication of poetic purpose, his recovered artistic identity in otherness, as "unicus," Damon's virtue will ever be the proximate deity of Milton's being. So the shepherd returns full of confidence and joy to his earthly tasks and trials ahead of him: no longer "ite impasti agni" but "ite lachrymae." Damon soars in the lively imagination of the artist's mind above, dashing with his foot the splendid colored arc of the rainbow. The sense of Damon's vir-tus (manly virtue) as admired hero, as the leader, is just suggested in his company in heaven: "heroumque animas inter, divosque perennes" (l. 205).

Diodati's loving superintendence is assured in "dexter ades." This answers the plangent lament of 38: "quis mihi." The more retiring boy was terrified without the guardianship of the adored hero and is now returned to that warm and secure protection. By virtue of the double song of Epitaphium Damonis, joining the pastoral dirge drawn from Theocritus XIII to the consolation of art from I, the young Damon, recipient of those witty, intimate poems of Milton's salad days, will always be remembered in the words of bucolic innocence, while Diodati, the man of extraordinary virtue and grace, will be ever-present as the mature poet's artistic ward.

Lines 215–19 take the poem into the heady delight and wild celebration of mystic rites. The love they celebrate together is service to the Hebrew god and there is the riotous ringing of cymbals and the victory of the world's redeemer. Death and its pall of melancholy are thrown aside in prospect of the radiant godhead. The palm of triumph is held in his hand, his head bears the luminous crown of sainthood. The strains of the Grecian lyre, the pastoral mode, are mingled freely and voluptuously with the victory song of Israel. The conformation of the bacchic rapture, the poet's afflatus, to the divine mystery of Christian faith is exactly phrased in the juxtaposition of pagan with divine vocabulary: the "furit lyra" of the rhapsodist is framed in the "choreis beatis" of Christian election. The wild fury of the orgy is grafted to the thyrsus of Israel. The privilege of the intellectual elect, steeped in the learning of Greece, is mingled freely with the assurance of the Puritan chosen few, thus adducing in one the poet's sustaining strengths and substantial consolation in art and faith. This is no failed song surely, but the first, glorious intimation of a poetic supremacy forged, I believe, in the crucible of otherness.

In an article about Milton and Diodati, Shawcross begins at the end of the epitaph — with this great poetic finale. He entitles his article "Psychobiographical Perspective — Milton and Diodati: An Essay in Psychodynamic Meaning."[27] The title alone does almost more damage than good I fear. Instead of an attempt to recover the beauty of a rare love, this heavy-handed treatment puts Milton on the couch. Shawcross writes:

> At the conclusion of the *Epitaphium Damonis*, a Neo-Latin elegy on the death of his friend Charles Diodati, John Milton makes a curious pagan-Christian collocation:
>
>> You, encircled around your head with a shining crown and riding in happy bowers entwined with palm leaves, shall pursue eternally the immortal marriage where song and mingled lyre rage with blessed dances, and festal orgies revel under the Thyrsis of Sion. (215–19)
>
> Diodati, now an angel of pure air (203–4), is haloed and resident in the happy bowers of paradise. Earthly bowers of earthly bliss are made, we know from *Comus*, of "hyacinth and roses" (male and female symbols); in contrast such bowers as Diodati's are created by "Flowers of more mingled hew," entwined with palm leaves— the palm of the victor's struggle, of the multitude singing before the throne of God (Revelation vii.9). But Diodati does not simply rest in his bower: he is "riding" ("gestans"). The word has the obvious meaning of spinning round in his heavenly orbit like all angelic intelligences, but also the commonplace physical meaning of sexual intercourse.

And so it continues until the end. There he argues, concerning Milton and his father: "Milton writes: 'Now since it has fallen to me to have been born a poet' (*Ad Patrem*, 61), a line susceptible of more meaning when we consider physical-emotional-psychological make-up and categoric role-playing."[28]

There is something wearying about this sort of post-Lawrentian discovery of sex everywhere and amateur psychology in all places. The Empire State Building must be a symbol of the grossest phallic obsession and the whole of Manhattan island no more than a shameless orgy of indulgent tower worship — high, unassailable, erect and massive. Whereas, of course, it is no such thing, but merely the need to provide office space for lots of people in a very restricted area. One is reminded a little of the bathos in *Northanger Abbey,* the hope of uncovering a gruesome hoard turns to no more than reels of laundry lists. In reading Milton psychodynamically Shawcross argues well that the friendship between the two young men was full of homoerotic desire but one tends to say, "So what?" Rather than exhibiting the beauty and wonderful strengths of the rather neglected Neo-Latin elegy, this type of analysis, however well meant, tends to attract the wrong sort of attention to the work. To begin by suggesting that there is double entendre threaded throughout the text is not difficult: one can read sex into a Mexican landscape of cacti or a Swiss scene of wide lakes and huge mountains. To suggest that Milton is leering at a secret readership with notions of being ridden by Diodati seems unlikely and a little damaging to the text, not to mention its place in a tradition. As for "categoric role-playing" I, for one, am puzzled as much as I am challenged by the prospect of "physical-emotional-psychological make-up." Shawcross does not show how the poem itself, or the writing of poetry, or the relationship between art and life is associated with a love of deep and enduring intensity. Nor does he seem to feel the pain of loss or the profound relation between the poem and the cruel passage of grieving a loved one. Death features very seldom in his commentary. This article tends to make sensational what should be treated with the utmost care and circumspection. Love that was carefully and tenderly placed in a learned language, protected from prying eyes and vulgar interpretation, deserves to be read most sensitively within the tradition as well as within the poet's oeuvre as a whole. Probably I have nowhere near attained this degree of sensitivity in reading the poem in my slow and close way. Milton's erudition, like Gray's, is terrifying and one frequently feels like an invasive barbarian. But of one thing I am sure. I believe John Milton loved Charles Diodati and that he recorded that love in what is probably his most personal and beautiful work.

The most tenuous underlying suppositions in a psychodynamic reading are that sex rather than love is primary and that sex itself is a universal: it is a biological given, a contained and identifiable impulse which finds
expression (or repression) in outer social forms. I think the complex
nature of a shifting relationship has to be read in terms of the social con-
ditions of the day. Milton's love for Diodati should not be determined as
a mere impulse but as the function of a conditioning social imperative.
Thus Sinfield cautions in reading *In Memoriam*:

> As Jeffrey Weeks explains [*Sex, Politics and Society*, 1981], it is a mis-
> take to conceptualize sex as a dehistoricized "driving, instinctual
> force, whose characteristics are built into the biology of the human
> animal, which shapes human institutions and whose will must force
> its way out, either in the form of direct sexual expression or, if
> blocked, in the form of perversion or neuroses." The view which cor-
> responds to the materialist emphasis taken in the present study, and
> which is offered by Lacan, Foucault and interactionist social scientists
> like J. H. Gagnon and William Simon, sees "the individual as a prod-
> uct of social forces, an 'ensemble of social relations,' rather than as a
> simple natural unity" (Weeks, p. 3). In this view sexuality is not a
> given which must find its way to the surface by one means or another,
> it is, rather, something which is constructed in determinate historical
> conditions.[29]

Not that this view has to be accepted as wholly final. The way in
which Sinfield lists modern theorists as unquestionable authorities alerts
one to a degree of authoritarianism and thus some underlying uncertainty.
Equally, when he avers that it is a "mistake to," one is wary of the finality
of his sentence. In the area of love and mourning, of great dedication to,
and admiration of, another human being, the pain of loss and the inexplicable force of attraction towards another man in particular, it is wisest
to avoid any such categorical theoretical matrices.

There is a further complicating factor that persuades against any dog-
matic fixity. Tennyson pertinently warns: "that this [*IM*] is a poem, *not*
an actual biography. ... 'I' is not always the author speaking of himself,
but the voice of the human race speaking through him" (*Memoir* I.304–5).
Of course it is grandiose of him to imagine himself as the sibylline voice
through whom the universal unconscious speaks in mysterious murmurings. It is irritating. But the distinction between author and speaker is a
needed reminder, if an old one. Shawcross dangerously conflates Milton
and speaker. Milton's elegies, English and Neo-Latin, are fascinating in
their reception, as testimony of proscribed passion, but also in public as

prescribed texts. The same may be said for Gray or Tennyson. It is precisely the tension between personal, lyric intensity and achieved impersonality of a public tone which is reflected in the complex voice of the poet who needs to find, and does find, a strategy for saying and yet not saying, that ties these three major poets and their works in a remarkable way. This ambivalence and fluctuation is essential and needs to be kept in mind in consideration of such fine and famous texts: "For words, like Nature, half reveal / And half conceal the Soul within" (*IM* 5.3–4).

CHAPTER TWO

A Secret Sympathy

Richard West and Thomas Gray

> By night we lingered on the lawn,
> For underfoot the herb was dry;
> And genial warmth; and o'er the sky
> The silvery haze of summer drawn.
> And calm that let the tapers burn
> Unwavering; not a cricket chirred;
> The brook alone far-off was heard,
> And on the board the fluttering urn.[1]

Roger Lonsdale, in one of the most illuminating articles on Gray, suggests that the poet's "dimly understood sense of a private predicament" was possibly the "real spring of his creativity."[2] Looking to the latter part of Gray's life (at fifty-four), Lonsdale quotes two passages from Gray's letters to a young man, Charles von Bonstetten, to whom Gray had become deeply attached. I requote in full:

> Never did I feel, my dear Bonstetten, to what a tedious length the short moments of our life may be extended by impatience and expectation, till you had left me: nor ever before with so strong a conviction how much this frail body sympathizes with the inquietude of the mind. I am grown old in the compass of less than three weeks. ... I did not conceive till now (I own) what it was to lose you, nor felt the solitude and insipidity of my own condition, before I possess'd the happiness of your friendship.[3]

And a week later:

> My life now is but a perpetual conversation with your shadow.—The known sound of your voice still rings in my ears.—There, on the cor-

ner of the fender, you are standing, or tinkling on the Pianoforte, or
stretch'd at length on the sofa.— Do you reflect, my dearest Friend,
that it is a week or eight days, before I can receive a letter from you
and as much more before you can have my answer, that all that time
(with more than Herculean toil) I am employ'd in pushing the tedious
hours along, and wishing to annihilate them; the more I strive, the
heavier they move and the longer they grow.[4]

And finally, in May 1770:

I know and have too often felt the disadvantages I lay myself under,
how much I hurt the little interest I have in you, by this air of sadness
so contrary to your nature and present enjoyments: but sure you will
forgive, tho' you can not sympathise with me. It is impossible with me
to dissemble with you. Such as I am, I expose my heart to your view,
nor wish to conceal a single thought from your penetrating eyes.[5]

Heath-Stubbs in the preface to his *Thomas Gray, Selected Poems*,
reaches a similar conclusion to Lonsdale:

[His] poetry is, at first sight, wholly literary in inspiration — a poetry
turned in upon itself, itself its own inspiration. But this is only a half-
truth. What gives it its lasting appeal (as also with Gray's letters) is the
sense, surely, that its formalities contain within themselves a deep
undercurrent of emotions not made wholly explicit. These emotions
were rooted to a very great extent, in Gray's relationships with his
friends — with West, with Walpole, and with Mason who became his
biographer. But above all, in his letters to Charles Von Bonstetten (the
young Swiss who visited Cambridge in Gray's later years) he comes
near to speaking out, and speaking something very like the language
of passion.[6]

Heath-Stubbs then quotes from the same passages that Lonsdale cites.
Lonsdale wisely warns, however, against using these words for the wrong
reasons: "This one, sad, unignorable exposure of the heart does not provide us with a key which unlocks the secret of Gray's poetry."[7] (A mistake, perhaps, that Shawcross makes.) What follows is as crucial for
understanding Gray and his poetry as that bright ember of Milton's love
for Diodati that still glows through *Epitaphium Damonis*. Lonsdale
significantly points out that this single exposure of Gray's heart near the
end of his life "may suggest why his poetic career as a whole had become
a process of escape from a dimly understood sense of a private predicament, which was in itself the real spring of his creativity."[8] It is important

to examine how this sense of otherness, of difference, impelled the poet, how the artist won a poetic self from the trial of this difference. The biographical details do not explain Milton or Gray, but certainly help to assess the peculiar quality of their predicament and genius. We would be much the poorer, for instance, in our understanding of Tennessee Williams if we did not have his own statement about some of the forces that molded his being and his writing life. In it, there are strong similarities to the early life experiences of Milton and Gray. Williams writes:

> At the age of fourteen I discovered writing as an escape from a world of reality in which I felt acutely uncomfortable. It immediately became my place of retreat, my cave, my refuge. From what? From being called a sissy by the neighbourhood kids, and Miss Nancy by my father, because I would rather read books in my grandfather's large and classical library than play marbles and baseball and other normal kid games, a result of a severe childhood illness and of excessive attachment to the female members of my family, who had coaxed me back into life.[9]

It is important that, if we go back to Lonsdale's quotation above (but now in full), the word "escape" is prominent and in a remarkably similar emotional context:

> This one, sad, unignorable exposure of the heart [the May letter to Bonstetten] does not provide us with a key which unlocks the secret of Gray's poetry. Yet it may suggest why his poetic career as a whole had become a process of escape from a dimly understood sense of a private predicament, which was in itself the real spring of his creativity.[10]

The sense of otherness, of literature and writing as an escape from a world that seemed so alien and hostile in its gender prescriptions and expectations, is common to Milton and Gray. How far society will allow such men to express their hurt at this alienation, if such expression takes the form of a critique of the prescribing society, is a true test of humane values. The intrusion or admission of such revealing critiques of the oppressive and judgmental nature of normative regulation is complex. It usually obliges both the critical writer, negotiating an understanding of othered writer and othering society, and the creative writer, speaking out about his or her predicament, to play a diplomatic game. So it is telling that, as much as the final expression of passionate affection for another man occurred at the end of Gray's life, in a letter, with the recipient of it far away on the Continent, so the explication of Gray's poetry by Lonsdale includes this central communication at the very end of the article. It is almost as if the critic and poet alike have bowed to public censure and tucked away, as the addendum to their work, what should be the start. The key phrases in Gray's letters quoted above have all the freshness of adolescent passion told of for *le premier temps* to another: "I never felt how horrible life was till you left', 'I didn't realize till now what it was to lose you," "being so happy with you made me understand how lonely and awful it is without you;" "I live on pictures and memories of you," "I imagine you here, I see you, I hear your voice", "it is unbearable without you;" "I can't pretend to you," "you see right into my heart," "'you know how I really feel." These are love letters if the language is stripped of the cumbrous and securing abstract nouns such as "inquietude," "insipidity" or the carefully controlled syntax of balance and answer. All that is not said is "I love you." But it is stated almost the more loudly through the masking devices of gracious correspondence etiquette between two men writing to each other. Below the surface formality is the pulse of real love denied expression, gagged, quieted. The deliberately calming language is the author's life jacket but his noose as well. Gray nods to the propriety of the establishment and (in a painfully negotiated obfuscation of the self) counts himself a part of it.

Similarly Lonsdale himself, writing in 1973 and published first in no less prestigious or nationally established journal than *The Proceedings of the British Academy* is under the same strictures of majority social conformity as the Oxford don and respected poet of 1770. Gray, like Housman, is bound to a double life of private desire and public denial. Gray became an institution and paid publicly and was penalized privately at the same time for cutting off the recognition and expression of his love. But what choice did he have in even tentatively formulating the real nature of his heart's affections let alone appropriating some ground for their expression? Gray and his greatest poem are institutionalized, taken over by the nationalist interest as a reward (and a searing punishment) for his fastidious masking of the inner life that he was obliged to close up. Lonsdale's sensitive concluding paragraph, held over in the best traditions of British propriety, serves as an *apologia pro vita Graiae*; it hints in the most discreet English way at the heart of Gray's true passion but leaves the hint tentative and apologetic:

> I have myself been concerned only to suggest that poetry which might seem "complacent" in its "massive calm" was in reality neither complacent nor calm; or, at least, that such calm as it ever achieved was

the result of a personal and poetic struggle that cannot but be moving, if viewed with the sympathetic imagination which was its unifying theme.[11]

Not surprisingly, Milton and Gray sought out particularly treasured friendships with men who were cheerful, kind, confident, and more securely mature than themselves. Such bonds were doubly coveted as they realized something of the acceptance never felt among the *vulgus* who, though perceptibly a *vulgus*, were still enough of a complete majority to be society, the establishment, admission to which was not granted to men who seemed to them pale and tender flowers such as Gray. This sharp barb of exclusion cut into their self-respect and psychological well-being. The wonder of their intellectual resilience is that they turn a social handicap into a literary virtue. Rejection makes them alive to the pain of exclusion, prompts them to question the whole system of values otherwise assumed to be correct in their society.

In accounting for his retreat into letters, Tennessee Williams goes on to link his desire to succeed in this one safe area of the intellect with the vulnerability that follows admitting dedication to a particular goal. Williams further associates his fear of failure with the fury, violence and criticism of his society that is exhibited in many of his plays. As a typical example of this process— from exclusion to anger—he cites the case of the end to his first published work, a short story:

> I drew upon a paragraph in the ancient histories of Herodotus to create a story of how the Egyptian queen, Nitocris, invited all of her enemies to a lavish banquet on the shores of the Nile, and how, at the height of this banquet, she excused herself from the table and opened sluice gates admitting the waters of the Nile into the locked banquet hall, drowning her unloved guests like so many rats.[12]

At heart, Gray's *Elegy* is as much a radical indictment of the hubristic, unreflective, selfish and barbarically destructive values encoded in his society's desiderata as Johnson's mournful satire of the same wrongheaded impulses in *The Vanity of Human Wishes*. Too often the *Elegy* suffers, ironically enough, and fascinatingly enough, from too much social prescription and almost martial recognition. Too often its calm surface structure is read as a breviary of life truths, a sort of handbook of verities pleasingly compiled. Too seldom is it seen that the pain of enduring society that unquestioningly venerates gaudy achievement and egocentric opulence causes the poet to question the fundamental tenets of his society. It is major revisionist thought actuated by an aching sense of otherness. The poem formulates a desire to revoke the thoughtless *mores* of a crude, clutching society and put in their place the culture of the heart. The unknown, the poor, the illiterate laborer are associated with the other. The poet's own otherness reaches towards the unrecognized of society in indictment of the hegemony. Here already are strong precedents to Wordsworth's leech gatherer. Gray argues from the margins of the marginalized, turning an apparent weakness into a strength:

> Let not Ambition mock their useful toil,
> Their homely joys, and destiny obscure;
> Nor Grandeur hear with a disdainful smile,
> The short and simple annals of the poor.
>
> The boast of heraldry, the pomp of pow'r,
> And all that beauty, all that wealth e'er gave,
> Awaits alike th'inevitable hour.
> The paths of glory lead but to the grave.
>
> Nor you, ye Proud, impute to These the fault,
> If Mem'ry o'er their Tomb no Trophies raise,
> Where thro' the long-drawn isle and fretted vault
> The pealing anthem swells the note of praise.
>
> (*Elegy*, 29–40[13])

Gray desires that the memorial of a life ought not to be the material edifice of a vain Ozymandias but the smaller ambit and more precisely demanding scrutiny of those immediately about one and close to one: the Theocritean ethos. To say that at least one person has genuinely loved you, that one other human being feels the loss of your "Cecropios sales," "blanditiae," becomes a far more enduring monument. To win the memorial of another's heart as the end goal of life is to radically adjust the criteria for human excellence and to cause human beings not to strive to excel over one another, not to impress and dazzle their fellow human beings in hegemonic competition, but to accept the slight bounds of their few friends, the modest precincts of their kith and kin. To have as a wanted epitaph nothing so much as the words graven in someone else's living heart, "much loved," is to require human beings to resign hubris by the wish to please, help and love: "He gain'd from Heav'n ('twas all he wish'd) a friend." This is the argument for community that makes Gray's *Elegy* some of the greatest poetry ever written: more appropriate in the materialist efflorescence of our fin de siecle world than ever before. The poet asks searchingly of the reader the perennial and uncomfortable questions: What are you doing and why? What are you striving for and why? Who are you, actually? In his graveyard meditations he holds up the stenching, chapfallen skull to force us to reexamine fundamental assumptions. I cannot imagine any society more in need of this drastic anatomy than this materialistically clogged and obdurately unconcerned world of ours. It is sad that some read the *Elegy* as no more than a sort of Polonius-like run of glib truisms. That interpretation misses the plea and suffering that underpin and integrate the whole work. The poet seeks that other country built upon the enlightened hope of reciprocal concern and mutual dependence. The unspeakable loss of one true friend who really understood and granted him moments of life, flickerings of that emotional identity that Milton so treasured in the company of Diodati, causes the poet to comprehend the primacy of this life-giving love in the architecture of a civilization.

The very deprivation of these men's emotional lives caused by their otherness and resultant exclusion, their sensitivity in an insensitive environment, prompts them to perceive the need for a radically new community, one not of social coercion but of emotional liberty, not to sink into hopeless cynicism, but to rise above the narrow means of a greedy society and imaginatively conceive of a better place, another country, with a finer set of empathetic values in which the memorial of the heart is the true gauge of human achievement. The central stanza of the epitaph to the *Elegy* encapsulates these criteria of friendship, the heart's devotion to love, generosity and identity. Cruel loss of the one humanizing and enlivening bond accorded to such a social outsider is reduced imaginatively through a burning critique of unfeeling pomposity, the rage of power and unchecked avarice. The challenge of an altruistic concern for the condition of others is as firmly rooted in the humanist wisdom of his poetic predecessor Pope, and the tradition that he represents, as it is in those beneficiaries of such thinking in the century to follow such as Shelley. What else is Gray asking but what Shelley so lyrically requires of a better world of men?

> The great secret of morals is love; or a going out of our own nature, and an identification of ourselves with the beautiful which exists in thought, action, or person, not our own. A man, to be greatly good, must imagine intensely and comprehensively; he must put himself in the place of another and of many others; the pains and pleasures of his species must become his own.[14]

It is curious that Lytton Sells, in what is supposed to be a major critical review of Gray, *Thomas Gray: His Life and Works*,[15] writes so unsympathetically of Gray and his work. Over and over again the emphasis of this critical biography falls judgmentally on the desiccation of Gray's life and the tenuity of his poetic output. With an obtuse monotony Lytton Sells castigates Gray for his reliance on sources:

> But it remains a fact that the Elegy has been admired by poets greater than Gray: by Byron, Tennyson and Edward Fitzgerald. The ornate and studied language, the lapidary phrases, perhaps also the flavour of Miltonic diction, no doubt account for this admiration. Like many readers, they were less concerned with ideas than with language; and one suspects that it is, in the main, the beauty of the language that has made the Elegy so popular, its readers not realizing how little was of Gray's own invention. The most quoted line is indeed a paraphrase of a verse of his friend, Richard West —"The paths of glory lead but to the grave[16]."

This paragraph is littered with questionable assumptions. The word "greater" assumes a ranking of authors that turns on some closed system never opened to the reader but left *ex cathedra*. Whether Fitzgerald should be ranked against Gray is worrying to start with and to decide summarily that he is simply greater than Gray is objectionable. That a mind as brilliant and incisive as Byron's should focus on the language and neglect the ideas of the *Elegy*, as if searching mechanically for rhetorical tropes and tricks in a poem that is no more than a collection of shining techniques and flourishes, seems daft. The assumption that there are ordinary readers who can see only the clever effects and then that band of informed and discerning readers such as Lytton Sells, who see more deeply into the cheat of Gray's derivative verse, is arrogant. Worst of all is the crude imputation that Gray stole his best line from a dead friend. In fact this appropriation and reworking of a deceased loved one's work is the subtle intertext of love's commitment. The commemorative poetic marker that is threaded into the formal verse is a tribute as well as a key to the real emotional impulse of the poem as a whole. As insensitive, if not more so, is the following:

> The bulk of the Elegy, that is the first 92 lines, mingles thoughts and expressions known to be those of his friend with certain of his own; but for the most part they are borrowings from the Latin, Italian and English poets— too many indeed.[17]

Surely Lytton Sells realizes that the poet is arguing for an acknowledgment of our fellow man, and so obviously would value the *learning* of his fellow man and have the good manners to acknowledge his debt to him? His poetic practice is a reflection of his poetic concern. Surely Lytton Sells knows that Gray writes in a tradition of learning in which it is essential to the spirit of intellectual interdependence that poetry is a part of others' thought, not some raging excursus of private genius? To brand Gray as unoriginal is to miss seriously the point of his argument for intellectual community of the text and social community in the argument of the *Elegy*. Surely Lytton Sells knows that the bucolic tradition centers on the importance of the little people in checking and upbraiding the hubristic adventurers and tyrants lurking in us all? Surely he might have guessed that Gray, like Milton, is so painstakingly observant of the wellconnected page because the world of letters, the adherence of like minds intellectually linked across centuries, is the one world in which they enjoy free citizenship, in which they can shine and enjoy their own identity? If Gray wrote little I would scarcely see this as a fault or a problem. I would rather have only the *Elegy* than the whole of *Lamia* and I think even Keats himself might agree. We do not have much of Johnson but we are happy to have the Juvenal imitations in particular. How can we revere the monitory significance of Wordsworth's appeal for self-reflective humanity in *Resolution and Independence*, his proximity to the outcasts of society as valuable, his apt admonishment to the arrogantly young, to himself, and still fail to see the same felt concern for community in the *Elegy*? What makes the apparently solemn and marmoreal completeness so febrile and taut with experience is the realization that Gray himself, as poet, is the sufferer of that lonely wilderness existence of a Cumberland beggar or a single leech gatherer. Gray's grasp of the radical isolation of life and the pain of singularity and difference is the very mainspring of his poetic output. Writing is his gift for it, is the great redemptive means of redressing the shortcomings of a purblind society and holding up the bright hope of a better place and people. For what else does Dickens argue for again and again but the memorial of the heart, in one great novel after another, against the rapacity and coldness of a materialist, snobbish society? What else does George Eliot plead when Eppy's golden locks replace Silas's consuming avarice for gold? Lytton Sells should have realized that Gray does not silently steal from West, but pays back the memory of a beloved friend by situating his companion's thoughts within the structure of one of the finest elegiac memorials ever written.

All through his life Gray longed for the secure amity that is founded in love and unquestioning intimacy. He longed for the fraternal union he once, so briefly, enjoyed as a boy and young man, the acceptance so poignantly described by West in a letter of November 1735 which memorably intimates the sense of protected youth exposed to the glare of the larger world:

You use me very cruelly: You have sent me but one letter since I have been at Oxford, and that too agreeable not to make me sensible how great my loss is not having more. Next to seeing you is the pleasure of seeing your handwriting; next to hearing you is the pleasure of hearing from you. Really and sincerely I wonder at you, that you thought it not worth while to answer my last letter. I hope this will have better success in behalf of your quondam school-fellow; in behalf of one who has walked hand in hand with you, like the two children in the wood,

> Through many a flowery path and shelly grot,
> Where learning lull'd us in her private maze.

The very thought, you see, tips my pen with poetry, and brings Eton to my view. Consider me very seriously here in a strange country, inhabited by things that call themselves Doctors and Masters of Arts; a country flowing with syllogism and ale, where Horace and Virgil are equally unknown; consider me, I say, in this melancholy light, and then think if something be not due to
> Yours[18]

Gray longed for this same oneness sadly glimpsed again only towards the end of his life in the happy hours of study with the talented young Bonstetten. The start and close of his life are in the parentheses of companionship which leave the main a bleak waste. He longed his whole life to recover that innocent companionship of his youth. He yearned to requite the gaping experience of an unexpectedly alienated and alienating adulthood, the othering effects of his serious and well-stocked intellect and the loss of his beloved Favonius. (Tennessee Williams might well have thought of his father's classical library as a private maze where learning lulled him.) It seems remarkably unsympathetic and harsh that some critics should charge Gray with emotional desiccation and too small an output.

Gray's wistfully nostalgic poetic remembrance of his school and school years, his *Ode on a Distant Prospect of Eton College*, perfectly captures the poet's sense of an untroubled youth interrupted by the biting miseries of adulthood:

> Ah happy hills, ah pleasing shade,
> Ah fields belov'd in vain,
> Where once my careless childhood stray'd
> A stranger yet to pain!
>
> (11–14)[19]

The "quadruple alliance" of the Eton school friends—Walpole, Ashton, West and Gray — told so much, in its witty mimicry of the great political alliance in Europe, about the secluded and happy imaginings of these four brilliant boys. Gray's position in the group, his identity among such close and like-minded friends, assured him of "a momentary bliss" (16). His otherness was unexposed to the blasts of social conformity so that, looking back, he could from the experience of exclusion and loneliness watch himself as a carefree youth with the overseeing eye of adult pain:

> Alas! regardless of their doom,
> The little victims play!
> No sense have they of ills to come,
> Nor care beyond to-day:
> Yet see how all around 'em wait
> The Ministers of human fate,
> And black Misfortune's baleful train!
>
> (51–7)[20]

The abrupt confrontation of his isolation in a prescriptive social environment, a nature not suited anyway to barging a way through to eminence, but most of all the death of his particular friend, West, intensifies the bitter truths of his own Elsinore, that once had all the outward appearance of joyful prospects. The *Elegy*, then, mourns West, Gray's loss of youthful security and the destructive folly of ambition and avarice. Just as the young Danish prince is suddenly faced with the ugly facts of concupiscence and power plotting, the harsh dealings of adult affairs, wrenched away from the private meditations and security of university life, so Gray has to confront this social maelstrom of competing passions and animal appetites and sift for himself some reason for being. Milton's relation to his secure paternal world of Horton is remarkably similar. The loss of West, like the loss of Diodati for Milton, is the catalyst for a torturing introspection and ruthless examination of the self now naked and vulnerable without the protection of a Horton or an Eton. The retreat of youth is over and, with it, the reclusion of private imaginings. Gray's *Elegy* impels the writer to recover meaning from the chaos of bereavement — not the bereavement alone of one person, but the loss of an identifying soul and time. The anguish of otherness forces Gray to quarry a new personhood from the single seam of ore remaining: Walpole and he had quarreled, West was gone and his happy years were fled. He was, like Milton at a similar age, utterly alone.

A letter to West in 1742 (May 27) reveals something of Gray's bemusement at the alterations of adulthood among his school fellows:

> I shall see Mr ** and his Wife, nay, and his Child too, for he has got a
> Boy. Is it not odd to consider one's Contemporaries in the grave light
> of Husband and Father? There is my Lords ** and ***, they are States-
> men: Do not you remember them dirty boys playing at cricket? As for
> me, I am never a bit the older, nor the bigger, nor the wiser than I was
> then: No, not for having been beyond sea.[21]

This sad confusion at the adult world and the changes it brings to many
from boyhood to manhood (set in gentle irony that in at least some degree
glances back at the author), his standing still amid the throng as bewil-
dered outsider, may give another sense to the purely pastoral nostalgia of
retreat usually seen in his famous phrase "far from the madding crowd."
However painful and alienating the experience of this crucial break may
have been between youth and adulthood, loss and redefinition, it had the
benefit of sparking a rigorous scrutiny of life about him. His poetic delib-
eration of his own state of otherness allows him, by his very isolation, the
space to speculate on the human condition and locate within its fluctuations one fine point of redeeming significance, a remarkably sturdy existential moment: the criterion of individual concern. In searching out some
resilient meaning, Gray works for the age he lived in as well. At the epicenter of his own pain, caused so ironically by the adversity of society's
difference, he formulates a raison d'être that encapsulates much of the best
thinking of that society at that time: "He gained from Heaven ('twas all
he wish'd) a friend." In a letter to West (Dec. 1735), Gray speaks of his
appreciation of West's care for him with a typical lightness that belies the
depth of his attachment:

> However, as the most undeserving people in the world must sure have
> the vanity to wish somebody had a regard for them, so I need not
> wonder at my own, at being pleased that you care about me. You need
> not doubt, therefore, of having a first row in the front box of my little
> heart, and I believe you are not in danger of being crowded there.[22]

It is too easy, as Heath-Stubbs pertinently remarked, to miss the tur-
bulent strength of such emotions and such devotion beneath the glacial
surface structure of *Elegy*. The verse form of his *Elegy*, the quatrain structure, is like the intensifying pattern of the insistent, almost liturgical,
somnolence of the short paragraphs and regularly repeated refrain of *Epitaphium Damonis*. It has an anesthetizing effect, so that the raw pain of
the mourner is drugged by the steady meters. Tennyson's *In Memoriam*
most powerfully exemplifies this healing, soporific effect of the quatrain form. The curious amalgam of styles and conventions brought to

harmonious unity in *Lycidas* is taken over and further stylized in the *Elegy*, to the point that there is a danger of taking the inscrutable placidity of the form literally. But, of course, this funeral mask, this solemnity of meticulously arranged and scrupulously selected allusions, is the very thing to keep away the *profanum vulgus*. With such a literary antecedent Gray need have no more recourse to the learned language to procure that gravity of form which will ensure dignity of reception and literary permanence for the probity of a rare love. The assimilation of the seminal Hylas complaint into a set register of melancholic reflection marks a major assimilation and transformation of the elegiac form. As in *Lycidas*, the English is public and moves stiffly to preclude the jibes of the uncouth and the interpolations of the unlearned. This is full-dress mourning and the long slow movement of erudite lines insists on and enforces an air of gravity. The degree of social criticism in the dramatic contrast between stanzas eight and nine echoes strongly the "blind Fury" and "blind mouths" sections of *Lycidas* (64–84 and 102–31), thus further safeguarding the poem from charges of peculiar sentimentality or excessive affection for another man. The antihubristic stanzas on fame link directly to those in *Lycidas*; only the theme has been expanded to re-echo social indictment and the private desire to "burst out into sudden blaze" (*Lycidas*, 74). Cromwell, "guilt[y] of his country's blood," functions retrospectively to adjust the sense of unrecognized, "wasted" talent in the famous fourteenth stanza ("Full many a gem").

How we read *Lycidas*, however, or Gray's *Elegy* or the vital correspondences between them, turns much on a lively and open-minded appreciation of the intertextuality of the Latin poems by each poet. Understanding how intensely Milton loved Diodati, how conscious he was of his difference, knowing the depth of Gray's love for West and the wretchedness of the bleak isolation he realized at his death, cause us to reread the major English texts of established greatness—*Lycidas* and the *Elegy*. Canonizing these poems as great texts, as a part of a hegemonic intellectual and cultural *imperium*, is to do them a disservice; it is to mistake the superbly cogent and erudite poetic expression in *Lycidas* and the *Elegy* as testimony of the English culture and nation that nurtured the poets. So the poets' original need for a language that is immaculately normative to enclose a nonnormative anxiety over existence has unfortunately led to the poems being adopted as triumphant artifacts, trumpets of imperial greatness and proof of nationhood to be blasted in the ears of lesser languages and lesser people usually by particularly mediocre minds: servants of jingoism. Nothing, nothing at all could be a more ironical reversal for either poem, set as they are to indict a careless and bombastic hegemony, calling for the responsible conscience of the individual to be awakened by love for his fellows through a sober contemplation of life's brevity. To free these poems from the well-meant but unhelpful misappropriation, it is necessary to reintegrate the origins and the nature of this highly stylized elegiac form and, more pertinently, the writers' need to develop it. At root, I believe, this form is a masterful construct of unarguable social conformity and radically private difference. The Latin poems which are at the root of each poet's emotional and intellectual lives tell of this submerged impetus without which the *Elegy* or *Lycidas* are dead art forms, grotesques of literary greatness wheeled out to puzzle young readers and cow foreign students with the glare of British erudition. Milton is so moved by the death of King because literary endeavor is such a necessary part of his life; it is his reason for being. As for Tennessee Williams, learning and writing are a refuge, an escape for men such as Gray or Milton.

The grotesque, unnatural fact of youthful expiry sets upon Milton particularly and causes him to reconsider the whole nature of being, his justification for living and, thereby, the goals of his life. It is hard to get at the force of this painfully recovered intellectual autonomy without the record of his *Epitaphium Damonis*. In the same way we are required to consider very closely the relation, frequently questioned or marginalized, between Gray's "Sonnet: On the Death of Richard West" and the *Elegy*. Behind this English elegiac sonnet are the superbly beautiful Latin lines addressed to West at the start of the fourth book of Gray's once envisaged *De Principiis Cogitandi*, dedicated to West but abandoned after his young friend's death. These lines are seldom translated for consideration of Gray's poetry, seldom referred to in critical appraisal of, or even in connection with, the *Elegy*. In the 1814 edition these Latin lines are the last to appear in the whole volume. They should, of course, appear very near the start, next to the quotations from his letters to Bonstetten. In these lines we find phrases of regard as tender as those to Diodati in the *Epitaphium*. The poet is "ictus amore" (struck with love) for his beloved Favonius, "dilecte Favoni." The real pulse of the poet's affections is buried, and has been buried, far below the surface attractions of the great elegiac text that generations of English people, colonists and colonized, have learned by rote for the sake of selected, epigrammatic truths or, rather, degraded truisms.

Because of the transforming force of Milton's early work, Gray can cast the fuller weight of his poem upon the vernacular, which now has the precedent and form engrafted upon it, while burying the real lament in the undisturbed woof of its verbal tapestry. Even in the sonnet on the death of Richard West, the immediate and inconsolable grief is made glassy and formally obscure to an extent. Nowhere do we find the gentle tones of love's immediate expression as in the "ictus amore" of its Latin shadow text. Even the title of the Latin lines is not made manifest as a tribute of poetry in love to a friend — it is safely hidden as the proemium to a book of philosophical speculation.

In the English sonnet to West, however, we still see the Theocritean tradition, transposed into Milton's Latin *Epitaphium*, coming through in English:

Sonnet
(On the Death of Richard West)

In vain to me the smileing Mornings shine,
And redning Phoebus lifts his golden Fire;
The Birds in vain their amorous Descant joyn;
Or chearful Fields resume their green Attire:
These Ears, alas! for other Notes repine,
A different Object do these eyes require.
My lonely Anguish melts no Heart, but mine;
And in my Breast the imperfect Joys expire.
Yet Morning smiles the busy Race to chear,
And new-born Pleasure brings to happier Men:
The Fields to all their wonted Tribute bear:
To warm their little Loves the Birds complain:
I fruitless mourn to him, that cannot hear,
And weep the more, because I weep in vain.[23]

Lines 9 and 10 of *Epitaphium Damonis* describe how the wheat pushes up brilliant green, completely regardless of the misery and sense of a breach in nature experienced by the poet. So here in line 4, "chearful Fields resume their green Attire." The unmoved world of nature and the lonely lament of the bereaved Hercules from Theocritus's Idyll XIII reappear in the English of this sonnet at line 7: "My lonely Anguish melts no Heart but mine." The sense of himself being out of time with the larger structure of things is in a way the poet's unconscious expression of that otherness in his makeup that sets him so painfully apart. The dissonance between the uninterrupted daily pattern, the announcement of each new day, and his own cruel disruption is symptomatic of a larger estrangement from his fellow man and life so that "In vain to me the smileing Mornings shine,/And redning Phoebus lifts his golden Fire." The beneficent face of creation, that sense of natural purpose granted to the *pecus* members is denied him and especially so when that one validating and harmonizing agent of his life has vanished. The sonnet begins and ends with the phrase "in vain" and it is repeated again in line 3. Just as in *Epitaphium Damonis* Milton contrasted his own lonely predicament against the backdrop of animals in nature herding together, so here Gray purposely and effectively opposes his own desolation with the morning song of birds filled with amorous desire. The loss of his own love and the impossibility of marriage and a secure nest stand out grimly and starkly against the unquestioning fullness of nature's cycle among birds and animals. The replenishment of nature within these easy patterns seems cruel against the difference of the poet's state. The return of the "smileing Mornings," or the fields that cheerfully "resume their green Attire," tell of this cyclic completeness of which the poet's otherness and unexpected loss of a soulmate have no part. Even within the poem itself, Gray shows this repetitious, consoling pattern from which he is isolated by taking up the loci of the first line — morning, fields, birds— in the opening lines of the sestet. The amorous descant of the birds' early song gives way to their care for "little Loves" in the nest in line 12. This recalls the image of birds finding their mates in *Epitaphium Damonis*. Here the cycle of nature is juxtaposed against the poet's grief to show the depths of his melancholy and affliction, but also to suggest the rift between himself and the flourishing world. The loss of West prompts as much a temporarily anxious lament as it seems to bring into definition a state of physical and metaphysical isolation and otherness previously submerged in the subconscious but now an abiding fact. Even taking into account that some scholars show the sonnet was probably written before West died, the argument for Gray's depression as suggested above seems all the stronger: he felt and finally accepted his alienation.

The form of the sonnet traditionally articulates the passions of the heart but there could hardly be a more anguished cry of such alienation than the last line, not merely a lover's complaint but testimony of inexplicable difference. The world is ever distant to his plight. Lytton Sells, not interested in this, nor seeming to care for the genius that turns quite a boring line of Cibber into a memorable articulation of the double pain and so almost self-generating sense of disjunction, notes only that "it is to be regretted that Gray used Colley Cibber's words, from his adaptation of *Richard III*: 'So must we weep, because we weep in vain'"."[24] Lytton Sells seems to be deaf to the cries of loss and estrangement. All he can do is detect borrowings. The emotional force of its grieving formulation is unmistakable, however, and memorable. This sonnet forcibly perpetuates the agony of loss in the Hylas idyll.

By contrast, in the *Elegy*, we can see how the poet almost obsessively pushes the immediate or detectably first-person tone into that particularly didactic, lapidary and epigraphic detachment which Tennyson perfects later. An obtrusively instructional tone closes over the first-person voice: concernment and definition are meticulously shaded out in many of the excisions and alterations from the first versions of the poem. For the public English readership the lament has to be immaculately meditative.

In the Latin *Ad Favonium*, however, there is a powerful return to the tender lyrical quality of *Epitaphium Damonis*. The protective solemnity of meditative prospects is melted to a quiet, tearful poem of extraordinary intimacy. Here is the gentle love of *Epitaphium Damonis* and the letter to Bonstetten. There is the same admixture of tender trust and boyish admiration for a personal hero discernible in Milton's epitaph to Diodati. Here he is himself, he finds an answering self that allows him to achieve quiet assurance and dignifying security. It is everywhere in the poem's soft cadences but so apparent in the emotional attachment sensible in "dilecte Favoni" (13). Here follows the text and translation of *Ad Favonium* as it appears in Starr and Hendrickson's edition of the poems:

Liber Secundus
De Principiis Cogitandi

Hactenus haud segnis Naturae arcana retexi
Musarum interpres, primusque Britanna per arva
Romano liquidum deduxi flumine rivum.
Cum Tu opere in medio, spes tanti et causa laboris,

5 Linquis, et aeternam fati te condis in umbram!
Vidi egomet duro graviter concussa dolore
Pectora, in alterius non umquam lenta dolorem;
Et languere oculos vidi, et pallescere amantem
Vultum, quo nunquam Pietas nisi rara, Fidesque,

10 Altus amor Veri, et purum spirabat Honestum.
Visa tamen tardi demum inclementia morbi
Cessare est, reducemque iterum roseo ore Salutem
Speravi, atque una tecum, dilecte Favoni!
Credulus heu longos, ut quondam, fallere Soles:

15 Heu spes necquicquam dulces, atque irrita vota!
Heu maestos Soles, sine te quos ducere flendo
Per desideria, et questus Jam cogor inanes!

At Tu, sancta anima, et nostri non indiga luctus,
Stellanti templo, sincerique aetheris igne,

20 Unde orta es, fruere: atque oh si secura, nec ultra
Mortalis, notos olim miserata labores
Respectes, tenuesque vacet cognoscere curas;
Humanam si forte alta de sede procellam
Contemplere, metus stimulosque cupidinis acres,

25 Gaudiaque et gemitus, parvoque in corde tumultum
   Irarum ingentem, et saevos sub pectore fluctus:
   Respice et has lacrymas, memori quas ictus amore
   Fundo; quod possum, juxta lugere sepulchrum
   Dum juvat, et mutae vana haec jactare favillae

ON THE ELEMENTS OF THOUGHT
BOOK II

So far had I advanced in my zeal to uncover the secrets of Nature,
and, the vocal instrument of the Muses, had been the first to lead a
clear brook from the Roman river through British fields, when thou,
the hope and inspiration of so great a task, didst leave in the midst of
the labour and conceal thyself in the eternal shadow of death! With
my own eyes I had seen thy breast gravely stricken with cruel pain, a
breast never insensitive to another's pain; I had seen thine eyes languish and thy loving face grow pale, whence naught but extraordinary
Devotion, and Trust, and deep love of Truth, and uncorrupted Honour used to breathe. At length, however, the merciless cruelty of lingering sickness seemed to be departing, and I hoped for the
restoration of rosy-cheeked Health, and thee along with it, beloved
Favonius! Fondly trusting, alas, the vain sweet hopes, the unavailing
prayers and vows! Alas, the sunny days, now filled with grief!
Deprived of thee, I must pass them in longing and vain complaints,
weeping all the while.

But thou, blessed spirit, hast no need of my lamentations; thou
enjoyest the starry region and the fire of the pure aether from whence
thou wert born. But Oh! if thou art free from care yet not completely
beyond the reach of mortal concerns, and if thou dost look back with
compassion upon the labours that once were so familiar and hast
leisure to think of trifling cares; if, perchance, thou dost contemplate
from thy lofty seat the human storm, the fears, the sharp goads of
desire, the joys and griefs, the tumult of anger that seems so immense
in the tiny heart of man and the savage waves that surge in the human
breast: then look back also on these tears of mine, which, stricken as I
am with love, I am shedding in memory of thee; I can do no more, so
long as my only desire is to lament here beside thy tomb and to
address these vain words to thy silent ashes.[25]

Just as Milton was conscious of amalgamating the particular aspects of
Sicilian idylls with the culture of Britain ("Sicilicum Thamesina per oppida carmen," *Epitaphium Damonis, l. 4*), so Gray realized how important
it was to effect the rich confluence of these streams. In lines 1–3 he tells
of his previous plan to write a book of Lucretian scope concerning the work

of British philosophy "primusque Brittana per arva / Romano liquidum" (2–3). Looking back from the far end of the twentieth century, through Tennyson's superb and seemingly effortless achievement in *In Memoriam*, it is easy, perhaps too easy, to disregard the fundamental work of his predecessors who did so much to integrate the classical and vernacular spheres.

The inspiration for Gray's projected large work, *De Principiis Cogitandi*, and the assuring presence that is behind the confidence in "Primusque," is, of course, Gray's intimate friend, West. When "in opere medio" this love ends in death, the work dies too. The other books of the bold Lucretian project were never written. As in *Epitaphium Damonis*, the equation is similar from the beginning Thyrsis bids the flocks "ite procul" and thus dismisses his work here. Loss of Diodati paralyzes his will and purpose. Here Gray fails to imagine the world without West. That young friend was the "spes tanti et causa laboris" (4). In a way, given the peculiar significance of his literary works, writing is to Gray, as it was to Milton or Williams, a refuge, where he could be himself. By saying that West is the mainspring of that writing, Gray tells of the extraordinary depth of his love for West. He is part of, or possibly the unrealized core of, his inner being. The sense of dereliction is taken up in the second-person verbs "linquis" and "condis" endorsed by the emphatic, personal nominative "tu" and reflexive "te", expressing an immediacy and remarkable softness. The gentleness greatly accentuates the sense of abandonment as his companion buries himself in an "aeternam … umbram" (5). The slight recrimination of West's earthly departure in the middle of Gray's work, "opere in medio" is observable in many lines of *Epitaphium Damonis,* especially the formulaic repetition of "quis … mihi:" "Where does this leave me?" It is rare in *Lycidas* and hardly perceptible in the *Elegy*. It is the Hylas strain of inconsolable searching and longing. In the English laments this is so nicely glazed over that one only detects the urgency of the emotions by asking why the tone is so perfectly controlled.

In line 6 of the address to Favonius, Gray introduces the mood of absolute trust and intimacy which distinguishes the poem. There is a mood of hushed privacy between the two men. This sense of the poetry receding into the guarded chambers of the heart is signaled by the first person, underscored so definitely by the "egomet." This stresses the particular closeness of actual experience — Gray has seen his beloved West "concussa" by "dolore." But West's nature, that is precious to Gray, is one that is never slow to feel the pangs of another's hurt. This compassionate and warm nature, like Diodati's, is of a more expressive and giving kind that naturally attracts to it the more withdrawn and hesitant emotions of men such as Milton or Gray. The repetition of "vidi" (6 and 9) stresses the personal witness, the proven record of time and love shared. Gray is proud to speak of this precious oneness. West's kindness, his altruism and ability to reach out to another's suffering, are perfectly conveyed by the parallel between his own poem and concern for others "in alterius." West is very much one who is "tender for another's pain" (Eton ode, l. 93).

The matched endings in "dolorem" exactly catch this reciprocal equation of suffering and sympathy. The warmheartedness of West glows for the soul that admired it so much and is by nature timid to show his own heart for fear of hurt. In this capacity for relieving pain and for his ability to share pain Gray is in awe of West. The admiration of the other's ease and emotional empathy expresses his own awkwardness and inner timidity. Doubly therefore West is a part of Gray's being, he is an alter being, another half who completes and defends his own fragile self. When, in English, in the *Elegy*, Gray comes closest to speaking of the loss of this love, he does so in some lines, significantly rejected from the final version, that show pathos more beautifully blended than anywhere else in his work. Mason writes:

> Before the Epitaph, Mr Gray originally inserted a very beautiful stanza, which was printed in some of the first editions, but afterwards omitted, because he thought it was too long a parenthesis in this place. The lines however are, in themselves, exquisitely fine, and demand preservation:
>
>> There scatter'd oft, the earliest of the year,
>> By hands unseen are show'rs of violets found;
>> The redbreast loves to build and warble there,
>> And little footprints lightly print the ground.[26]

In the choice of "show'rs of violets," the anonymity of "hands unseen" and the diminutive "little footprints," the poet tells of the tenderness and completing admiration for his beloved Favonius. The fact that Gray does not make it plain that the *Elegy* is a lament for West is itself highly significant. The internal evidence, however, reading the *Elegy* as a recognition of the preeminent need for the memorial of the heart alone, ties it to West. In the Latin, Gray captures the soft, almost tangible quality of this devotion as Milton often does in his *Epitaphium Damonis*. As Tennyson longed for the touch of Hallam's hand one last time, so the desire to be near West, to be comforted by his warm and kindly nature, is expressed in the pitiful cadence of "Et languere oculos vidi, et pallescere amantem / Vultum" (8–9).

The loving face, the precious eyes, remind us of the life of this most admired friend, yet the double infinitives of "languere" and "pallescere" sound the interruption of death, the decay behind the bloom of youth. "Languere" recalls "languescent lumina morte" in Catullus lxiv.188. Ariadne, stranded on Naxos and abandoned by her beloved Theseus, laments her passion and grieves over the desolation all about her: a landscape that is the shape and form of her own shattered feeling for the handsome Athenian (186–91). Ariadne cries against the injustice of Theseus's callous treatment just as Gray bewails the cruelty of fate that snatches away the one person who completes and inspires him. This allusion to Ariadne, distraught and alone in a foreign place, without him to whom she had given her whole heart, is a valuable dimension to the nature of Gray's bereavement. His sense of loss seems more crippling than Milton's. He is reconciled to its privation rather than determined to resolve the agony. The fire of remonstrance that we find in early parts of *Epitaphium Damonis*, the rage of Hercules, is transmuted to an acceptance of the finality of West's death. Gray closes the door softly on that part of his heart. He does not fight the adversity of it with puritan zeal but retires in melancholy.

Gray's love for West, like Milton's for Diodati or Tennyson's for Hallam, is fired by the love of imitable virtue. Aspiration for the sheer goodness of Diodati drives Milton to commemorate him through his intellectual and religious sense of election in his work. But Gray pales himself, "pallescere," and takes up no arms against the injustice of outrageous fortune. Instead he eyes the vanity of human activities with a sadness, considering how frantically human beings chase after trifles. Diodati's love is a refining love as it so works on his mourning friend as to steel Milton's purpose to codify the qualities of Diodati in his verse. The remembrance of his love is a monument to unmatched probity. So too West is ever to be a high-water mark of the excellence of life in Gray's view of things. But Gray pines for a love that refines away the dross of wealth, "the pomp and power." In a typically eighteenth-century way, Gray's experience of the refining love gives him an absolute respect for the modest dimensions of human existence so that the small violets strewed about and the tiny prints of the robin's feet in the snow are emblematic of Gray's profound appreciation of the reality of small lives which make up the stream of life. His love teaches his heart to look past the "noble rage" and seek reality in the simplicity of lives whose achievement is measured by reciprocated kindness and friendship's tender, sustaining care. In this of course his choice of the bucolic tradition is correct as so much of the Theocritean wisdom rests on attention to the epic virtues of non-epic figures. The character of a goatherd is selected as a miniature of life led along the "cool sequestered vale" which upbraids the desolation caused by a proud Agamemnon, a stubborn Achilles, an arrogant Theseus—or "Some Cromwell guilt[y] of his country's blood."

Given Gray's society, its strictures on a man such as Gray, his clear awareness of the loss of West, the unlikelihood of ever finding such a relationship again, his dignified adjustment to the illusory possession of love but absolute devotion to the reality of its brief appearance in men's lives seems as much a triumph over fate and melancholy as Milton's. The nature of that adjustment to bereavement is so eloquent of the character of the energetic Puritan and the gentle eighteenth-century academic. Gray's life is not so much attenuated or desiccated by grief as framed by it. His immediate knowledge of it puts into perspective the hustle and bustle of those thoughtless adventurers and unreflective materialists about him. West's love refines and defines Gray's mature poetic self as much as Diodati's did Milton's.

Against the senseless tide of vanity remains the redeeming virtue of West's character, never mentioned in the public verse of the *Elegy* but commemorated with all the depth of private dedication and exquisitely chosen literary allusion that befits it. Where Milton cites the exemplary character of Diodati at the prose start to his *Epitaphium Damonis*, Gray incorporates West's character into the very texture of the poetry. This is an important middle stage towards that perfectly assimilated *admiratio virtutis et imitatio* in Tennyson. The close relation between boyish wonder at the nature of the admired friend and personal integration of that character is an essential part of the rites of consolation. Helpless grieving gives way to a useful living out of the deceased's virtue. The cross of four cardinal virtues in West's nature, "Pietas, Fidesque, amor Veri et Honestum" (l. 9) centers on the verb "spirabat." The imperfect aspect bears precisely the sense of the habitual and constant. Those traits are ever discernible in his gentle face. But, of course, "spirabat" is transferred by the testimony of the living poetry to the *imitatio* of the poet's own dedication in such love and to such virtue. The Horatian resonance in "fides" and "veritas" fills out the "laudatio amici amati." The interconnectedness to an ancient text claims for the poem the *aeternitatem scriptoris*. As much as Horace relies on the power of verse to console Virgil grieving for his friend Quintilius (*Od.* I.xxiv.7), so Gray rests on the hope of literary continuity.

This finely crafted ode of Horace's displays the same crucial transformation of helpless grief into a living commemoration. At first Horace is at one with the weeping bachelor poet and asks where one can set a limit on lamentation for such a dear individual. Horace invokes the powers of "lugubris cantus." Again Horace searches for an equal in virtue for the lost Quintilius. The poem itself, however, neatly replies to these questions. With that exact symmetry for which so many of the odes are prized, the second question is answered at line 10, the middle line of the twenty-line piece: "You yourself Virgil are the embodiment of such virtue." The world therefore is not deprived but has a successor to that goodness, one anxious to perpetuate it in life. This reversal from inconsolable loss to fully consolable reality is made with a tact that is equaled only by artistic virtuosity. "Flebilis" of line 9 is altered to "flebilior" of line 10. The compliment to Virgil is sustained by placing the name politely at the end of the line. The first question of "quis modus et pudor" is answered by the latter half of the ode. Decent bounds to mourning are set by the gods themselves; the religiously weighted "nefas" shows the limits of mortal powers. Yet, mention of Orpheus reminds Virgil of the redemptive power of song which, like Horace's own verses offered in love, endure beyond the grave and are preserved in accordance with their worth. Horace recalls Virgil to his craft and a steady estimate of his own use to the living. Quintilius is not dead but alive in his friend and his friend's work. The perpetuity of letters then enforces the crafted care of these lines of Latin written by Gray some 1600 years after Horace. The first noun "pietas," poised between the double negatives of "numquam ... nisi?" the insistence in the epithet "altus" and the resonance of the Horatian allusion — all consolidate the inscriptional strength of this testimony to an admired virtue.

Horace's consolation is offered, however, to another. It is not the lyric "I," the suffering of a Hercules, and certainly not the actual record of personal grief and loss. Gray's lines in *Ad Favonium* are. Below the lapidary proclamation of West's merit runs the lyric voice of a lover. Lines 11–13 move with the speed and impetus of private grief. The current of this sadness is taken up in the pathos of recollected hope, that this dear one may be restored, that "demum" the ravages of the "morbi tardi" may be checked. The light of hope seems to shine as the "reducem" is followed by "iterum" and concluded with the brightness of "roseo ore." The plaintive "speravi," attached to the optimism of "roseo" yet restrained by the inevitable gloom of the aorist "visa est cessare," is held over, like a sob, to the start of line 13. Thus the desire to be together with West is modulated in the tenderness of impossible passion. The climactic and painful address in *Ad Favonium* catches up the strain of helpless regret and endlessly fond wishing familiar from *Epitaphium Damonis*. Orpheus stretching out for the vanishing form of Eurydice, the half-drowned call of Hylas to his forlorn Hercules, the distressed lament of Milton — so much is embodied in the superbly elegiac fall of these central lines, cast so hauntingly in the half light of hope and hopelessness, in the valediction to West who was in every sense "dilecte Favoni," the beloved spirit, breath of the poet's own being.

At line 14, however, the dream of a recovered friendship is shattered. "Credulus" placed at the start of the line tells at once of the poet's altered perspective. The long Lucretian work will never be completed; the hope and reason for it have vanished with West's life. "Credulus" is the first sign of the resignation to what Sidney calls the uncertainty of life. The blow of this sudden death alerts Gray to the dreamlike quality of his optimistic youth. He was in fact "credulous." The eighteenth-century concern with scale, with the need to upend the hubristic disproportions created by an inflating ego, to correct the individual in terms of the community, can be traced from this point on in the poem. The gullible, unteachable Gulliver, who forever places himself and his own at the center of everything, the folly of egocentricity and parochialism can be seen here. Johnson's unmasking of the vain and pitiably shortsighted little passions that beat in us and throw up so much dust in the faces of others is part of Gray's sobering reversal of youthful wishing. Johnson's own stab at the foolish desire for great schemes in his introspective and searching Latin poem Γνωθι Σεαυτον is close to Gray's abandonment of the Lucretian work. Gray is at one with the thinking of such men in seeking consolation. He turns the aching at his soul into a radically self-reflexive examination of his own smallness in terms of the whole. The meditative distancing is a turning point in the poem and marks the attainment of his own remarkably dignified resolution of grief. The formulation of this view of things is as intensely personal and new as it is founded on a far-reaching body of ancient and contemporary wisdom.

The first of three sighs in "heu" (14) is significantly linked to "credulus," not the sadness of West's demise. Gray is mourning the loss of naiveté and the callow assumptions of the young. No more will he be able to "wile away" the long days. As Rowse pointed out about Milton, Gray too has lost his youth and is cast loose in the desolation of the rapacious adult world.

"Fallere" directly recalls lines 45–7 of Epitaphium Damonis. But at this stage in Gray's poem, the use of "fallere" has the real sense of falsifying time's progress. The nostalgic "ut quondam" casts the idyll of timeless leisure and perpetual love into a past world, the Sicilian dream as insubstantial as the heat that quivers over the herby scrub. The enclosure of time by death leads to the disclosure of the tenuity of happiness, the incidental nature of love and the provisional quality of life itself. But this very sobering and saddening recognition of things turns Gray in exactly the opposite direction from Milton. Where Milton determined not merely to "meditari grandia" but to embark with purpose on a task of epic strength in memory of the epic virtue of his male friendship, Gray resorts to the Alexandrian wisdom of life in miniature, the beauty and virtue not of significant, heroic lives but of the insignificant and apparently unnoticed lives of Everyman. Here, in celebrating the humble lives of the real world, he is at one with Johnson on one side and Wordsworth on the other. He realizes the enduring value but painful brevity and rarity of the sort of love he in particular and, by poetic extrapolation, human beings in general are granted. Although he sees the illusory quality of the idyll, at the same time he realizes that the happiness of youth is for himself, and for many perhaps, to be the single sustaining moment of identifying happiness in his life. The pity of it has turned to gentle gratitude for at least that little given. In a way he has framed his own idyllic love in the sober black frame of mortality's random strokes.

"Nequicquam" takes up this very sense after the second long sigh of "heu" (l.15). "Nequicquam," between "spes" and "dulces," the dappled nature of life's joy forever offset by the dark splashes of misery is realized in exquisite word painting. Gray is a master of this aspect of Latin verse structure. The eclogue world of youth, that green haven of innocent happiness, is both exposed as transitory and memorialized as the only time of completeness and happiness. Gray knows that the relationships enjoyed at the boys' school of Eton cannot be extended into real life. The rest of his life will be, he says (and he was right), made of "sad days, which he is forced to spend in weeping and in empty complaint and longing." Gray realizes the acute pangs of otherness without bitterness and appreciates the one good, redeeming love of his youth. In this resignation and gratitude he evinces an extraordinary personal probity of spirit and a powerfully mature understanding of the mixed state of life, "more to be endured than enjoyed."

As in Milton, the classical allusions are used with a formidable accuracy so that the immediate scene is suddenly given an alluring backdrop which leads the eye ever further. Here Gray's phrase "longos ... soles" (14) recalls lines 51–2 of Virgil's Eclogue IX. Moeris departs from the green world of the country farm and mourns the loss of the feathery grasses, the springs hidden with leaves and the songs that immortalized them. He is resigned to the iniquity of things yet mourns his lot in a dignified and yet, for that, more movingly elegiac strain. Lines 51–4 deepen the tone of the eclogue with a *haut bas* solemnity. Moeris remembers that so many of his youthful days were lost in singing just as Gray's early years were spent in the carefree security of the love of his friend and the enjoyment of poetic song. But, Moeris sighs, time bears all before it — even the songs and the once-sweet voice of the youthful singer. This gentle melancholy is the hall-mark of Gray's adaptation to the death of West. Without bitterness he accepts the iniquity of life. Although Moeris acknowledges that song has no power over the draconian laws of state (11–13) he ends the eclogue by praising the potency of Menalcas's poetry. Gray, though no longer set to write an impressive Lucretian verse treatise, finds deep solace in the expression of his grief in learned song.

If not the physical preserve, then even more passionately perhaps the memory of Favonius will be the guiding star of the bleak years ahead. He will be the "sancta anima" who will ever remind his mortal companion of the existence of that complete amity of the soul, that peace of the heart. The direct address to his beloved is marked by the strong "at" of line 18. The unusually emphatic "tu" introduces the tender strain of personal speech never allowed to appear even in the *Elegy*. Even in the sonnet to West this verbal caress is similar to the lyric warmth of lines 121–3:

> Large was his bounty, and his soul sincere,
> Heaven did a recompence as largely send:
> He gave to misery (all he had) a tear,
> He gain'd from heav'n (twas all he wished) a friend.

In position too, Gray's lines function similarly: as a bridge to apotheosis of the admired friend. At the moment of nearest intimacy, as if the expression of this love were expiatory, the shift to valediction can take place. In every sense I believe West was "dilecte Favoni" and "sancta anima" to a man who felt estranged from the exchange of passions between men and women in the society about him. The ineffable rapport and assuring one-ness of his youth was not a passing stage but the enduring and redeem-ing time of emotional vivacity. The rest is, for him, islanded by otherness, another type of stranded Ariadne, his heart no more than ashes.

The phrase "nostri non indiga luctus" is taken from the second *Geor-gic*, line 428. This is a crucial reference in the Gray poem as it places West within the sober bounds of the *beatus ille* tradition. He is revered here as that happy man who has learned the right values of living a modest and virtuous life. This is the touchstone of Gray's thought and the criterion against which he denigrates the boundless, bloody, consciousless ambi-tion of the unreflective tyrants in the *Elegy*. The bright apple trees are symbols of the prosperity which flows from wisdom and flourish "ad sidera raptim / vi propria nituntur" ("hardly in want of our care"). So the blessed soul of West soars by its natural virtue to the stars, not needing the lamentation of Gray. By this correspondence to the Virgilian source, West is importantly linked to a passage which celebrates the world as it should be, upheld by the fructifying virtue of humble and simple living. The contrast to this image of right living follows immediately. Riotous disorder and injustice reign as ruthless self-concern is unleashed. No one can read this passage without seeing at once the connectedness to the *Elegy* and, more sadly, the timeless verities portrayed almost in vain by one generation of poets after another keen to recall us prophetlike to the benefits of community. In Virgil's praise of the simple life at 72–4 we have the eternal pattern of Wordsworth's *Michael*. The grave dignity of the freeholders is both a moral and a political enfranchisement of the individual who works in modesty and anonymity: plain living and high thinking. That golden phrase of the *beatus ille* tradition at 459–60 centers the character of West within these admirable bounds of quiet humanity and redemptive love. West will ever be Gray's happy man, by comparison with whom the silly baubles of ambition, the heady temptations of pride and wealth, are exposed at a glance. West's own lines, reviling the pomp and soul corruption of earthly wishes, are incorporated into the *Elegy* at lines 33–6. This inclusion binds the *Elegy* powerfully not only to the personal significance of West's memory, but also to the resonant Virgilian thought behind it.

Eric Smith may discount Mason's conclusion that the *Elegy* was written largely under the effects of West's death, but internal evidence such as that above persuades me that the loss of Favonius is inextricably woven into the fabric of the *Elegy* (not least through the poetic tribute of assimilating several of West's own poetic phrases). Strange that Smith should find too little internal evidence:

> Yet the evidence of a close and contemporary connection between West's death and the *Elegy* is very far from conclusive. Mason believed that the poem was written in 1742 in its first version, with a stoical conclusion arguing for an influence of the "sacred calm" of evening, "a grateful earnest of eternal peace," on the mind of the speaker, "before the happy idea of the hoary-headed Swain, Etc. suggested itself to him." He thought it was concerned with West. There is nothing finally to refute the idea, though, in this version, one cannot feel that there is internal evidence to support it.[27]

The Latin lines to West record the impact and effect of West's death on Gray and show the direct lyric expression underlying so much of the thinking in the *Elegy*. It is surely important then to keep the biographical elements alive in the *Elegy* and the Latin verses go some way toward sustaining that link. Just as *Epitaphium Damonis* provides a more plangent record of the dilemma of youthful expiry confronting the young poet, so the lines to Favonius are a private record of grief and adjustment to its sudden blow; the intrusion of biography can appear in Latin but is seldom allowed to surface in the more accessible vernacular.

The description of the beloved's apotheosis in *Epitaphium Damonis*, as here, of the elevation to a heavenly tutelary state, is neither just an obscure remnant of Neo-Latin nor a sort of *deus ex machina* resolution to the poem's argument. The celestial presidence of Diodati or West is an image of the poet's successful transformation of helpless grief into a useful assimilation of, and dedication to, the virtues of the deceased. West is with him. The immediate physical presence and companionship of Charles or Richard is intensified into a redemptive living out through art of the character of these much-admired friends. In some ways Milton or Gray become Diodati or West. The "sancta anima," the fleeting breath of the dear friend, imparts something of itself to the living correspondent artist. The departed friend is immortalized both in the life of the other and in the perpetuity of art. Gray, like Milton, lays claim to the ancient power of song, such as attributed to Menalcas in Eclogue IX or the first Theocritus idyll. But Gray's lines have none of the climactic triumph of Milton's *Epitaphium Damonis*. The almost frenzied assertion of a glorious personal poetics of resistance does not appear in Gray's mournful resignation. He speaks from the underworld of melancholy, destined to pace for the duration of his life a mortal precinct that is in so many ways utterly unamenable. The Puritan poet's energetic opposition, *contra mundum*, stated with such heroic confidence and purpose, is here altered to a sadly distanced perspective of the littleness of human affairs distorted by egocentric pride, to billowy passions within tiny frames. West's soul that is blissfully "secura" in the upper realms of light, looks down on the pitiable, all-too-familiar little round of human vanities. The phrase "tenuesque vacet cognoscere curat" confirms the earlier allusion to Virgil's *Georgics* and thus the *beatus ille* tradition.

Gray does not assume any superior position over human affairs by some sort of vicarious elevation to West's station; this would be to claim the superior surveillance of an Epicurean godhead. Rather the death of his particular friend has caused him such acute pain that he is forced, like Milton, to reassess his entire reason for being. His otherness prevents him from any comfortable relaxation upon the consolatory devices of the normative society about him. In each case, the poet turns instead to the citizenship of the literary world for a foundation of his position: who he is and why he is an artist. The adjective "tenues" is not cynical of the "curas" of mankind but rather a deeply sympathetic response to helplessly vulnerable mankind, so easily inflated with oversized passions, grotesque and unseemly. West's death is the sobering lesson of mortality, the focusing reminder, the memento mori death's head that adjusts the wild outrage of human anger, indignation, love, and so on. Gray realizes too well that no amount of bookish philosophy can calm the human breast without dehumanizing the subject, but he finds a resolution to his grief in contemplating the controlling perspective of death over human wishes. It is primarily in the community of death that the community of life is founded. This is the impassioned plea of the restrained and dignified *Elegy* whose central criterion is so perfectly restated in Gray's lines to Bentley:

> Enough for me, if to some feeling breast
> My lines a secret sympathy *impart*;
> And as their pleasing influence *flows confest*,
> A sigh of reflection *heaves the heart*.[28]

To win a friend, to have deserved the love of a West and to reciprocate that love in one's own life and work, is perhaps a fine achievement in life. As soon as the consideration of common mortality levels the hubristic aspirations of the private self, the appeal of a shared humanity, the community of a small number of mortal beneficiaries, replaces the vacuum of self-concern.

Both Virgil and Wordsworth turn to images from the insect world to illustrate the possibility of exemplary community. The metaphor of insects works to shame the clumsy selfishness of human beings and to remind us of our own diminutive proportions compared to the next order, of angelic creatures, above us. In this way Gray is a vital link in the perpetuation and dynamic reinterpretation of the *beatus ille* tradition. Gray as sufferer of bereavement and the isolation of otherness is consoled by the imagination of a better place, a community of human beings educated to the needful reciprocity of life. The great projects of ambitious youth, set out to dazzle all, are exposed by death's random strokes. The benevolent face of Favonius looking down over the all-too-familiar struggles ("labores") and concerns ("curas") of humans links *Georgics* IV.177, *Lycidas* 74 and the *Elegy* 57–64. The gentle deflation of mortal business is extended over 22–6. The "humanam procellam" that West will view from alta de sede" is much like the description of bees at war in *Georgics* IV.67–87. The famous Virgilian passage describes in mock-heroic mode the haughty preparation of the angry forces: they are thicker than hail, or acorns shaken from a great oak. The kings move through the ranks of bees "ingentis animos angusto in pectore versant" (83). Like the foolish courtiers of a Popean scene, great passions move in comically diminutive breasts. The reversal comes when Virgil states that a simple handful of dust will quiet the contest. So too lines 23–6 show the grave disjunction between the high passions of insectlike human beings who fail to reflect on their imminent and sudden extinction. Gray does not laugh like a Democritus at this as a distant folly; he is no Lucretian observer from on high. Rather he feels firsthand the disproportionate grief that wracks his insignificant self, looks back on the proud projections of youth with a wry smile. The Virgilian oxymoron between "ingentes animos" and "angusto in pectore" is mirrored in Gray's line 25, "parvo in corde tumultum." But the verb "contemplere" controls the deflationary technique so that the incongruities of human passions are not marked, but mourned. Gray wins back the mood of Virgil's sympathetic sense and imparts to it as well the chief burden of his own sadness. Traditional material is thus charged anew with poetic life, "sic vivat" thus it helps the poet to use verse to measure and observe his own feelings.

The employment of Latin is complex here; it is not simply a private code. The generic wealth of Latin surpasses English and offers Gray an easier way to express himself. The art of writing in another language is itself fascinating, as if the poet can speak with another voice, not just linguistically but psychologically too. The learned language is also traditionally employed for the marmoreal finality of epitaphs. So Johnson insisted on Latin for Goldsmith's tablet. The Neo-Latin of a bilingual poet such as Gray is also constantly held in intertextual tension against the English verse. So at lines 25–6 the phrase "parvo in corde tumultum / Irarum ingentem" corresponds to large sections of the Elegy. Between the force of emotions felt by humanity, the harsh stabs of lust "stimulosque cupidinis," or the savage currents of the heart ("saevos sub pectore fluctus") and the minuscule nature of man in the larger scheme, is a disjunction exactly examined in Georgics IV. 67–86. Human beings, pathetically top heavy with self-importance, turn about the fragile whims of the private ego. The Virgilian passage could be cited as a fundamental intertext for both Gray poems. It roots Gray's thought in a definitively eighteenth-century adaptation of classical sources which rests on an appreciation of the urgent need to hold in check the impetus to egocentricity. As in the Virgilian passage, this psychologically pernicious force is also recognized as a potentially destructive political vortex: unless the ego is conditioned by objective consideration, the consuming appetite of self will not only corrupt the mental well-being of the individual but thereby destroy the possibility of healthful community.

It is useful to illustrate this point in miniature by contrasting Gray's reception of *Georgics* IV with Milton's. Condee and Keightley find the phrase "ignavumque procul pecus" at line 25 of *Epitaphium Damonis* strange. It is, however, taken from *Georgics* IV.168: "ignavum fucos pecus a praesepibus arcent." To Milton then, the bees are the divine emblem of redemptive labor; they are the good elect kept apart from the lazy/ignorant mob by the cleanliness of their lives and purity of their deeds. The sweet honey of their toil is the provision of goodness to the world. To Gray, however, the bees remind men of their brief existence, their smallness and the need to establish community. There is a world of difference between the anxious zeal of "redemptive labour" and reflective imagination, the "quiet tolerance" of "useful toil." One speaks in the absolutes of revolutionary fervor, the other in the provisional terms of postrevolutionary moderation.

The plaintive tone, begun at line 18 and sustained through the lachrymose contemplation of our little passions, is stilled to a funereal finality by the imperative "respice" of 27, which echoes the subjunctive of 22. The frequentative form suggests an initial, lively attentiveness but now with "respice" one senses the wrench of a valediction. The enlivening force of a tutelary spirit superintending the small labors of the living is altered to a last call to witness the merit of these real tears and the tearful memorial of the verse itself. The finely placed "et" before "has lacrymas" recalls the perfectly idiomatic strength of the Latin verse syntax by which the object is deferred and thus the sentence is slowed to suggest the poet's mournful reluctance to close the work, bid farewell and articulate the last remembrances of Favonius still clinging to his heart. (Closing the sentence is a type of emotional closure; the word is a separating power.) Similarly the enjambment of "fundo" across to line 28 replicates the poet's soft lamentations. But the phrase "ictus amore" most powerfully imitates the hidden wounds of love. Here at last is the explication of, and testimony to, his love for Richard West. The soul cannot rest, the poem cannot be completed, the poet's self will not be annealed until the writing inscribes the final admission of a precious and rare passion. In retrospect, Gray realizes the vanity of life without West and in retrospect he must testify to the beauty of the personal rapport and sympathy; he must find a verbal equivalent that balances it with poetic dignity. The quality of these lines is particularly close to that of Tennyson's *In Memoriam*. Gray develops the received form into a slow-moving and worthy verbal cortege to the memory of his dear West. In *Epitaphium Damonis*, and here, there is an almost palpable need to bury the beloved, to bury, in the living soul, the character of the remembered companion. Poetic burial is a poetic transformation of desolation into consolation through the integrating force of art. The completion of these verse rites is the completion of the poet's recovered poetic self.

Writing out grief the poet is made whole by his craft. The phrase "quod possum" (28) takes up this implication of the poor singer paying tribute to the best of his ability. The resonances in these final lines go far beyond the concluding section of the English sonnet to West, although the two are bound together. In the English the strongest mood is created of an exclusion from nature: the ordinary cycles leave him to "lonely anguish" while "to warm their little loves the birds complain." Even in this disparity between the world and himself, in the clear portrait of othering grief, there is not the exquisitely controlled melody of the Latin. This last cadence from "respice" onwards to the end is one of the great achievements of Gray's Latin verse. As much as the phoenix section of *Epitaphium Damonis* measured the Renaissance virtuosity of Milton, so here the sad catch in the voice at "quod possum" and "dum vivat" holds back the last strains in exact articulation of almost unbearable sadness and tells of the eighteenth-century concern with restraint. This concurrence of melancholy voice and poetic music adumbrates the transference of grave loss to artistic autonomy. These last lines form an entablature of grief which marks as great a moment in this poet's achievement of maturity as *Epitaphium Damonis* does in Milton's. The picture of the poet "weeping beside the sepulchre of West" is conditioned by the phrase "dum vivat." At last the bereaved must quit the lifeless tomb and incorporate the living spirit, the "sancta anima Favoni" into his art and life. The phrasing of the beautiful "iuxta lugere sepulchrum" has the pictorial quality of a Roman funerary bas-relief. There is all the tenderness in it of a husband's final farewell to a beloved wife's spirit. In tone, cadence and vocabulary this is the poetry of the classic love elegy. Gray's formidable scholarship is reserved for the concluding phrase. Not here the neatly conclusive final lines of the sonnet to West. Instead there is the terrifying sight of man's impotence before the extinction of life and love. Man, that wondrous being, and all his blithe exchanges of affection are taken down to silent ashes. The juxtaposition of "mutae vana" tells of the mute West and the vain grief of his earthly friend. It is undercut by the potent force of verse that speaks for the dead, redeems his loss and ensures the permanent record — in the poet's heart and those of his many readers — not the vanity of grieving.

Gray draws on Propertius II.i.87 for this final salutation at his friend's tomb: "taliaque in lacrymans mutae jace verba favillae." Propertius explains to Maecenas that he cannot sing of great wars and heroes. His gift is to sing of his love: "ingenium nobis ipsa puella facit" (4). Propertius wittily shows that love is at the start of the *Iliad*. Great matters are born from trifles. But like Theocritus, Propertius claims a greater significance for the apparently little things. The macrohistory of dates and battles is rated less than the micro-history of the home and the heart. The current of human events is not charted according to kings and emperors but through the moments of being between people. The connections to Virgil's *Georgics*, *The Vanity of Human Wishes*, *Ozymandias* or the leech gatherer are powerful. The poem of small things, finely wrought in the Callimachean tradition, is the same detailed cameo of domestic truths found in Austen too. The contrast between "intonent" (l. 40) and "angusto pectore" points to the same deflation of great events seen in *Georgics* IV. (Woolf would also approve, I think.) So too, at line 45, Propertius turns to the battles fought in his narrow bed as the real subject of his poetry. Here "angusto" and "proelia" contrast not merely as a witty jibe but as a searching examination of what really is important. What is history? he asks. Is it in fact the national struggles chronicled in wars and sieges or is it the record of private life, the record of the heart? Possibly it is more important to follow the selfconfrontation and self-knowledge in a single hearse than to number the horses at Waterloo; the proper study of mankind is after all mankind. Propertius sings of his passionate love: "laus in amore mori: laus alter, si datur imo / posse frui" (l. 46). His whole reason for being is love, and Propertius shows that love alone of all things cannot be healed by human cures. When, therefore, it is asked of the poet how he spent his life, what is the justification for it, he replies that it must be stated, "breve in exiguo marmore" that if he died the cause must be a "dura puella." The marble tablet must be "exiguus" to suit the modest claims of the "little" life led not for military glory, dazzling wealth or fame set to "burst out into sudden blaze" but for the love of another human being. Gray's appropriation of the Propertian line captures therefore with exquisite accuracy the central concerns of the poem's argument: the epitaph to his love for West and the correct scale of things. The primacy of the human heart as a criterion for useful living is what exposes the folly of that destructive desire to dominate and impress others. So the conclusion to the *Elegy* itself or Gray's superb last lines in his *Stanzas to Mr Bentley* reiterate the poet's belief in a radically alternative measure of achievement.

At the center of his thought is his absolute knowledge of a rare love sustained and experienced between himself and the gentle Favonius. West's lines at the end of his poem *Ad Amicos*, sent to Gray in July 1737, articulate the same criteria for living:

Yet some there are (ere spent my vital days)
Within whose breasts my tomb I wish to raise.
Lov'd in my life, lamented in my end,
Their praise would crown me as their precepts mend:
To them may these fond lines my name endear,
Not from the Poet but the friend sincere.[29]

Ad Amicos is a fine reworking of sections from Tibullus's fifth elegy in book III. Without the intertextual evidence of the love elegy's intense presence in Gray's own work and indirectly from West as seen, the *Elegy* becomes no more than a polished reassertion of inherited verities, Polonius-style. Actually the public performance of the Elegy's superbly controlled language and images is directed by the remembrance and integrating force of an enduring passion. The learned language of Latin both keeps away the "profane crowd" of prurient gossip and allows the poet to connect his argument directly by classical allusion to the love poetry he is really writing. He does not want to draw our attention to great battles or modern heroes nor can he mock the folly of inflated pride in witty lines of satire. His concern is to center our attention on the lived experience of those rare moments of empathetic love between one human being and another: this to him is reality. Were he to write these lines to Favonius in English, his allusions would have to be to English love poetry (as Tennyson used the Shakespearean sonnets) and so open the way for those spies of gross misinterpretation looking with glee for the different or the odd. Instead Gray employs Latin to assure the presentation of dignity and truth for a pure affection which deserves serious regard.

Ironically, the English *Elegy* is cast in such impeccably conformist structure and has been so revered by conformist society that any intrusion of the biographical, let alone Lonsdale's argument that the wellspring of its inspiration is otherness, is rejected at once. However the internal evidence of the Latin directs us to the love poetry that really forms the center of Gray's being. The loss of the one love of his is the real cause of his extraordinarily succinct assimilation of belief in the classical sources, grounded in the little life which consoles his otherness. Through his writing of this love he finds a poetic autonomy and sureness of being that weights his greatest work with a probity which has from the time of its publication won universal respect. It may be time now to reread the work in a spirit of understanding a love that sublimates his poetry and should equally win our universal respect. It is an essentially humanizing love that prompts the poet to envision a society of larger sympathies and worthier criteria of real greatness. The loss of West is plangently caught in a moving phrase in Gray's letter to Ashton after hearing of the death of his dear Favonius:

> This melancholy day is the first that I have had any notice of my Loss in poor West, and that only by so unexpected a Means as some Verses published in a Newspaper (they are fine & true & I believe may be your own). I had indeed some reason to suspect it some days since from receiving a letter of my own sent back unopen'd. The stupid people had put it no Cover, nor thought it worth while to write one Line to inform me of the reason, tho' by knowing how to direct, they must imagine I was his friend. I am a fool indeed to be surprised at meeting brutishness or Want of thought among mankind; what I would desire is, that you would have the goodness to tell me, what you know of his death, more particularly as soon as you have any Leisure; my own Sorrow.[30]

"This melancholy day" seems doubly bleak as so much of the grief of it was feared and forecast so long before. One cannot read the words "this melancholy day," which spell the youthful, cruel fate of kindhearted West, without remembering West's own protest at the imminence of death. In 1737, in *Ad Amicos,* he writes:

> alone I stand
>
> Like some sad exile in a desert land;
> Around no friends their lenient care to join
> In mutual warmth, and mix their heart with mine.
> Or real pains, or those which fancy raise,
> Forever blot the sunshine of my days;
> To sickness still, and still to grief a prey,
> Health turns from me her rosy face away.
> Just heav'n! What sin, ere life begins to bloom,
>
> Devotes my head untimely to the tomb;
> Did ere this hand against a brother's life
> Drug the dire bowl or point the murd'rous knife?
> Did ere this tongue the slanderer's tale proclaim,
> Or madly violate my Maker's name?
> Did ere this heart betray a friend or foe,
> Or know a thought that all the world might know?
> As yet just started from the lists of time,
> My growing years have scarcely told their prime;
> Useless, as yet, through life I've idly run,
> No pleasures tasted, and few duties done.
> Ah, who ere autumn's mellowing suns appear,
> Would pluck the promise of the vernal year;

Or, ere the grapes their purple hue betray,
Tear the crude cluster from the mourning spray.
Stern Power of Fate, whose ebon sceptre rules,
The Stygian deserts and Cimmerian pools,
Forbear, nor rashly smite my youthful heart,
A victim yet unworthy of thy dart;[31]

His pleading prayer granted him a further five years, keeping away
the fateful dart. Nevertheless he died without Gray at his side and the
notice of his death was conveyed in the most callous way. West's apology
for living a "useless" life is, however, undercut by the fact of Gray's dev-
astated heart and the poetic memorial he raised. Where West had hoped
to erect a living headstone in the affections of those who treasured the life
of a kind and true friend, he succeeded. Far from being a useless life, his
time on earth had been emblematic of the values that Gray reveres for
him in his *Elegy*. Between the dazzling, worldly life of Walpole and the
quiet, difficult time of a gentle person unfairly dogged by illness, Gray
eventually chose the reserve of private significance rather than the driving
need of men such as Walpole (senior) to wield the "rod of empire."

The *Elegy* holds in tension the world of Walpole and achievement
versus the tranquil insignificance of West. It is, of course, not poetically
portrayed as a simple dichotomy but rather argued back and forth to show
a far more Keatsian dialectic. Between the recluse and the loud statesman,
there is a maze of complicated intervention in which choices are continually qualified and reconsidered. But in assessing the proximity and impact
of West and Walpole in particular on the poet's consciousness, the growth
of his attachment to West and the sudden quarrel with Walpole, it is hard
not to see the *Elegy* as in some ways dismissing the public world of Walpole, which had once so captivated the young Gray, and embracing the
criterion of "enough for me, if to some feeling breast / My lines a secret
sympathy impart" (*To Bentley*, 25–6).

Raymond Bentman writes of this sympathy which had to be secret
in a signal article of 1992.[32] In a valuable summary of secondary sources
Bentman first cites one of the finest Gray scholars, Roger Martin,[33] and
ends with the work in Rousseau's book on the Enlightenment.[34] The title
of Bentman's essay, or rather the coda to it, "hopeless love," raises some
difficulties however. It is too easy perhaps to cast Gray as a tragic romantic whose love gained no fulfillment and whose life was blighted. This
would be to see only one side of a many-sided concern. West's love was
hopeless in the sense of scant or any physical substantiation but surely the
eventual and triumphant recognition of his love and character in Gray's

heart is anything but hopeless? The "feeling breast" becomes a signifying criterion in Gray's life and, through his poetry, in the thinking of many others. West's death, I believe, has a vital consummation in the poetic life of Gray. There is a danger in recounting the history of Gray as an empty failure in which authority and hegemony completely beat him and his mind and love into submission and silence. This is neither accurate nor helpful regarding the complex power structures of resistance which Foucault charts so carefully.

The secret sympathy among members of the quadruple alliance, their large role in hegemonic life, the fact that their letters and poetry stand on the shelves of libraries around the world point to a successful insurgence into othering territory. The very adoption of a term of political power, the alliance, recalling European strategies of war, tells clearly of the members' certain grasp of the contest about and within them. The correspondence, in every sense of the word, struck among these four men proves admirably resilient and ingenious in crossing, transgressing and subverting social boundaries.

It is similarly incautious possibly to regard sexual identity as monolithic and final. I am therefore wary of Bentman's phrase "Some evidence of Gray's sexual orientation."[35] There is a hint of pathologizing a case. Again the phrase suggests a binary opposition. I am sure that the question of identity is less bluntly oppositional and more, as indeed several theorists hold, of a kaleidoscope of social indices, private history, historically bound perceptions, religious faith and so on. Nor do I see the use of proving "Gray was gay" or that "Gay was gay." This type of isolation and reductivism seems too brutally teleological. There is no revivification of the predicament, no recognition or celebration of the resistance, the redemption of the self or the winning of identity. There is too little of the phoenix which ends Milton's epitaph poem to Diodati. What marks the three poets in this study is the vitality of this rebirth of an identity and a superbly deft appropriation of audience.

We are back in some ways to the problem of Nichols's "empty dream" and "failed song." Although there *is*, obviously and seriously, a grim record of isolation and loneliness, there are many substantial counterattacks from the psyche and writing talents that refuse to be failed or empty. The resilience of the inner being and the discovery of an authentic identity needs to be held in tension against the agony. For, in many ways, the identity which does fight back is a bolder and more authentic one than the self which is replete and unchallenged in the comfort of social acceptance and congruity. Death and literary endeavor, mourning and love, abjection and self-assertion — all these factors create minor polarities that qualify and displace any simple binary argumentation or conclusionary impulses in studies of these three writers of genius.

The assumptions behind a phrase such as "evidence of sexual orientation" can be displaced in many ways and exposed as questionable. To what extent identity is not simply sexual selfhood but part of a social matrix is argued by Sinfield and discussed at the end of chapter 1 above. One need not go far to find many other ways of shining a torch straight through the seemingly impermeable conclusiveness of equating the self with the sexual. Memory is but one more example.

Martin translates into beautiful French a famous line from Gray's letters: "Notre mémoire voit plus que nos yeux dans ce pays."[36] It already has a Proustian ring. The self as memory is a particularly acute aspect of identity formation in these three poets because in each case memory of the beloved and the shock of untimely death accentuate the agony of alienation. Time spent in intimate consonance is thus a locus of meaning. The countryside becomes a landscape of remembrance, perfectly sustained in the setting of a country churchyard at dusk. In Virgilian mode the yew tree in *In Memoriam* becomes a beacon of meaning. Rural scenes are invested with memory:

> Witch-elms that counterchange the floor
>   Of this flat lawn with dusk and bright;
>   And thou, with all thy breadth and height
> Of foliage, towering sycamore;
>
> How often, hither wandering down,
>   My Arthur found your shadows fair,
>   And shook to all the liberal air
> The dust and din and steam of town.
>
> (89.1–8)[37]

Similarly Eton is an informing memory to Gray. Here again, of course, the experience is not whole and complete. It is dangerous to romanticize the memory. Time at Eton might have been idealized in retrospect, yet the fact that the four boys needed to form an alliance suggests considerable disharmony, just as the fissures among the men in later life testify to the inner politics of this group. Thus there are contesting elements in the geography of the self. One could coalesce parts too: the memory of sexual fulfillment at boarding school or the elision of memory elsewhere. But the complete privileging of one aspect of identity formation over others seems to blunt the investigation of an emergent self or hamper the useful recuperation of a poet's work in the light of any such emergence.

Bentman spends the middle part of his article placing Gray in the context of sexual proscriptions of the day. This is fine work. It is essential to know what punishment and what laws applied. But this again has the danger of a unilateral oppression. It is such a model of the doers versus the done to that can obfuscate some of the resistant reflexes in the psyche. There is also a difficulty knowing how consciously the poet identified himself with such outlawed individuals. The poetry here suggests that Milton is not as deliberate and selfconscious as Tennyson in the strategy of saying while nonsaying. The use of another language might be read as a more substantial avoidance of public or even private negotiation of identity than the conscious manipulation and daring of Tennyson. The surfacing of this conscious self in an open contestation of the speakable may support the notion of homosexuality only being invented in the nineteenth century. This then troubles retrospectively the simple association of criminology records with the othered self and its resurgent impulses in earlier centuries. The fluidity of the socialized other may match the ambivalence of the allusive subtext running through *Epitaphium Damonis*. It may prove of the highest difficulty to estimate the extent to which legal proscriptions of the day intruded upon the self. It is probably impossible to contextualize sexuality simply by reading of the prosecutions of the day. The use of highly socialized terms from one century for the inner being of someone from another century cannot be implemented without the risk of banality. The collocation of contemporary records of prosecution and literary texts almost has to result in vacuity:

> In this oppressive climate, direct influences on Gray of the contemporary antisodomitical publications are difficult to prove because he would not have talked about material that forced him into silence. We know that he read Pope's *Epistle to Dr Arbuthnot* (TW 9). He would most likely have seen the numerous reports of the Dutch massacres. Beyond this evidence, we can only rely on the fact that he grew up in a powerfully antisodomitical ambiance.[38]

This tells us little of the inner tensions and struggles, the pressures and counterpressures of the imaginative poet. It is useful to know how many were killed or vilified but it does nothing to suggest the resourcefulness and dignifying strength of a soul and identity that fights back. We may be told how many Jewish people were massacred at Auschwitz but we have recourse to Anne Frank's diary in order to perceive something of the inner beauty and resourcefulness that negates the essence of the term "totalitarianism." Where there is authority there is resistance and in mapping the sites of resistance one negates the impression of a cogent and totally

imperious hegemony. To overemphasize a polarity of authority and subjection in relation to the private imagination and literary endeavor of the
other there is little but the extrapolation and endorsement of a false total-
ity of power. It perpetuates a propaganda of supervision that never existed.
To show up the almost credulous reading of a Milton poem or the successful invasion of Victoria's heart with the mourning song of one man
for another is to underline the fiction of this absolute control. To imply
powerlessness is to deny humanity and admit a degree of societal mar-
shaling that never existed. To recuperate the potency, the incursionary
strategies and ingenuity, not to mention the sheer poetry of the love elegies I look at, is to prize open the gap between two readings of the phrase
"consolation of otherness:" "ways of consoling otherness" versus "being
other is a consolation in life." Read one way it is assumed otherness *needs*
to be consoled; read another way, being othered is a considerable consolation, the self enjoys an *advantageous* situation. This ambivalence is central to my argument. How quickly we assume the other requires mending
or pity, or how slowly we realize that otherness advantages the resistant
imagination, may be an index of some of the social conditioning of our
own time — the policing of the mind and the failure of such attempts to
police.

Bentman may talk of raids on molly houses but we may also talk of
literary raids, and much more successful ones, upon the somnolent minds
of a smug, so-called majority that likes to think itself unified, whole and
inviolable. It is time to smash up the myth of a hierarchy of sexual authority that ranges from the fucker (hetero male) to the fucked (hetero women)
to the fucked up (gays). It never existed. Milton, Gray and Tennyson
infiltrated the system that others only imagined was a system. It is not the
time simply to languish in the agony, sufferings and loneliness of gays: iter-
ating injustices may do no more than entrench the belief that there *was*
an all-powerful system that did things to some people who did nothing
back. The fact is these poetic texts are some of the greatest artistry and
intellectual endeavor of each century. They are proof of an intellectual
assault that renders vapid and limp the protestations of a *vulgus* which
read with one eye closed while Milton, Gray and Tennyson were smiling,
the printing presses were rolling, and little boys and girls recited the *Elegy*
for competitions on Parents' Day.

Shatto and Shaw,[39] in their impeccably scholarly introduction to *In
Memoriam*, distinguish clearly between opposing elements of empti-
ness/failure and festal triumph. Much of the above has dealt with the danger of focusing entirely on one pole of gay experience — loss, cruel
isolation, melancholy. But this sadness, which Shatto and Shaw characterize

as deriving from the Greek form of *epicidion*, is opposed to the joyous tone of the *genethliakon* which, of course, is the literary type of the triumphant conclusion to *Epitaphium Damonis*. But it is also the poetic expression of a triumph of the imagination and private identity over the punishment/abjection motif, the *De Profundis* aspect of Wilde's life. But we need to see the glittering success of Wilde's career and self as well. There is the revered corpus of his works, the acclamation of generations of readers and the critical centrality of his thinking today. All this, aside from the pleasure of his plays performed, testifies to the *genethliakon* part of his achievement. Tennyson and Milton, in their poetic incorporation of the celebratory form, rejoice not only in a resuscitation of their mourning spirits but in a reformation of their inner being.

This recovery of identity is a remarkable achievement of mind and soul. The almost ecstatic tone of the poetry is rare in quality:

> Thy voice is on the rolling air;
>   I hear thee where the waters run;
>   Thou standest in the rising sun,
> And in the setting thou art fair.
>
> What art thou then? I cannot guess;
>   But tho' I seem in star and flower
>   To feel thee some diffusive power,
> I do not therefore love thee less:
>
> My love involves the love before;
>   My love is vaster passion now;
>   Tho' mix'd with God and Nature thou,
> I seem to love thee more and more.
>
> Far off thou art, but ever nigh;
>   I have thee still, and I rejoice;
>   I prosper, circled with thy voice;
> I shall not lose thee tho' I die.[40]

This is love poetry by any name. Alfred Tennyson loved Hallam from the bottom to the peak of his being. The sense of Hallam's benevolent surveillance from heaven above allows Tennyson to appropriate the Christian purity and worth of his love. This is possibly the most radical intervention of love over social proscription and testifies to the resilient force of Tennyson's marriage of true minds that affords such a reclaimed identity. This love is neither a crime before men nor a sin before God, *neque crimen neque peccatum*. Milton's steps from love to Love erode any such charge. In a way it is most dangerous even to entertain terms such as "crime" or "sin." This again is the trap of binary poles, of imagining total empowerment versus utter subservience. Trying to refute the vocabulary of such charges openly in rational debate merely endorses the claim that there may be charges to be answered. Refutation grants credence to the proscription. Poetic celebration, however, of the love that must be sung, precludes the possibility of prohibitive positioning. Marriage of the mind and soul is brightly celebrated in the verses of these male love elegies. There are memorable echoes of the *genethliakon* in the distinct parallels that exist between celebratory verses from *In Memoriam* and the jubilant bacchanal which ends *Epitaphium Damonis*:

> Ipse caput nitidúm cinctus rutilante corona,
> Létaque frondentis gestans umbracula palmae
> Aeternùm perages immortales hymenaeos;
> Cantus ubi, choreisque furit lyra mista beatis,
> Festa Sionaeo bacchantur & Orgia Thyrso.

A recent book on Gray takes up, again, the strain of agony and melancholy to the exclusion of this triumphant note.[41] Gleckner's title for the book is *Gray Agonistes*. His emphasis falls squarely on the suffering with little sense of Gray's ingenuity or social circumspection. The title also indicates how much is made of the Bloomian notion of a later writer struggling against the ghost of an antecedent genius, in this case Milton. Gleckner suspects there is a Miltonic strain somewhere but searches too hard for epic comparisons. He is sometimes obliged to connect bizarre pieces in search of collocations:

> Retrospectively viewed from the shortly to appear Eton College and Favourite Cat odes, the intersections of *Paradise Lost* and *Agrippina* indeed take on a borrowed power. I have in mind here such passages as, from *Eton College*,
>
> > Some bold adventurers disdain
> > The limits of their little reign
> > And unknown regions dare descry
>
> and Gray's later reference in the ode to the dire fate awaiting those whom "Ambition … shall tempt to rise." And in the Favourite Cat ode, we find in its cautionary moralistic conclusion: "one false step is ne'er retrieved," one should be "bold" only with "caution";
>
> > Not all that tempts your wandering eyes
> > And heedless hearts is *lawful prize*. [my italics]

Such retrospectivity on Gray's part, visible here but in rudimentary form, is in fact a crucial characteristic of his subtextual autobiography. Moreover, as I have noted before, his self-referentiality is informed centrally by a swelling chorus of echoes of and allusions to Satan's—and progressively to Milton's own—ambition and transgressiveness.[42]

The critic is not at his best here. On page 119, however, Gleckner does mention links between Milton's *Epitaphium Damonis* and the *Elegy* as well as other extraordinary similarities between the lives of the two men. But Gleckner spends too much time trying to force connections with *Paradise Lost* to attend thoroughly to the numerous interdependencies between Milton's funerary verses and the *Elegy* or the role of Latin as a subtly deflective medium. He is not able to concentrate fully on the double voice of the main texts. Although Gleckner refers quite widely to the Gray/West letters and the Latin poems reproduced there, he does not chart the details of some of Gray's early slights to West. He does not always follow the chronology closely enough to detect minute yet significant phrases. He is not able therefore to trace the smaller but significant shifts between Walpole's influence and West's. In fact he scarcely admits such a polarity.

But Gleckner, I believe, does provide some of the finest and most compelling readings of the *Elegy*. Throughout his book he insists on the currency of the *Lycidas* text in Gray's thought. The watery grave of Lycidas and the Hylas myth are not overtly connected but Gleckner weaves in Milton's English death song as an essential part of Milton's predicament of life. He does so with great skill and accuracy. He supports Weinfield who argues for the presence of West throughout the great *Elegy*.[43] Gleckner is at his best in the following passage which is lengthy but well worth quotation. He moves effortlessly among associated texts of Milton, West and Gray.

> [In] West's *Ad Amicos* … there *is* (not merely a hope that there will be) someone "within whose breast my tomb I wish to raise." Gray's, of course, is that breast, not merely "some kindred spirit['s]," the breast not of "the Poet but the Friend sincere" (CTG, 64). No "struggling pangs of conscious truth to hide" here, no "blushes of ingenuous [i.e., honourable] shame" (*Elegy*, 69–70) to repress; rather, with no "denial vain, and coy excuse" here is Gray speaking out in Milton's "lucky words" of him who was "nursed upon the self-same hill, / Fed the same flock, by fountain, shade and rill." The imagined language of Gray's "hoary-headed swain" is thus transformed via *Lycidas* from pure observation ("oft have we seen him"—West *or* Gray) to Milton's plurally governed recollections, as in

> Together both, ere the high lawns appeared
> Under the opening eyelids of the morn,
> We drove afield, and both together heard
> What time the gray-fly winds her sultry horn,
> Batt'ning our flocks with the fresh dews of night.
>
> (*Lycidas*, 25–29)

Together both, both together we — "But O the heavy change, now thou art gone, / Now thou art gone, and never must return" (*Lycidas*, 37–38). Thou, thou, I alone, and "what now is to become of me?" as Milton writes in *Epitaphium Damonis*. "But now alone," he continues, "I wander through the fields, alone through the pastures; where branches deepen the shadows in the valleys, there I wait for evening. Over my head rain and the east wind make a moaning sound, and the forest twilight is shaken by the swaying trees."

I cite especially "what now is to become of me?" not only for its appropriateness to Gray's "existential situation" (Weinfield's phrase, page 97) but because Gray himself pointedly alludes to it:

> One morn I missed him on the customed hill,
> Along the heath and near his favourite tree.
>
> (109–10)

For "customed" Gray originally wrote "accustom'd," evoking not so much "th'accustomed oak" of *Il Penseroso* (whose context does not support the allusion) but the "accustomed elm" under which Thyrsis (Milton) and Diodati (Damon) used to sit together, and to which Milton returns after coming home from Italy only to learn "that his friend was gone." In addition, and more powerfully since it directly addresses West, Gray clearly is recalling in lines 106–14 of the *Elegy* his own translation of Propertius's Elegy 2.1, which he had sent to West a month before his death:

> Today the lover walks, tomorrow is no more;
> A train of mourning friends attend his pall,
> And wonder at the sudden funeral.
>
> (96–98)

The "Epitaph," then, is at once Propertius's "short Marble" that but "preserve[s] a Name, / A little Verse, [his] All that shall remain" (100–101), Milton's *Epitaphium*, and the "tomb" West "wish[ed] to raise" in Gray's breast.[44]

We can only applaud: all the texts are related closely and illuminate each other. The palimpsest of one poet's suffering and loss is read through the poetry of another. The triumph of the creative imagination is cele-brated even if Gleckner does not distinctly place the festal tone in con-text or argument. Of course, Gleckner's reading cries out for the integrating source reference of the Hylas myth. Milton's revolutionary alteration of this myth to a text of agonized *private* experience is *the* major step in constructing the first model for the male love elegy in English. Similarly Gleckner needs the later references of Tennyson's lone yew tree in contemplating the significance of Milton's single elm surrounded by sweet memory. Most regrettably, he cannot focus on the particular rela-tion of these mourning songs because of his determination to prove strong links with *Paradise Lost* and several other contexts, such as Young's *Night Thoughts*. His canvas is not large enough for sketching such connections. But in his writing as quoted above I think Gleckner does frontier work in connecting sections of a superb tradition in English poetry. Strangely, in his 1997 book Gleckner takes up many of the strands of Bentman's 1992 essay but nowhere seems to refer to it or quote from it. I cannot account for that.

Naturally, in showing up weaknesses in both works, I invite a com-mensurate scrutiny of this work of mine. That is as it should be. There are countless points of contention. One can imagine some of them. "Too little queer theory." "No theory." "Where is Matthew Arnold and '*Thyr-sis* — A Monody to Commemorate the Author's Friend, Arthur Hugh Clough, who died at Florence, 1861'?" "How could you omit such an obvi-ous connecting text?" "Where is Shelley's *Adonais*?" "Who says Milton is that distinct about the Hylas referent anyway?" "How can the allusions be conscious yet the poet remain uncertain about his own identity?" "There are terrible and serious gaps in the fundamental assumptions." "One does not argue with the book in its detail, but more sadly, with its ill-conceived beginnings." "There is far too little Greek." "There is too much Latin." "Where is Walt Whitman?" "Or Kit Marlowe?" Such are just a few obvi-ous possibilities for critique and one does not need to be that enterpris-ing to mimic the voice of a crotchety reviewer. But this brief contribution of mine is no more than part of the stream of critical appreciation which winds its slow way from Mason to Martin, to Bentman, to Gleckner, to me and on, certainly, to new scholars. They will undoubtedly detect weak elements in my work but I hope they may discover some new critical ter-ritory as well. At the very least, there is one claim to which I hold here: the significance and centrality of the male love elegy as a form that incor-porates some of the most important thinking and poetic expression in English.

CHAPTER THREE

Points of Resistance

Gray's Letters

Thyrsis

O easy access to the hearer's grace
  When Dorian shepherds sang to Proserpine!
    For she herself had trod Sicilian fields,
  She knew the Dorian water's gush divine,
    She knew each lily white which Enna yields,
      Each rose with blushing face;
  She loved the Dorian pipe, the Dorian strain.
    But ah! but of our poor Thames she never heard!
    Her foot the cummer cowslips never stirred;
  And we should tease her with our plaint in vain.

Well! wind-dispersed and vain the words will be,
  Yet, Thyrsis, let me give my grief its hour
    In the old haunt and find our tree-topped hill!
  Who, if not I, for questing here hath power?
    I know the wood which hides the daffodil,
      I know the Fyfield tree,
  I know what white, what purple fritillaries
    The grassy harvest of the river fields,
    Above by Ensham, down by Sandford yields,
  And what sedged brooks are Thames's tributaries.
                                        (91–110)
                                    Matthew Arnold

Looking back over Gray's correspondence that ended with West's death in 1742, it is easy to see two very different Thomas Grays. In writing to or being with Walpole, he adopts a completely different persona, register and even, one suspects, being, from when he communicates with West. Gray, as the son of business people, is in awe of the prime minister's son; he takes on the loud and jovial confidence of high circles. When writing to West, he is often shy and always in confidence. It almost seems that he is exploring two aspects of the self. Occasionally, when hard under the character of Walpole, he can be patronizing or neglectful towards West. But as the years pass, his correspondence with West increases—correspondence not only of letters but about Letters and about locating a certain identity of the self. West's death seems to project Gray into a formal articulation of this identity and to posit a tribute to that probity which he learned to discern in West and which he raised for all to see in his immortal *Elegy*.

The very first of his letters (in Toynbee) is to Walpole and in it we see the persona of a highspirited Gray, using the energy of satire which we know he can master and enjoy at times:

> Sr, do you think, that I'll be fob'd off with eleven lines and a half? after waiting this week in continual expectation, & proposing to myself all the pleasure, that you, if you would, might give me; Gadsbud! I am provoked into a fermentation! When I see you next, I'll firk you, I'll rattle you with a Certiorari: let me tell you; I am at present as full of wrath and choler, as— as— you are of wit & good-nature; though I begin to doubt your title to the last of them since you have balked me in this manner: what an excuse do you make with your passion-week and fiddle-faddle, as if you could ever be at a loss what to say; why, I, that am in the country could give you a full & true account of half a dozen Intrigues, nay I have an amour carried on almost under my window between a boar & a sow, people of very good fashion, that come to an assignation, and squeak like ten masquerades; I have a great mind to make you hear the whole progress of the affair, together with the humors of miss Pigsnies, the lady's Confidente.[1]

This is the poet of delightful invention and subtle irony that we know from the cat drowned in a goldfish bowl. The letter is, in Toynbee's note, written "in a round schoolboy hand" and "must have been written during Gray's holidays from Eton in 1734[2]." Toynbee also notes carefully the quotation from Congreve's *Double Dealer* in the high spirits of "I'll firk you." There is a wit and joie de vivre here that accords carefully with the character of the recipient, almost as if Gray has the capacity to become the person addressed. Or is he playing with roles for himself, testing the living out of parts of his own nature, or what he thinks/hopes may be himself? Could this literary experiment be the first rough work of finding his self or defining himself?

In October 1734 he writes one of his most amusing pieces ever, again to Walpole, figuring himself as Pru, a loving goddaughter, writing to her "honner'd nurse." It is such a fine piece of complicated irony and manipulation of the persona that it would not be fair to reproduce less than the whole:

> This comes to let you know, that I am in good health; but that I should not have been so, if it had not been for your kind promise of coming to tend me yourself, & see the effect of your own Prescription: and I should desire of you, so please you, as how that, you would be so good as to be so kind, as to do me the favour of bringing down with you a quantity of it, prepared as your Grandmother's Aunt, poor Mrs Hawthorn (God rest her soul, for she was as well a natured, a good Gentlewoman, as ever broke bread, or trod upon Shoe-leather; though I say it, that should not say it; for you know, she was related to me, & marry! Not a jot the worse, I trow) used to make it: now I would not put you to this trouble, if I could provide myself of the Ingredients here; but truly, when I went to the Poticaries for a drachm of Spirit of Ridicule; the saucy Jackanapes of a Prentice-Boy fleered at me, I warrant ye, as who should say, you don't know your Errand: so by me troth, away ambles I (like a fool as I came) home again, & when I came to look of your Receipt; to be sure, there was Spt of RIDICULE in great letters, as plain as the nose in one's face: & so, back hurries I in a making — Water-while, as one may say, & when I came there, says I; you stripling, up-start, worsted-stocking, white-liver'd, lath-backed, impudent Princox, says I; abuse me! That am your betters every day of the week, says I; you ill-begotten, pocky, rascally, damned Son-of-a-Bitch, says I — for you know, when he put me in such a perilous Passion, how could one help telling him his own why, twould have provoked any Christian in the world, tho' twere a Dog — to speak; & so if you'll be so kind, I'll take care you shall be satisfied for your trouble: so, this is all at present from
>
>> your ever-dutifull & most
>> obedient & most affectionate,
>> Loving God-daughter
>> PRU: OROSMADES[3]

The sheer delight that Gray shows in mimicking the intonations of his character, made up as it is from texts as diverse as *Romeo and Juliet* or the widow Blackacre of Wycherley's *The Plain Dealer,* goes far in creating the fun of the letter. His gleeful suggestion of the coy and self-righteous together with the crude and abusive attains its own specific credence. It may be telling that, amid the ingenious build-up of the satire, Gray takes the persona of the younger and subservient character writing to the more experienced and knowledgeable nurse of his childhood. In much of their relationship before the break-up, Gray plays the same part. By Walpole's side and in Walpole's shadow, he travels about Europe and is received as the friend of the prime minister's son. If Gray is tinkering with a role, that of witty companion, we know that the tussle for selfhood and self-discovery may have been, among other things, what led to the quarrel. Gray is, as he writes in verse to Walpole in December 1734, at this early stage of his life and in the full glare of Walpole's company, "That little naked, melancholy thing / My Soul, when first she tryed her flight to wing[4]." In the early part of this verse dedication to Walpole we see a Gray who may already sense the loneliness, the sadness of his own state but who longs all the more for that gregarious liveliness of the more public character:

> From purling Streams & the Elysian Scene,
> From Groves, that smile with never-fading Green
> I reascend; in Atropos' despight
> Restored to Celadon, & upper light:
> Ye gods, that sway the Regions under ground,
> Reveal to mortal View your realms profound;
> At his command admit the eye of Day;
> When Celadon commands, what God can disobey?
> Nor seeks he your Tartarean fires to know,
> The house of torture, & th' Abyss of Woe;
> But happy fields & Mansions free from Pain,
> Gay Meads, & springing flowers best please ye gentle Swain.[5]

Celadon is the name given to Walpole by the members of the little dead poets' society of the quadruple alliance. His name is equated by Gray with joy and light — away from the gloom of introspection, the bright world of society as opposed to the inner world. But Gray's earnest desire to escape the melancholy cast and situation of his own character is perhaps too openly revealed by the over-happy, too-loud idiom of these early letters to the muchadmired Walpole. Behind the dour lines of "That little, naked, melancholy thing / My Soul" lies the worrying shadow of Hadrian's lines to his soul, as Toynbee accurately reminds us: "Animula vagula blandula / Pallidula rigida nudula." A classic example of the powerful use of allusion in poets such as Gray or Milton, this literary reflection exactly restates the dichotomy of social verve and optimism in life versus the cold hand of mortality. We know from Cicero's use of the diminutive in his letters *Ad Familiares* how much more ingrained this form is in the idiom of Latin than in English. In this example the suffix in "vagula blandula" enforces the sense of winning innocence (little, sweet soul), while the same ending in the second segment, in "pallidula" and "nudula" sharpens the note of insignificance (small, trifling soul). The answering diminutives tell of the smallness and cruel brevity of existence against the deceptive charm of vivacity: the seductive "vagula blandula" are undercut by the harsh reality of "pallidula rigida nudula." Gray's little, naked, melancholy soul, his own anxious spirit, already tainted by intimations of loneliness and difference, gasps for the verve and gregarious oblivion of Walpole's social sense, for Celadon's "upper light." These elements, of course, of the enticing activity and pomp of the busy and competitive world versus the sobering anonymity of mortality, run in tension through the *Elegy*. Already here we see the prefiguring of the dialectic of introspection versus the social sense.

The early adventures of his soul, although described with a Popean verve that testifies well to Gray's technical skill, yet recall the tone of the dark fourth canto of *The Rape of the Lock*, thus betraying a predominantly gloomy, melancholy outlook. His soul

> Began with speed new regions to explore,
> And blunder'd thro' a narrow Postern door;
> First most devoutly having said its Prayers,
> It tumbled down a thousand pair of [Stairs],
> Thro' Entries long, thro' Cellars vast & deep,
> Where ghostly Rats their habitations keep,
> Where Spiders spread their Webs, & owlish Goblins sleep.
> After so many Chances had befell,
> It came into a mead of Asphodel:
> Betwixt the Confines of ye light & dark
> It lies, of 'Lyzium ye St James's park:
> Here Spirit-Beaux flutter along the Mall,
> And shadows in disguise scate o'er ye Iced Canal:
> Here groves embower'd, & more sequester'd Shades,
> Frequented by ye Ghosts of Ancient Maids,
> Are seen to rise: the melancholy Scene
> With gloomy haunts, & twilight walks between
> Conceals the wayward band: here spend their time
> Greensickness Girls, that died in youthful prime,
> Virgins forlorn, all drest in Willow-green-i
> With Queen Elizabeth and Nicolini.[6]

Technically, of course, we see the hand of the consummate versifier in such light yet perfect touches as the enjambment in "light & dark / It lies." Here Gray distinguishes himself as worthy of emulating Pope. In concern though, there is a troubled complexity of repression that powerfully recalls lines in the fourth canto of *The Rape of the Lock*. Images of unfulfillment congest into a sense of arrested emotional growth. Gray's own foreshortened or precluded desire seems betrayed by the tone of crepuscular sadness. This has important implications for the *Elegy* and our reading of the twilight melancholy of its setting. Gray has so often been criticized for the desiccation of his spirit. It seems unsympathetic, to say the least, that this so-called deficiency should be seen as an inherent fault of his character rather than the blighting effect of social proscription which I believe it largely was. Lytton Sells can be relied on, in his compendious review of Gray's life and works, to show unconcern and coldness for his subject — ironically so, when this is what he magisterially determines to be Gray's shortcoming:

> His most evident failing was a deficiency of heart. He appears to have felt no love for any one person after the death of West, and of Mrs Gray (which latter he felt less keenly), except possibly Dr Wharton and his family. Even before his mother's death, he had begun to suffer a desiccation of the spirit. Bonstetten put his finger on this moral malady, this 'misère du coeur,' which was due, he supposed, to Gray's never having been in love[7].

Lytton Sells seems to be entirely indifferent to, or ignorant of, the cruel predicament of otherness in which Gray found himself. It explains so much, such as the closure, rather than deficiency, of heart after the loss of West. Where Lytton Sells judges, he might have understood and looked into the role of writing and letters in consoling this profound anxiety. Bonstetten too, shows an extraordinary, culpable lack of feeling for the person he accuses of lacking feeling. Gray — poet of national renown, even of international repute, don at Cambridge, figure of social standing, was hopelessly constricted from pursuing the passion within — he could only long for another country in which there was humanity enough to allow its expression.

Lytton Sells is not finished with his heavy-handed condemnation though:

> It [Gray's never having been in love causing his desiccation] was certainly part of the truth, though the trouble lay deeper. His cold-blooded account of the trial of the Scottish Lords contrasts strikingly with Walpole's more generous attitude. Cole was shocked, in 1770, by his indifference to the indecency of Dr Long's burial. It throws light on this aspect of Gray's character to record that he appears to have felt no obligation to society, or to his fellow men in general. Pembroke

Hall and its servants might have existed for his sole convenience. It is difficult for a reader of his letters to avoid comparing them with those of his lifelong benefactor, Horace Walpole. To Walpole much certainly had been given by nature; but how much did he give in return! Unfailing generosity, and wit, and good humor; untiring activity in politics, in literature, in versatile accomplishments, in encouragement to Gray. Gray's attitude is hardly expressed by fancying that it was simply one of detachment. His intense dislike of persons who had done him no injury, as, for example, the Duke of Newcastle — a man of exemplary personal character — has already been mentioned. His vitriolic attacks on Lord Sandwich and Lord Holland appear symptomatic of some mental, as well as moral, disorder.[8]

If we read back from the significance of West's life to Gray and the excruciating social constraints impinging on Gray, then it is rather unfair to judge him as "cold-blooded" or to fail to understand the intense pain and hurt of the poet's soul. To suggest that he was blindly selfish in his college seems unsubstantiated. To claim that his letters compare badly against Walpole's is hardly supported by our study so far of only the first few of Gray's letters. We discover wit, imagination, affection, if a little clamorous, for Walpole, and the gathering ennui of a psyche that detects an incipient alienation. Nowhere does his correspondence fare ill against Walpole's. When Lytton Sells reaches the acme of his attack and claims that Gray was disordered mentally and morally then we realize that he is clutching so desperately for a coherent reading that he has forced his view to the limits of inaccuracy and distortion. Gray was certainly not mentally disordered.

Lytton Sells is searching so hard, and yet a clue to Gray's emotional life is right under his nose. On the very next page after his little tirade Sells notes: "A competent Latinist, he [Gray] expressed his feelings more easily in Latin than in English. The last section of the 'De Principiis Cogitandi' expresses a more natural and more moving tribute to West than does his sonnet."[9] At this point Lytton Sells's critical impulse is unerring. He has found the quick of Gray's hidden, hurt desires— the pulse of his romantic existence. He is as crucially accurate about the use of Latin here, to express a secret truth, as A. L. Rowse is in telling of Milton's exquisite lines to Diodati in Latin. Tennyson speaks in his day with equal tenderness and unfailing emotional truth but in the confirmed and, by that time, established and thus protective form of English male love lamentation. Latin, revered in the intellectual colony of England, enjoyed such impeccable regard that it could be used as social surety for expressing feelings that social arbiters would otherwise have condemned in English.

It is significant that, as Tennyson used much of the ambivalent Shake-spearean sonnet sequence in his funerary poem, Gray, at the end of these early, short verses to Walpole, casts his farewell in the terms of love images:

> Believe, that never was so faithful found
> Queen Proserpine to Pluto under ground,
> Or Cleopatra to her Marc-Antony
> Or Orozmades to his Celadony.[10]

By implication Gray is the feminine and adoring, while Pluto, Mark Anthony and Walpole stand sternly male. Milton to Diodati and Tennyson to Hallam assumed similar roles.

Even if a large part of the adoration stated is self-conscious irony understood by both parties, there remains unmistakably the language of love amid the jocular good humor and funny exaggeration that we know Gray in good spirits could master:

> After having been very piously at St Mary's church yesterday; as I was coming home; somebody told me, that you was come, & that your servant had been to enquire for me: whereupon throwing off all the Pruderie & Reserve of a Cambridge Student, in a great extasie, I ran in a vast hurry to set Bells a-ringing, & kindle a thousand Bonfires— when amidst these Convulsions of Joy, I was stopt by one of our Colledge, who inform'd me that a fine Gentleman in a laced hat & scarlet Stockings wanted me: so, you may conclude, as soon as I set eyes on him, I was ready to eat him for having your Livery on; but he soon checked me by acquainting me twas not You, that was come; but — Your Service: now undoubtedly after being so terribly bauked; one could not have lived, but by the help of Hartshorn, HungaryWa-ter, & your Journal, which gives me a greater Flow of Spirits than ei[ther of them.] [But, dear Celadon], nothing gave me half so much pleasure, as to find; that after the toil of the day was over, you could be so good as to throw away a moment in thinking of me.[11]

Below the banter and elusive, at least partial, role play of the fainting damsel awaiting news of her beau, there is the clear and sober acknowl-edgment of deep affection. The relationship which gives emotional mean-ing to Gray at this time is the one with Walpole, and the beacon of this identity shines plainly in the phrases "nothing gave me ... so much plea-sure, as to find ... [that you were] thinking of me." Here are the terms of perennial commitment of one human being to another — the love that secures, binds and grants meaning to life. The playfulness of Gray's inven-tion of metaphors for this commitment is itself, looking back over his life, a powerful testimony to the confidence and joy that he felt in his dedication to Walpole at this time. Even here, though, beneath the fun, there is an element of absolute truth. There is really the cunning of passion that artfully sets its admission aside by the device, in this instance, of a Turkish tale:

> When the Dew of the morning is upon me, thy Image is before mine eyes; nor, when the night overshadoweth me, dost thou depart from me. Shall I ne'er behold thine eyes, until our eternal meeting in ye immortal Chioses [bowers] of Paradise; and sure at that hour, thy Soul shall have need of Ablution and the sight of Israphiel, the Angel of examination: surely, it is pure as the Snow on Mount Ararat, & beautiful as the cheeks of the Houries: the Feast of Ramadan is now past away, & thou thinkest not of leaving Candahar; what shall I say unto thee, thou unkind one? Thou has lost me in oblivion, & I am become as one, whom thou never didst remember: before; we were as two Palm-trees in the Vale of Medina, I flourish'd in thy friendship, and bore my head aloft: but now I wander in Solitariness, as a traveller in the sandy desarts of Barca, & pine in vain to tast of the living fountain of thy conversation: I have beheld thee in my Slumbers, I have attempted to seize on thee, I sought for thee & behold! thou wert not there! thou wert departed, as the smoke, or as the Shadows, when the Sun entreth his bed-chamber: were I to behold thy countenance, tho' far off; my heart should bound as the Antelope; yea! My soul should be as light, as the Roe-buck on the hills of Erzerom.[12]

Gray and Walpole had been like two palm trees at Eton. They had grown in friendship and the security of affection. The safe world there had allowed them to flourish. Gray's *Ode on a Distant Prospect of Eton College* is grounded on the melancholy retrospective that we glimpse in this letter — of two friends once entire and complete in a little world which abruptly ends and leaves them separate and exposed. The world into which they were issued, challenging and exciting to many, was alien and alienating to Gray in particular who mourned the security of his male group. It is telling that Walpole later in life simulated a replacement group of male friends in his Strawberry Hill circle and never married. In many ways this friendship with the delicate Chute and others stood in for the Eton world of their idyllic youth, a sort of perfect Arcadia. The images of wandering in solitariness in deserts and pining are strongly reminiscent of the Hylas lament. The search for an identifying relationship, another place of safety and friendship, is taken up in the very next letter, one in which the start is a quotation, altered from the first eclogue of Virgil. Thus the pastoral motif, functioning as a recollection metaphor, a phrase of alienation, is sustained quite smoothly through the correspondence: "Tityre, dum patulae recubo sub tegmine fagi." Being the first line of the first eclogue, it stands by synecdoche for the entire sequence. Although this allusion is undercut by Gray's witty remarks immediately below it, again showing the self-conscious irony, there is a powerful sense of the irony as a screen against admissions of affection that may be too frank:

> Though you'll think perhaps it's a little cold weather for giving oneself languishing airs under a tree; however supposing it's by the fireplace, it will be full as well; so as I was going to say — but, I believe, I was going to say nothing, so I must begin over again — .[13]

Gray's letter to Walpole of January 21, 1735, continues the complex celebration of a romantic friendship:

> I, Orozmades, Master of the noble Science of Defense, hearing of the great reputation of thee, Timothy Celadon, do challenge & invite thee to contend with me at long-love, great-affection, or whatever other weapon you shall make choice of, in Kings-Colledge Quadrangle, a Week hence precisely — .[14]

The witty flourish is complicated by some possible double entendres but mainly by the perceptible sincerity of "long-love" and "great-affection." As in previous letters, the real burden of the emotional correspondence is discovered after the diversionary opening:

> I hate living by halves, for now I lead a kind of I dont know how — as it were — :in short, what the devil d'ye mean by keeping me from myself so long? I expect to be pay'd with interest, & in a short time to be a whole thing, whereas at this present writing, I am but a
> DEMI-OROZ:[15]

"Demi" is a shortened form of the phrase "demidium animae meae" which opens letter 5 of December 1734: Toynbee notes that it is taken from Horace, *Odes* I.iii.8. The romantic simplicity of the statement that Walpole is the completing half of Gray's consciousness is a fine formulation for the marriage of true minds— two human beings who are so naturally drawn to each other that, despite the storms of disagreement and agitation that lay before them, their amity of the mind held fast and constant through it all. The conceit in "keeping me from myself" is a superb equation of the identifying correspondence of being that sustained both men. Their unity is not only a dignifying existential element but most importantly a signifying aspect of a particularly precarious life amid the alien corn. In Walpole's gregarious, busy life and mind, Gray finds, or at least at this time in his life thinks he finds, that compensating being who fills the sense of isolation and vacuity in his own.

As so often in the work of Milton, Gray and Tennyson (if less eruditely so) the allusion carries much of the main emotional freight. Here the classical reference, embedded below the occasionally lighter surface structure of diversionary wit, bears urgently the sense of tremulous anxiety that Horace felt for the safe return of Virgil, his other half in mind and spirit. It is not that Horace simply wishes to have his good friend back, as if this were a wholly altruistic concern and one predicated on separateness; this would underline a type of arrogant independence which Horace's love of Virgil circles far beyond. Horace needs Virgil as part of his very self—the completing consciousness of a beloved companion. In Gray this inner calling—longing—is more complicated by the profound alienation he feels in the larger world, outside the safe bounds of Eton's little Arcadia. This alienation is seldom evidenced by the poet of carpe diem. Such a distinction, I believe, is crucial in determining the melancholic hue of so much of Gray's work or the elegiac force of so much of *Paradise Lost* or the almost inconsolable quality of that greatest lament— *In Memoriam*. So much of the sad, crepuscular imagery of a paradise irretrievably lost, of the Arcadia of the soul vanished, has to do with the bewildering loneliness of otherness experienced by these major establishment, or establishment-made, poets. In trying to recover something of the exact nature of each poet's particular isolation, it is useful to consider the force of the imaginative reflex and envisaging of a consolatory reason for being discovered by each poet. The dream of youth, of reclining under the deep shade of a spreading beech tree ("recubo sub tegmine fagi") in the carefree and unmindful assurance of companionship, the cicadas singing loudly in the quivering haze, is finally a mirage which has to be painfully reconstructed in the terms of a strange and hostile world. In these early letters of Gray the tone of witty humor abounds and testifies predominantly to a consciousness still tied to the dream world of the eclogues. The real terms of hostility and experience have yet to strike the unsuspecting undergraduate: "Alas, regardless of their fate / The little victims play."

Letters 12, 13 and 14 sustain the tone of playfulness, even flirtatiousness. Gray takes on different voices in order to entertain overtly and covertly to express his constant longing for Walpole. As in the first letter, Gray uses a significant phrase from *Henry IV, Part II*, to complain of Walpole's long absence: "when these two eyes behold, I question, whether I shall believe them: three months is a long while, for a poor lone woman to bear; and I have born & born, and been fub'd off, & fub'd off from this day to that day by you, thou Honeysuckle Villain."[16] Even allowing for the irony of play in adopting the persona, there remains a fond solicitude which is just perceptible through the nagging words borrowed from Dame Quickly. "Honey-suckle Villain" somehow tells of Gray's captivation: he assumes again a feminine character in establishing the terms of their relationship at this point.

These terms are exactly reversed between Gray and West at this time. Gray is sought and West is the neglected and pleading correspondent. Gray is dismissive of West's solicitations and writes harshly of them to Walpole in letter 16: "I received a long letter mighty pretty, in Latin, from West yesterday; partly about butter'd Turnips, partly about an Eclipse, that I understood no more than the Man in the Moon; he desired his love to you in English."[17] The patronizing sarcasm in "long," "mighty" and "pretty" is measured out in the cruel allusion to West seeming to write harebrained nonsense. The final jab of "in English" appears to be particularly gratuitous, implying that at least here he is comprehensible.

Walpole's first letter to Gray reproduced by Toynbee is full of the world: Walpole's travels in Europe, the sights, some clever allusions, but little else. Generally the letter reads much like the journal of a tour and Walpole writes with remarkable indifference to the adoring Gray. There seems to be a scale of admiration or definite pecking order among the young men in which the roles of hero and hero worshiper are understood tacitly. Walpole may be dismissive of Gray much as Gray is towards West. This seems to accord with the ranking of prowess that takes place at some boys' public schools.

From the bottom of this scale comes West writing his first letter preserved in Toynbee (no.18); the one in Latin which Gray scorned is lost. The tone is noticeably different from that of any of the complex and highspirited pieces between Gray and Walpole discussed so far. Here the letter from West is immediately direct, solemn and, not to be disguised, markedly more mature. He speaks in a dignified way and quite plainly of his affection for Gray. Set against what we know Gray was saying about West behind his back, this maturity and sincerity are remarkably, and ironically, sobering in deflating those who are higher up than he in the established ladder of admiration.

> You use me very cruelly: You have sent me but one letter since I have been at Oxford, and that too agreeable not to make me sensible how great my loss is in not having more. Next to seeing you is the pleasure of seeing your handwriting; next to hearing you is the pleasure of

hearing from you. Really and sincerely I wonder at you, that you
thought it not worth while to answer my last letter. I hope this will
have better success in behalf of your quondam school-fellow; in behalf
of one who has walked hand in hand with you like two children in the
wood,

> Through many a flowery path and shelly grot,
> Where learning lull'd us in our private maze.

The very thought you see tips my pen with poetry, and brings Eton to
my view. Consider me here in a very strange country, inhabited by
things that call themselves Doctors and Masters of Arts; a country
flowing with syllogisms and ale, where Horace and Virgil are equally
unknown; consider me, I say, in this melancholy light, and then think
if something be not due to,

> Yours.

Here the language of sincere affection and love does not have to be decoded
from a mass of titillating wit; here the expression is consistent and all of
a piece. The simple symmetry of "seeing you" / "seeing your handwriting" and "hearing you" / "hearing from you" has nothing clamorous or
flirtatious about it. There is no attempt to win favor. Rather it is the plain
statement of one person's love of another. The word "quondam" rever-
berates with nostalgia as it speaks not only of the neglect West feels but
also the loss of a whole world. The adult sphere that he is now thrust into
seems a "strange country." In a few key phrases West articulates the essential elements of an experience that is central to the imaginative lives of
Milton, Gray and Tennyson alike, and possibly thousands of people whose
emotional lives are not congruent with the enforced majority model.
Everything in the letter speaks of the bewilderment and alienation of a
life so remarkably like that of Milton. Gray has not yet fully realized this
melancholy fact, blinded as he is by Walpole's worldly joie de vivre, but
the shadow is growing longer.

In letter 19 Gray replies to the lonely West and there is a complete
alteration in his register from that used for Walpole. Here it seems he is
for the first time (or at least the first allowed us by Mason and later Toynbee's construction of the letters) able to speak quietly and earnestly of his
connectedness to another person. It is in terms of this letter primarily that
one has to dispute vigorously Lytton Sells's facile dismissal of Gray's emotional life. There were few that Gray could relate to given the circumstances: the death of West left him friendless and adrift psychologically.
If his mature life was largely a lonely time, it is not to be imputed to him

as a fault but surely to be mourned. The connectedness he feels with West is immediately bound to a crucial existential metaphor used by Gray. Ironically enough the very isolation of his predicament (and Milton's and Tennyson's) forces him to confront the bleak condition of life far more startlingly than members of conformist groups who are in a degree falsely protected by the apparent security of that conformist system. A handicap is then made a virtue in taking the poetics of otherness directly, agonizingly, to the very epicenter of existence's meaningless vacuity:

> When you have seen one of my days, you have seen a whole year of my life; they go round and round like the blind horse in the mill, only he has the satisfaction of fancying he makes a progress, and gets some ground; my eyes are open enough to see the same dull prospect, and to know that having made four and twenty steps more, I shall be just where I was.[18]

The Sisyphus/Camus implications of this extraordinarily powerful metaphor of the blind horse in the mill are clear. The urgency, even extravagance, of Gray's courtship of Walpole's favor is also explicable in terms of this sober statement of his actual experience of emptiness. He courts Walpole in an attempt to escape his own painfully clear perception of the bleak expanse of the years of life. Walpole and the worldly distractions of bustle and social business seem to be one possible way of disguising the naked truth. Activity, pursuit of vanity, may appear to be a palliative against the dreaded nothingness whereby the blindness of the horse in the mill is itself a blessing which Gray cannot claim: he sees and it hurts intensely to do so. He sees partly because he is outside the comforting, yet beguiling, matrices of social conformity, and partly because he has a poetic gift of insight. In a way he is desperately trying to run from the exercise of this great gift. He is a bard and his deep engagement with the role of bard in later English poems is partly explained by the anguish of his early struggle in accepting the implications of a poetic self. The type of identity and dependence he claims with Walpole, recognizing him as his *demidium animae*, is by no means false, but it is too loud, too keen, to be the groundwork of real reciprocal truth telling. He wishes for that blindness, he hopes to lose his sight of life's aimless circle, in the delights and gregarious lightheartedness, call it frivolity, of much of Walpole's life. But West's maturity and clearheadedness are too consistent and incisive to allow Gray to escape — from either his perception of life's vacuity or his talent as a seer, a great poet. From this point on in the correspondence we witness a struggle between the poles of West and Walpole on the consciousness of an emerging poet. We also see the first grain of that single redemptive criterion, or reason for existence, the one stay against the harsh landscape of senselessness— the gaining of another human being's heart. In the *Elegy* this beguilingly modest requirement, this simple, rather frail defense against nothingness, against a darkening landscape, is rooted in the mild, undemanding, yet enduring affections of a true friend. This alone grants meaning. Gray writes to West:

> However, as the most undeserving people in the world must sure have the vanity to wish somebody had a regard for them, so I need not wonder at my own, in being pleased you care about me. You need not doubt, therefore, of having a first row in the front box of my little heart, and I believe you are not in danger of being crouded there; it is asking you to an old play, indeed, but you will be candid enough to excuse the whole piece for the sake of a few tolerable lines.[19]

Letter 20, which follows straight after the trenchant image of the horse in the mill, is written to Walpole and abounds in the sort of exuberance and too-loud exclamation noted already:

> A thousand thanks for the thousand happy New-Years you sent me, which, I suppose, a thousand good-natured people have made you a present of, in the overflowings of their zeal.[20]

The world of the prime minister's son is a luminous sphere of social glamor that proffers oblivion from the uncompromising truths of existential gloom and otherness. Gray is drawn to this circuit of activity, the "boasts of heraldry, the pomp of pow'r," more by the antagonistic urge of solitary introspection than by actual enjoyment of it. The tone of subservience to Walpole and what he represents of the world and of the fagging order of their schooldays is aptly shown in the forced levity of these lines from letter 21:

> Ashton terrifies me with telling me, that according to his latest Advices we are to remain in a State of Separation from you the Lord knows how much longer; we are inconsolable at the News, & weep our half Pint apiece every day about it; if you don't make more haste, instead of us you may chance to find a couple of Fountains by your fireside: if that should be our fate I beg I may have the honour of washing your hands, & filling your Tea-kettle every morning,[21]

By contrast in the next letter, to West, Gray attempts a little wit but soon speaks plainly of his need of him and sends some lines translated from Statius. It is telling that the world of letters, of that inner identity of himself as poet, is reserved mainly for writing to West. The confrontation of himself as poet is gradual and considerably nurtured by West's attention to writing. In this respect West's death is, like Diodati's and Hallam's, the particular event that impels the bereaved to dedicate himself to the literary life in which their friends had so much believed. Accepting the name and being of "poet" becomes a commemorative tribute.

Letter 23 demonstrates how subtly the process of literary identity between friends grows in a Pound/Eliot symbiosis of criticism and encouragement. There is a world of difference from the degree of abasement, even if allowed to be jocular, of the offering to fill Walpole's tea kettle. We witness the gradual unfolding of an authentic personality in the correspondence of friendship with West who writes of a translation of Statius sent him by Gray:

> I agree with you that you have broke Statius's head, but it is in like manner as Apollo broke Hyacinth's, you have foiled him infinitely at his own weapon; I must insist on seeing the rest of your translation, and then I will examine it entire, and compare it with the Latin, and be very wise and severe, and put on an inflexible face, such as becomes the character of a true son of Aristarchus, of hyper-critical memory. In the mean while,
>
> And calm'd the terrors of his claws in gold,
>
> is exactly Statius— Summos auro mansueverat ungues. I never knew before that the golden fangs on hammer-cloths were so old in fashion.[22]

In many ways West *is* an Aristarchus— he increasingly nurtures the young poet. The minute details of writing form the web of amity between the two friends and this same connectedness sustains, almost redeems, the friendship after West's death.

The gaiety and high spirits of Walpole's world are kept up in Gray's letters 24 and 25. The talk is of the town — the latest opera, and tales of an explosion in Westminster Hall. Gray attempts to sound like a man of fashion reporting the latest town gossip. But the raciness does not wear well on the melancholy consciousness of one who senses profoundly his otherness from the society of gloss and glamor. He describes the life of Walpole well as "a confusion of Wine & Bawdy & Hunting & Tobacco."[23] Nothing could be further from the quiet melancholy of West's existence. Sickly, unhappy in his home life and unsure of a career, he eyes the arrogance and frivolity of the passing show with an unfailing perspicuity.

Excused by circumstances from the comforting diversions and group pas-
times of wine, bawdy, hunting and tobacco, he is able to survey the pal-
liatives to the truth quite calmly — he sees the little ploys against reality
for what they are.

Gray fully realizes his inferiority in the ranking of Walpole's world
of loud and manly activities. In the bright sphere of upper-class values he
knows his incongruity. Yet he longs for inclusion. His awkwardness of
stature and lack of social skills are painfully obvious to himself. In the following sad lines in one of a whole sequence of letters to Walpole, the short,
fat poet parodies himself and his ill-fitting disposition:

> It rains, 'tis Sunday, this is the country; three circumstances so dull in
> conjunction with the dullness of my nature are like to give birth to an
> admirable production; I hope you will receive it, as you would a
> Michaelmas Goose from a Tenant; since I send it, not that I believe
> you have a taste for an awkward fat creature, but because I have no
> better way of showing my good-will.[24]

Similarly at Cambridge, Gray felt as much of an outsider as Milton had
done before him. He found the other students rough and full of childish
pranks. Writing to West in letter 33 he protests: "You must know that I
do not take degrees, and, after this term, shall have nothing more of college impertinencies to undergo, which I trust will be some pleasure to
you, as it is a great one to me."[25]

Other students regard Gray as a curiosity, an oddity. His difference
is almost chemically detectable to the majority and the response is immediate and sharp. We know about the tricks used to terrify him of a fire.
The tremulous and delicate poet is a stranger in this place of spirited youth
often intent on student fun, debauchery and drinking — much the same
list as Walpole's. The coincidence of pleasures explains much. Gray wishes
to be included yet is found to be, and feels, too different. He hardly rel-
ishes this exclusion and tries to ally himself with Walpole, who is his one
close friend from school with an entrée into this sphere of social (majority experience) acceptability. Being particularly sensitive, like Milton, he
reacts with anger to being an outcast and castigates the entire unsympathetic establishment for its barbaric lack of educated tolerance of otherness. He lambastes Cambridge in almost identical terms to Milton's as a
place of barbarity and unlearning:

> Surely it was of this place, now Cambridge, but formerly known by
> the name of Babylon, that the prophet spoke when he said, "the wild
> beasts of the desert shall dwell there, and their houses shall be full of

doleful creatures, and owls shall build there, and satyrs shall dance there; their forts and towers shall be a den for ever, a joy of wild asses."[26]

West, in reply to Gray, immediately adjures the Cambridge student never to neglect poetry as a stay in his life. This short passage marks quite distinctly a milestone in the commitment of a friend's concern for the identity and well-being of another. It is a crucial mark in the course of an emergent poetic self caringly nurtured by the love of West. The transfer of this affection determines a moment of definition for Gray. He may not have realized the significance of this trust in his talent as poet until after the break-up with Walpole and after West's death, when he was left entirely helpless for a meaning to his existence: "But wherever you go, let me beg you not to throw poetry 'like a nauseous weed away': Cherish its sweets in your bosom, they will serve you now and then to correct the disgusting sober follies of the common law."[27] That Gray did not yet fully appreciate West's altruism and devotion and that he still felt the need for, or hope of, escape into Walpole's brightly illumined public world is instanced by another of Gray's rather treacherous jabs at West to entertain Walpole, used probably in order to appear bored and superior. He appears instead merely ungrateful and immature: "I had a letter from West with an Elegy of Tibullus translated in it, t h u s l o n g [*sic*, to indicate tediousness]."[28] West, who was cast down by illness and poor spirits, lacking the solace of those benign social pleasures that are often enjoyed by the young and healthy, felt much as Gray would himself only after losing Walpole's company and West's life. West then is doubly betrayed by Gray's lack of sympathy and understanding. West is ahead of his beloved friend in the sufferings of the world and the expression of that pain.

After West's death, and looking back over some of these unkind slights to West, Gray may have had a lingering sense of guilt which possibly prompted him all the more to appreciate and revere his lost companion's early insight into the tenuity of life. Such remorse may have impelled Gray to invest his own *Elegy* with so much of West's poetic delineations. West sent Gray a fine poem entitled *Ad Amicos*. In it can be observed something of the mournful resignation of the *Elegy*. In *Ad Amicos* West ruefully tells of those more fortunate scholars who are allowed friendship, company and good health. West feels utterly alone, separated from the happiness of so many of the other students: "From you remote, methinks, alone I stand / Like some sad exile in a desert land." West's premonition of an early death, his suffering of the ravages of pain and sickness, make Gray's callous remarks particularly worthy of censure. Striking too is the maturity and control of West's verse; he is at this time Gray's superior in some ways. We see the shift from his imitation of Popean style to a bold reclamation of his own authentic poetic voice in a central part of the poem:

> How weak is Man to Reason's judging eye!
> Born in this moment, in the next we die;
> Part mortal clay, and part ethereal fire,
> Too proud to creep, too humble to aspire.
> In vain our plans of happiness we raise,
> Pain is our lot, and patience is our praise;
> Wealth, lineage, honours, conquest or a throne,
> Are what the wise would fear to call their own.
> Health is at best a vain, precarious thing,
> And fair-fac'd youth is ever on the wing;
> 'Tis like the stream, beside whose wat'ry bed
> Some blooming plant exalts his flowry head,
> Nurs'd by the wave the spreading branches rise
> Shade all the ground and flourish to the skies;
> The waves the while beneath in secret flow,
> And undermine the hollow bank below;
> Wide and more wide the waters urge their way,
> Bare all their roots and on their fibres prey.
> Too late the plant bewails his foolish pride
> And sinks, untimely, in the whelming tide.[29]

The alteration from the stunted exposition of moral truisms to the lyric passage of metaphor in which we can clearly hear the poet's tearful cry of despair is remarkable. I am not sure that up to this time Gray had ever written as fine a line as "wide and more wide the waters urge their way" as a moving evocation of time's inexorable erosion of life's granted vigor. The sense of betrayal that many invalids feel is present throughout this heart-felt passage. There is a real sense of flight upwards in poetic force from the line "Tis like the stream." The sudden curtailment of life from the insidious, almost actively conspiring forces below, the precarious nature of our hold on life, intensifies the loneliness of human fate. West, here, is close to the darkest passages of *Epitaphium Damonis* or *In Memoriam*. The gloomy outline of otherness only stretches the shadow further. West sees no other redemptive meaning to be raked from the ashes of this constant enervation than the few lights of real, enduring friendship struck along the quick way from birth to lingering illness or random death.

There are complex relations here. There is the saving force of friendship and the sublimation it allows in poetry or simply writing. There is the total belief of one human being in another and the trust that allows one to cast such love into writing. These elements, and the tensions between them, are well shown in letter 40, from Gray to West. The attempt at self-deception, of pretending a gay joie de vivre as is frequently undertaken in letters to Walpole, is thrown aside. Instead Gray is increasingly ready to admit and gradually confront the melancholy color of his disposition and alienated situation. Increasingly now it is to West that more letters and more emotionally frank ones are addressed in the correspondence. Interestingly we see Gray note clearly here, for the first time really, the sublimation of otherness in the consolation of friendship's love and in the writing out of pain and isolation:

> Low spirits are my true and faithful companions; they get up with me, go to bed with me, make journeys and returns as I do; nay, and pay visits, and will even affect to be jocose, and force a feeble laugh with me; but most commonly we sit alone together, and are the prettiest, insipid company in the world. However, when you come, I believe they must undergo the fate of all humble companions and be discarded. Would I could turn them to the same use that you have done, and make an Apollo of them.[30]

This is a central passage since it shows that Gray was fully aware of the transformation of pain into the cast of letters and it looks forward to his dedicatory lament to this stalwart friend in the *Elegy* itself. In this poem he does in fact turn these melancholy companions into an Apollo. The extraordinary congruence of experience among Milton, Gray and Tennyson is predicated on this transmogrifying of personal loss into the bright and evergreen bands of Apollo's servant-poets.

After two of the usual made-up jocular letters from Gray to his hero, Walpole, there appears a fine piece from West to Gray, in which West gently chides his friend for that disregard and neglect of which we know he does not hesitate to boast in letters to his socially more valuable friend, the son of the prime minister. Gray's neglect causes West real pain and the slight complaint that West makes is expressed as usual in admirably plain speech, exactly suited to the hurt he feels without ever appearing sentimental:

> Receiving no answer to my last letter, which I writ above a month ago, I must own I am a little uneasy. The slight shadow of you which I had in town, has only served to endear you to me the more. The moments I passed with you made a strong impression upon me. I singled you out for a friend, and I would have you know me to be yours, if you deem me worthy.[31]

West was in poor spirits at Oxford and even worse health. The break from close companionship at school, exacerbated by his unhappy family, cast him into deep melancholy. The black moment which is so evident at the early parts of *Epitaphium Damonis* and in many sections of *In Memoriam* is reflected mournfully in West's reworking of a Greek epigram (*Anth. Pal.* vii.170) into Latin. The tale of a boy drowning and then being clutched to his mother's bosom in the hope of life is deeply significant of the poet's own subconscious sufferings:

> Perspicui puerum ludentem in margine rivi
> Immersit vitreae limpidus error aquae:
> At gelido ut mater moribundum e flumine traxit
> Credula, & amplexu funus inane fovet:
> Paullatim puer in dilecto pectore, somno
> Languidus, aeternum lumina composuit.

I once saw a small boy playing along the edge of a river, when the winding flood of its glassy surface closed over him. But then the mother dragged him dying from the cold stream: in fond hope she warmed the still corpse in her embrace. Slowly the boy, now upon that beloved breast, languid in sleep, closed his eyes forever.

Here is the Greek from the *Anthology*:

Τόν τριετῆ παίζοντα περὶ φρέαρ ' Ἀρχιάνακτα
εἴδωλον μορφᾶς κωφὸν ἐπεσπάσατο
ἐκδ' ὕδατος τὸν παῖδα διάβρχον ἥρπασε νάτηρ
σκεπτομένα ζωᾶς εἴ τινα μοῖραν ἔχει
Νύμφας δ' οὐκ ἐμίηνεν ὁ νήπιος, ἀλλ' ἐπὶ γούνων
ματρὸς κοιμαθεὶς τον βαθὺν ὕπνον ἔχει.

Poseidippus or Callimachus

Gray noted justly, in Latin, that this translation was a "descriptio pulcherrima & quae tenuem illum graecorum spiritum mirifice sapit" "(a most beautiful description which captures the fine spirit of the Greek marvelously"). "Pulcherrima" and "mirifice" are entirely justified. In his choice of some words West may even exceed his original—the cruel hope in "credula" goes beyond the plain uncertainty of σκεπτομένα. The phrase "amplexu funus inane fovet" exactly extends the pitiful folly of the desperate mother's last embrace of her son's body. The fine arrangement of death/life wording creates a graphic mosaic of the elemental concerns of West's troubled being. The sense of drowning in life, dying in youth, killed in play, are all aspects of his larger poem in English (*Ad Amicos*) here brought down to a geometric intensity. The inevitability of death's implacable erosion is poignantly cast in "paullatim." West feels this tug of illness, the slow draining of life in his young body, and is suffused with angerless melancholy. Even the protests of the English poem give way here before the current of the cold tide that washes over the hapless boy at play on the river's edge. Just as in that extraordinarily lyric passage of the tree grown to height and beauty only to be cut off below by the water's eddies, so here the emphasis on the edge of the river captures quite accurately the impression of life led always innocent and unwary, played out on the unsuspected perils of dissolution, far more imminent than seen. The lively boy at play, so close to death, so unsuspecting, becomes fully and memorably emblematic as West fills an ancient epigram with the terror and pain of his own condition. In this way West does indeed "make an Apollo" of his suffering, as Gray stated. Poetry of this order sets a high standard for the grieving mourner to match in his commemorative verses. This is so with Diodati's intellectual pitch as well as Hallam's; the lost and beloved friends almost force the poets to become poets at the level of skill, ethical substance and intellect established by themselves. Here the ambit of friendship and writing intertwine in remarkable ways. If Gray's *Elegy* is the mark of Gray's achievement, it is virtually the poetic force of the bereaved that charges him to write to such a high pitch. Each writer is challenged by memory; of excellence to achieve excellence — of love to regain love.

Gray, however, before the loss of West, or the quarrel with Walpole, is still unaware of the erosion of life, of melancholy's dark power. If he suspects it, he loathes it and wishes to escape it or ignore it, and even thinks either option is possible. Against West's piteous lines of drowning in life, so akin in imagery to the loss of Hylas in the well, is Gray's persistent presentation of a certain arrogance of youth. But it is becoming more obviously now an attempt to keep up a cultivated harshness and tough indifference to circumstance when writing to Walpole and all he represents that is contrary to such melancholy strains. We are shown an unflattering view of this inexperienced Gray:

> now as for the transactions here, you are to be ascertain'd; that the Man at the Mitre has cut his throat, that one Mr White of Emmanuel a week ago drown'd himself, but since that has been seen a few miles of, having the appearance of one that had never been drown'd; wherefore it is by many conjectured, that he walketh.[32]

That depression in another and suicide should form matter for entertainment betrays an arrogance and callousness, or the pretended appearance of it, that itself betrays Gray's attempts to keep at bay the rising feeling of isolation and his low spirits, that otherness and weariness to which he admits almost exclusively to West. In his own image of the blind horse we see how nearly and threateningly the shadow of melancholy hung over his young heart.

In letter 47, Gray writes in Latin and does so to speak from the heart to the one person who he really allows such vulnerable admission. He thanks West for letters that are "mellitas," like honey, to him. Yet this sweetness is made bitter by the intrusion of West's illness. As with Milton in his *Lycidas*, Gray here regrets, and protests against, not only a specific intrusion of deforming disease but the grim margins of mortality on young life in general. They are the protestations of youth too against the grotesqueness of evil, death and sickness as phenomena on this earth. He resents the sheer obscenity of such facts. He exclaims, "oh morbum mihi quam odiosum!" "(oh illness, how hateful to me"). Sickness "qui de industria id agit, ut in singulos menses, Dii boni, quantis jucunditatibus orbarer!" "(which by its busy doings within a few months is able, o ye gods, to deprive me of so much joy!"). This is both the complaint of youth as well as horror at the mixed condition of life's cycle of decay and growth, corruption and generation. He grieves with Keats over the constant interference and intrusion — illness and good health, beauty and ugly age, completeness ever subverted, supplanted. He cites Lucretius IV.11.33–4 (where we today would probably call on Blake's "Sick Rose") in pointing to this horrifying mix of bittersweet, imperfect existence: "quam ex animo mihi dolendum est, quod 'Medio de fonte leporum / Surgit amari aliquid'" "(how I deplore that, 'from the very center of the fountain of our delights, rises up some bitter thing").

This sense of the uneven state of things moves to a constant tension between our desire to achieve on earth and the squalid nothingness of life here. This struggle between such poles is central to the thinking of the *Elegy*: "the dauntless breast" of "the little tyrant" versus "the destiny obscure" and "short and simple annals of the poor." Gray goes on in letter 47 to quote brilliantly from Juvenal X.169 and Virgil's, *Georgics* IV.562 to contrast sketches of Alexander the Great and Caesar with the dull tedium of life:

> Aestuas angusto limite mundi, viamque (ut dicitur) affectas Olympo, nos tamen non esse tam sublimes, utpote qui hisce in sordibus & faece diutius paululum versari volumus, reminiscendum est. You champ at the bit in this narrow little strip of earth, and make (as they say) your path to Olympus, but we, you should remember, are not so grand, as to wish to spend very much longer in this filth and shit.

Gray's genius for allusive precision, which has a remarkable creativity in itself, despite Lytton Sells's dismissal, is displayed in the recollection of Juvenal's famous picture of Alexander, intensely discontent with a small kingdom. Like so many military conquerors after him, such as Napoleon or Hitler, the great Greek leader stands for a frenzy of the human spirit at its most extreme, the folly of glory at its most exaggerated. Henry IV's speech over the body of Hotspur comes to mind when thinking of the epigrammatic "Aestuas angusto":

> *Hal* .For worms, brave Percy. Fare thee well, great heart!
> Ill-weav'd ambition, how much art thou shrunk!
> When that this body did contain a spirit,
> A kingdom for it was too small a bound;
> But now two paces of the vilest earth
> Is room enough.

Thus Juvenal identifies the quintessential and his words find application to point a moral and adorn a tale centuries later. His analysis of ambition, whether realized in a Napoleon upon his white steed, or Charles X in *The Vanity of Human Wishes*, comes to represent a pathetically hubristic streak in all human nature. We have to be constantly reminded of the brevity of our stay here. "Reminiscendum est" acts as a sturdy buffer to stop the upward force of inebriating ambition. Gray uses this contrast to point up a terrible danger — of losing hold of the present and perishing in blind pursuit of an earthly desire.

Gray advises West not to neglect his body — to balance his literary studies and high love of letters with a proper care for exercise and the outdoors. The advice may perhaps be a little hard since West really is ill and not of his own neglect at all. But Gray's sentiment and worry is strong and sincere. The fact that Gray is a little heavy-handed and underestimates the fragility of West is significant in several ways. But in a later letter (no. 53) the admonitory tone of "cura ut valeas" (see that you take care of yourself") tells of a real fondness and concern for Favonius's health.

In letter 53 Gray writes a fine Horatian-style ode (based on Odes II.vi) to West. They had planned to study law together after university. Gray tells of the courtroom world in which there is constant contention and squabbling. This first stanza is a witty reworking of the opening to Horace's original:

> Barbaras aedes aditure mecum
>   Quas Eris semper fovet inquieta,
> Lis ubi late sonat, et togatum

Aestuat agmen!

Gray

Septimi, Gadis aditure mecum et
Cantabrum indoctum iuga ferre nostra et
barbaras Syrtis, ubi Maura semper
 aestuat unda:

Horace

Cadiz, the place of peaceful retirement proposed by Septimius, is politely rejected by Horace who describes Spain as a scene of barbarism and warfare: the poet prefers cultivated Tibur. So in his lines to West, Gray turns about the proposal of shared careers at the inns of court to describe the study of law in the same terms as the uncouth world of legal squabbling. Horace's poem in turn rests on Catullus 11 in which the poet bids farewell to Lesbia and contemplates an escapist peregrination to all corners of the world with his companions Furius and Aurelius. What binds the three poems is the tension between contemplated travel abroad and life at home. For Catullus the truth about his *passer*/little sparrow girl is awful: life at home with his lover is unendurable and soon to end. For Horace there is the need to put off Septimius tactfully. Gray succeeds in drawing on the force of these foundation texts in filling the old life at home with much of the love imagery of Catullus's verse yet transposing the agony of an affair into the gentle agreement of true minds. The destructive eroticism of Catullus's passion for Lesbia is mediated to the quiet and beautifully enduring love of friends. Through the Horatian verse there is a calm yet recurrent irony in the poet's rejection of a suit for mutual retirement. There is something a little smug in his declaration of Tibur as his chosen home. In Gray's poem the switch from raucous courtroom to the green world is short of such sharp undercurrents; it is an appeal for the once enjoyed harmony of youth. Here is the text of the remaining stanzas, followed by Hendrickson's translation:

> Dulcius quanto, patulis sub ulmi
> Hospitae ramis temeré jacentem
> Sic libris horas, tenuique inertes
> Fallere Musâ?
>
> Saepe enim curis vagor expeditâ
> Mente; dum, blandam meditans Camoenam,
> Vix malo rori, meminive serae
> Cedere nocti;
>
> Et, pedes quó me rapiunt, in omni

Colle Parnassum videor videre
Fertilem sylvae, gelidamque in omni
Fonte Aganippen.

Risit et Ver me, facilesque Nymphae
Nare captantem, nec ineleganti,
Mané quicquid de violis eundo
Surripit aura:

Me reclinatum teneram per herbam;
Quâ leves cursus aqua cunque ducit,
Et moras dulci strepitu lapillo
Nectit in omni.

Hae novo nostrum feré pectus anno
Simplices curae tenuere, coelum
Quamdiú sudum explicuit Favonî
Purior hora:

Otia et campos nec adhúc relinquo,
Nec magís Phoebo Clytie fidelis;
(Ingruant venti licet, et senescat
Mollior aestas).

Namque, seu, laetos hominum labores
Prataque et montes recreante curru,
Purpurâ tractus oriens Eoos
Vestit, et auro;

Sedulus servo, veneratus orbem
Prodigum splendoris: amoeniori
Sive dilectam meditatur igne
Pingere Calpen;

Usque dum, fulgore magís, magís jam
Languido circum, variata nubes
Labitur furtim, viridisque in umbras
Scena recessit.

O ego felix, vice si (nec unquam
Surgerem rursus) simili cadentem
Parca me lenis sineret quieto
Fallere letho!

Multá flagranti, radiisque cincto
Integris ah! quam nihil inviderem,
Cum Dei ardentes medius quadrigas
Sentit Olympus?

To Gaius Favonius Artitius

O thou about to go with me to the barbaric temple which restless Eris always haunts, where legal strife resounds on every side and the toga-clad army swarms!

How much sweeter it would be to forget business and stretch at ease beneath the spreading branches of a sheltering elm and while away the idle hours with books and the humble Muse?

For now I often wander with care-free mind, while, as I meditate the soft Italian Muse, I scarce remember to heed the sickly dew or lateness of the night; and, wherever my feet take me, I seem to see in every hill a forest-clad Parnassus and in every spring a cool Aganippe.

Spring smiles on me, and gracious nymphs; my fastidious nose makes mine whatever the passing breeze of morning has stolen from the vio-lets, as I lie at ease on the tender grass, wheresoever a brook traces its light course and hesitates with sweet clashings at every pebble.

About the time of the year's renewal these simple cares engrossed my heart, as long as the brighter season of Favonius afforded cloudless skies: nor yet have I abandoned leisure and the fields, nor is Clytie more faithful to Phoebus (though the winds are rising and the softer summer is fading).

For I am his diligent and faithful slave, a worshipper of the orb that sheds splendour so lavishly, whether, as his car brings new life to the joyful labours of men, to meadow and mountain, he is rising and clothing the lands of the East in purple and gold, or whether he is about to paint his beloved Calpe with a more tempered fire: aye, to the very moment when, as the splendour grows dimmer and dimmer, the many-coloured cloud slips away like a thief and the scene fades into green shadows.

Oh, how blessed would I think myself (though I could never rise again), if kindly fate would permit me, sinking low in like fashion, to hide myself in peaceful death!

Ah, how little would I envy the god, blazing with many fires and crowned with unclouded rays, when the middle of heaven feels his flaming chariot.

ALCAIC FRAGMENT

O lachrymarum Fons, tenero sacros
Ducentium ortus ex animo; quater
Felix! in imo qui scatentem
Pectore te, pia Nympha, sensit!

ALCAIC FRAGMENT

O fountain of tears which have their sacred sources in the sensitive
soul! Four times blessed he who has felt thee, holy Nymph, bubbling
up from the depths of his heart![33]

Gray then describes the pastoral alternative beginning with the highly
evocative word "patulae" used at the opening of letter 9: it is a key to the
lost Arcadia of their innocent youth, the Eton kingdom that they once
knew. Held in tension then again is the strange and threatening sphere of
adult strife (of an Elsinore) versus the protected (Wittenberg) state of
unsuspecting youth; the law courts versus Arcadia. The romance of the
pastoral occlusion, that sylvan canopy of the spreading ("patulae") tree tells
of a past state of perfection particularly valued, in fact perhaps the only
reality for sons of otherness for whom the adult world is ever a clamorous,
alien landscape. By the equation of classical allusion, this rural place, the
green shade, represents the field of gentle poesy too, thus in few words
Gray subsumes the meaning of their youth as well as the redemptive meaning of the world of letters. It is the same as West's *locus amoenus* of place
and mind "where learning lull'd us in our private maze." In both these
spheres of experience, and the many bonds adjoining them, are the slight
signifying holds that procure meaning for a Gray or a Milton. This is both
a strength and a weakness. On the one hand large areas of consolatory
social acceptance and affirmation are denied Gray but granted without
question to many other citizens. On the other hand this very denial affords
a clear view through these often fallacious existential social assurances.
Otherness grants a unique, if pained, insight into the agony of existing.
Gray and Milton deploy this private pain in public voice.

The standard phrase "beguile the time" occurs here in the Latin to
suggest both the familiar somnolent retirement but also a means of cir-
cumventing, hiding from the adult, heterosexual world of time. The muse
will help to disguise hours of imprisonment: "sic libris horas, tenuique
inertes / fallere Musa." We are back to Tennessee Williams's library. Given
Gray's image of the blind horse at the mill — we know his acute awareness of vacuity, the sadness of accepting that at best we all beguile time,
our hours here — the phrase is complex. The sweet oblivion from cares of
the Elsinore world is captured in the soporific words "vagor," "blandam"
and "vix … memini." The Arcadia of reminiscence, of nature, companionship and poetry, is evoked well in this hazy forgetfulness through which
the poet wanders without care, unmindful even of the light dew that falls
in the night. Similarly the Arcadia of male love unanimity, of youthful oneness and sweet innocence, is perfectly revivified by the images of rural

seclusion — the paradise is a private garden of the remembered heart. Fundamentally, Gray is discounting the reality of the contentious and angry world of competition, reassuring West that he remains true to the bonds of their "private maze."

Melded to the truth of male love, identity is the controlling world of art that radiates through the false shadows of this ordinary place. So Arcadia itself, the place of reclusion, the green world, is charged by the immanence of Parnassus. Sidney would likely approve! Gray sees fertile Parnassus in every little hillock and discovers Aganippe in every spring. This dismissal of the busy London world, the adult whirligig, the heterosexual carousel, for the claims of art is crucial to Gray's aesthetic construct. Much of the *Elegy* takes on a new reading when cast in a Sidneyan light. "Far from the madding crowd" does not have to be just another *beatus ille* call for retreat. It may also reflect a melancholy resignation to a world seldom lit for him by an identifying reality. This accords well with the chronicle of Gray's actual life for which he too often receives criticism rather than understanding, not to mention sympathy. He and Milton feel far from the "pecus" or milling crowd of things from the start.

The language of ideal retreat is the language of a desired, here denied, perfect state: the controlling golden world mediates over the brazen world of this fallen plain full of contention, imperfection and incompleteness. Meaning is glimpsed in the desire: Arcadia, sketched in the impossible ideal of stanzas 2–6, is forever removed, unattainable yet corrective of this present state. This tantalizing view of a reigning Reality behind our own poor state is accentuated to a harsh distraction in the particular agony of the male love elegy in which the unilaterally declared, heterosexual state of official, majority experience isolates, or tries to isolate, the other. Much of this study aims to show how deftly these poets infiltrate and corrupt such barriers of deliberate or accidental, conscious or unconscious, prejudice. The central polarity of the *Elegy*, between fractious activity and quiet retreat, is exactly foreshadowed in the dramatic break between the harsh contention of the legal world in stanza 1 and the protective shade of Arcadia in 2. It is the dialectic of the Eton ode and the *Elegy*.

The aureate state of Arcadia is pointed out in stanza 4. Art alone, the closely linked tapestry of thought connecting poets and performers, attains that reality which Gray only at best seems to see —"videor videre." The companionship of letters, particularly shared between Gray and West, is a substantial bar to the sense of deprivation and barrenness. This consolation of letters, of the privately appreciated sphere of learned artists, returns in some ways the exclusion of the arrogantly dominant heterosexual hegemony. As with Milton, learning, to Gray and his small coterie of well-read scholar friends, is a bastion as well as a safe haven. The learned languages of Greek and Latin are particularly important in holding off the angry mob. The Parnassus of stanza 4, seen briefly in every hill, "in omni colle" is the very shape of that saving reality of art and learning that grows increasingly between West and Gray. Writing poetry, the achievement of poetry, as between Tennyson and Hallam, the intellectual melding of it, is the Parnassus that redeems an alien landscape. This union of the mind is a substantial consolation of otherness. Writing poetry becomes the writing out of the anguish of difference.

The languid, easeful quality of the country scene is taken deliberately beyond the beauty and tranquillity of any actual place. Stanza 5 describes an ideal *locus amoenus*. But it is not merely the perfection of nature that grants this idyllic state; it is the prospect of a country retirement shared with the beloved. The unanimity and untroubled states of Eton and boyhood are recaptured. Thus, at the heart of the poem, stanza 6, which describes extravagant bucolic peace, gives way to 7, which introduces Favonius's name and treasured companionship. The comparative in "purior hora" tells of the elevated clarity, the transforming beauty of the friendship. This raised consciousness, like the glimpses of pure Parnassus behind the hills about him, constitutes a countryside that is itself a locus for various redeeming sources of consolation. It seems ironic that a passion so frequently sneered at as unnatural should so easily find its identity and validation in nature. The passion for another, for the desired completeness and truth of art's world, for poetry and learning, is bonded to nature as an obdurate and revivifying metaphor. In stanza 8, Gray uses the word "fidelis" to speak of his devotion to "otia et campos"— untranslatable as "leisure" and open fields. The comparison of his faithfulness to heliotrope, once Clytie, turning her head perpetually to the sun, tells of his own dependence on the resources of nature and Phoebus's lyre. Both are held in thrall to the life-giving centers of their being. Arcadia, and pastoral vocabulary, the green shade and country retreat, acquire, for the male love oeuvre, a special significance fully recognized as a codified language which stretches from Theocritus to Marlowe to Whitman and beyond.

The parenthetical condition is one of the finest touches in the poem. The phrasing is sensual and fully elegiac, completely distant from the somewhat tart humor of the Horatian palimpsest. Devotion to nature will not be a mere youthful indulgence, a passing phase together with the dedication of youthful companionship. Arcadia and the love that it represents, the dream that it holds, will secure the poet through the harsh winds of age. Gray sees clearly the muted, unfulfilled yet melancholy compromise allotted his passions, but is sufficiently circumspect to see the gentle compensation of a shaded life "patulis sub ulmi." The resignation in "senescat / mollior aestas" reveals a sad acquiescence, even a longing for old age. This is close to the crepuscular shading of the *Elegy*. The inchoate aspect of the verb "senescat," to suggest the slow increase of years, takes up much of the sadness of Gray's relation to time and the years of adult life puzzlingly granted one who is condemned to an outsider's view of what to members of the social majority cannot be long enough. The ennui of otherness, the desolation of it and the sense of time's burden, is brought out in the longing almost for a less heated old age in which the passions that so unaccountably distinguish and torment him will have, hopefully, abated. (We know from the Bonstetten association, however, that the distinguishing passion will not gradually diminish with age.) The effective contrast between the threatening violence of "ingruant" and vulnerability of "mollior" accentuates the poet's clear perception of the buffeting winds of later life. There is a strong accord here with the scene in *Epitaphium Damonis* in which the two young friends take shelter in a cottage against the cold blasts outside. The fragility of male love experience and the hostility towards it are admirably felt in "ingruant" versus "mollior."

The remaining five stanzas sustain and elaborate on the metaphor of the faithful heliborc attending the progress of the sun. The poet is faithful to Phoebus, the god of poetry. Gray's transition here is remarkable for its precision. The classical allusion is as exact and potent as many of Milton's. In the general tension of Gray's correspondence, between the shy West and the brilliant Walpole, this dedication to poetry is something of another milestone in West's favor. The earlier patronizing tone has disappeared and there is a sincere bond struck in their union of writing. West's devotion to Gray and the poet within him begins at this point to take root noticeably. Much of the excitement of reading this neglected Latin poem is that of the archaeologist: there is a wonderful sense of discovery, of dusting off a relegated masterpiece and restoring its burnished whole. The image of Phoebus Apollo rising refulgent to clothe the landscape in purple and gold, the sense of regeneration in "recreante" and the joy in labors made "laetos"—all tell of the bright sun but, particularly, of the fructifying force of radiant poetry. The golden world of Reality appears in Phoebus as rays cast abundantly, a gift to the brazen earth. This true realm has to be striven for and held continually in the imagination. Gray swears his faith to it: "sedulus servo." He will forever revere this splendid orb held above the earth: "veneratus orbem / Prodigum splendoris." In many ways it is the promise of another country, the young poet's incipient consciousness of some place of tranquillity and love, of sunshine;

beyond this he is beginning to admit that the Walpole world of bustle and glamor can never be his. His inner battle, to accept this sad alienation and relinquish the active sphere reserved rather unfairly for the majority experience, is really over.

The climactic pitch of the Horatian poem, with its slightly tongue-in-cheek tone, or at best conciliatory flattery, moves in Gray's ending to a true vision of eventual oneness and glorious union with Apollo and the realms of light. It is a signal of release from this shadowy and unsatisfactory plain to reach up to the height of true artistic life and identity. The pace is marked in the "magis magis" of stanza 11. The desire to slip away quietly into death — to cheat ("fallere") the declining years — is much a part of the melancholy strain of the *Elegy*. The poet, sensing his difference in the world, does not look at death as the cruel termination of joy actual and full but as escape from a penitentiary. The word "fallere" is familiar from earlier poems in which time will be beguiled by various means. The need to outwit life, slip past it in a way, is captured in the cry of "o ego felix." The emphatic "ego" is the lyric height of the poem and tells of the pain of living. The concluding stanza is a vision of the poet himself enfolded in the glorious rays of Apollo's demesne — Olympus trembling at the chariot's burning weight. There is much of the celebratory festival that ends *Epitaphium Damonis*. Attaining the high realms of art after this life tells of a union with a controlling verity, a greater Reality only glimpsed at times through our imagination on earth. Art is the linking thread of Reality that binds the troubled mortal to the eventual state of life. Gray depends increasingly on this poetic unity with West. Their dedication to poetry is more and more a salvaging force in Gray's life. The elevated conclusion to the poem is no exaggeration of the significance of art in his being. As with Milton and Tennyson, this work of writing will be sacred, the one validating area of activity, sanctified by the trust given to them beyond the grave by those who believed in them as poets.

Without doubt the most personal, poetic and truly moving lines of this letter are not, however, in the poem at all but attached to it in some prose below: "bona tua venia sit si forte videar in fine subtristior; nam risui jamdudum salutem dixi; etiam paule moestitiae studiosiorem factum scias, promptumque, Καινοῖς παλαιὰ δακρύιος στένειν κακά" ("You must forgive me if I seem in fine a little sad; for I have said farewell to laughter and even, you should know, am made a little more studious of sadness and ready to weep fresh tears over old troubles"). The quality of "subtristior" is extraordinary in pinpointing the halfsadness and numbing melancholy of Gray's awakening consciousness of his predicament. There is the same wan qualifier as the prefix "sub" in the "paule" that leads into "moestitiae." So much of Gray's consciousness wavers between the Walpole world of extrovert enthusiasm and the West sphere of wistful introspection.

After this prose poetry occurs an Alcaic fragment. In Toynbee it concludes letter 52 whereas in Starr it is separated. In many ways, however, Toynbee provides a context which makes this fragment almost a final verse to "Barbaras aedes." Gray dedicates himself, in the fragment, as four-times happy if he can be one of those who sense in their heart the inspiration of the muse. Or is he trying to convince himself? The exclamatory "Felix!" seems to triumph over the mournful sense of release in quiet death at stanza 12. Poetry, he claims, raises the individual to that true state of harmony and oneness which is rarely enjoyed on an earth that is puzzling to the other. The sudden declaration of happiness in art is a triumphant conclusion to Gray's appeal to West, but the suddenness itself may be a monitory coda. Gray's correspondence with West attains a tone that is shared with none other. It is as if here only is he prepared to acknowledge the actual pain of his life's experience and call for an answering recognition. This consonance of spirit, and the reflex that operates between "subtristior" and a dedication to poetry, constitute substantial means of consoling otherness. But there is a break between the confessional prose lines and the poetic face. Gray is still holding back, hiding behind the muse. In the very next letter Gray takes up the witty, confident style of the early letters to Walpole. The contrast between this trifling, clever wit and the lyric intensity of his lines to West is remarkable and revealing.

Letter 57, from West, constitutes a poetic response and rebuke in some ways to Gray's Horatian imitation. It is a love poem. West insists that love must come first then the landscape may be transformed. He refers tellingly, in an intermediate letter (55), to "Barbaras aedes" as "your elegant ode." In reply to Gray's Horatian verses, West is far more emotionally responsive and spontaneous than Gray. Milton, Gray and Tennyson all follow a pattern of emotional timidity while their beloved friends, Diodati, West and Hallam, each show a more mature and ready expression of their feelings. The association of withdrawn poet and encouraging companion seems to bind each pair particularly closely. In his poetic response to Gray (letter 57), West signals an alteration directly in adopting the elegiac form, so invoking the languid beauty of Tibullus rather than the Horatian form called upon by Gray. Where Gray's "Barbaras aedes aditure" is clever and incisive in relation to the base poem, West is at once grateful and loving in his heartfelt response. This strikes at the core of Bonstetten's criticism of Gray — that he had never loved anyone. Between Gray's

"Barbaras aedes aditure" and West's reply poem, there is the difference between one almost stunted in emotional expression and the other who verbalizes love freely and in finely modulated verse. Where Gray sublimates his passion to intimation of a better world in which the patterns of love are free and true (here only glimpsed in art), West starts and ends his poem with the desire to embrace Gray and rest in his arms: "Amplector te, Graie" (l. 2) and "Illa intra optarem brachia cara mori." Where Gray displaces a socially proscribed passion and longs for another country, listlessly pining for justice somewhere, West immediately calls upon love as the inspiriting first force in nature. Between the friends there is a contest of souls; Gray prefers to discover Parnassus in nature, behind each little hillock some glimpse of nature, while West only finds meaning in nature when Venus intervenes and colors the familiar countryside with consciousness of the beloved. West is insistent, Gray resistant. Here is the poem and my translation:

ELEGIA

Quod mihi tam gratae misisti dona Camoenae,
    Qualia Maenalius Pan Deus ipse velit,
Amplector te, Graie, & toto corde reposco,
    Oh desiderium jam nimis usque meum:
Et mihi rura placent, et me quoque saepe volentem
    Duxerunt Dryades per sua prata Deae;
Sicubi lympha fugit liquido pede, sive virentem,
    Magna decus nemoris, quercus opacat humum:
Illuc mane novo vagor, illuc vesper sero,
    Et, noto ut jacui gramine, nota cano.
Nec nostrae ignorant divinam Amaryllida silvae:
    Ah, si desit amor, nil mihi rura placent.
Ille jugis habitat Deus, ille in vallibus imis,
    Regnat & in Caelis, regnat & Oceano;
Ille gregem taurosque domat, saevique leonem
    Seminis; ille feros, ultus Adonin apros:
Quin & fervet amore nemus, ramoque sub omni
    Concentu tremulo plurima gaudet avis.
Durae etiam in sylvis agitant connubia plantae,
    Dura etiam & fertur saxa animasse Venus.
Durior & saxis, & robore durior ille est,
    Sincero siquis pectore amare vetat:
Non illi in manibus sanctum deponere pignus,
    Non illi arcanum cor aperire velim;
Nescit amicitias, teneros qui nescit amores:
    Ah! si nulla Venus, nil mihi rura placent.

Me licet a patriâ longè in tellure juberent
    Externâ positum ducere fata dies;
Si vultus modo amatus adesset, non ego contra
    Plorarem magnos voce querente Deos.
At dulci in gremio curarum oblivia ducens
    Nil cuperem praeter posse placere meae;
Nec bona fortunae aspiciens, nec munera regum,
    Illa intrà optarem brachia cara mori.[34]

For what you have sent me, Gray, gifts of the delightful Muse such as the Arcadian god Pan himself might wish for, I embrace you and lay claim again to you with all my heart. Oh already my longing for you is too great!

The country does please me, and the Dryads have also often led me willingly through the meadows of the goddess where the stream runs with its pure fall or the oak, that chief splendour of the forest, shades the green earth. There I wander each new morning, there I find my way in the late of day. And when I stretch out on the familiar turf, I sing a familiar song.

But divine Amaryllis is not unknown in our woods.

Ah, if love is absent, the country cannot please me at all.

That god inhabits the plains, reigns in the deepest valleys, rules the skies and ocean. He tames the herd and bulls, and the lion of savage seed. He tames the fierce boars in revenge of Adonis. And see, the grove is full of warm love and countless birds rejoicing together under every branch in tremulous song. Even the unfeeling plants in the wood strive to marry, even the flinty stones Venus is said to quicken. He is more unfeeling than stone or oak, who refuses to open his whole heart to true love: I would not wish to entrust a sacred pledge into his hands, nor expose the secrets of my heart to him. He does not know friendship who does not know tender love.

Ah! if there is no Venus, the country cannot please me at all.

Let the fates order me to lead my life far from my motherland in some foreign country. As long as your beloved face were present I would not appeal against the gods with any complaining voice. Oblivious of care, resting in your lap, I would desire nothing else to please me. Not ambitious for the good things of fortune nor the gifts of kings, I would choose to die in those beloved arms.

It is a love poem. The fact it slipped through Mason's surgical fingers proves the social respectability and sanitizing force of Latin. It also shows the use of the learned language as secret courier, transgressive medium. This linguistic subterfuge substantiates Foucault's famous statement: "Where there is power, there is resistance ... a plurality of resistances ... spread over time and space. And it is doubtless the strategic codification of these points of resistance that makes a revolution possible."[35] It is unhelpful to wallow simply in the sensationalism of listing gay poets. Foucault strikes at the complexity and ingenuity of the contestation which we find precisely in the details of strategic evasion, encroachment and radical subversion in Gray, Milton and Tennyson. It is precisely in the social politics of readership exchange between proscribed poet and prescriptive society, in the ambivalence of public figure and private self that we may observe the sites of primary revolution. These minutiae of neglected Neo-Latin are Foucault's "points of resistance."

West not only insists on the truth and importance of love but on Gray's need to accept and recognize that love. The refrain underlines this concern and makes it clear that this is a reply poem to "Barbaras aedes." It may be that Gray is not fully conscious of his erotic self or that he is, and is ahead of West already in realizing society's implacable constraints. Or a more emotionally mature West is ahead of a timid Gray. Or there is something of both. Certainly the language of spontaneous and unmistakably sincere love is evident in West's opening lines "amplector te, Graie, & toto corde reposco / Oh desiderium jam nimis usque meum" (3–4). The concessive force of "et" that starts the catalogue of rural delights tells of West's careful distinction between the transferred Sidneyan sublimation and real, embracing love between two human beings. "Et" suggests that he too loves nature but that all the beauties and prettiness of purling streams are as nothing, even if Parnassus does intrude in poetic vision here and there, when love is absent. Nature is sterile and empty without the investment of shared affection. West's weariness of a landscape without personal identity is felt strongly in the repetition of "illuc ... illuc" in line 9 and "noto ... nota" in line 10. The scenes are familiar and dull if love is not there, "ah, si desit amor, nil mihi rura placent."

The tedium of life without passion moves to a complaint, however, in the next catalogue of country scenes from 13 to 21. Love reigns in highest heaven and deepest ocean, it tames bulls and fierce lions. Tellingly, West describes love as "ille [qui domat] feros, ultus Adonin, apros." Love is that power that tames the wild boars, in vengeance for Adonis. The figure of a beautiful youth gashed by savage beasts, themselves now softened by love, bespeaks the poet's own lacerated feelings of unrequited love. The image prepares well for the pained complaint given voice by the repeated forms of "durus" that begin each line in 19, 20 and 21. "Etiam" too is repeated in lines 19 and 20 to accentuate West's accusation: "even unfeeling plants in the forest writhe in married union, Venus even is said to animate the hard, lifeless stones—but harder than the very rocks or tougher than the oak—is that person who refuses to love from his real heart." What is significant is what is not said: Gray is harder than a stone in his refusal to love. How far Gray is culpable is hard to assess: whether he was fully conscious of his sexuality; whether it lay toward West or Walpole, whether he saw and felt all yet realized the impossibility of the situation. The safe reading, of course, is that there is no silent accusation of Gray but that the whole is a complaint from West about his own desire for the love of a woman. In that case lines 23 to 26 deal with West's own desire, ending with the cry: "ah! if there is no Venus, the countryside cannot please me." This reading has some obstacles though, especially the triple "durus" of 19 to 21. Why would he accuse himself of a stony heart, or who is the lady of an unfeeling soul?

The end section moves towards the earlier possibility of an unspoken rebuke to Gray for his cerebral distance or frightened evasion. Possibly it had not occurred to West, or any of the three consciously, that West may love Gray and Gray love Walpole. Gray himself may, in trying to avoid a recognition of his state, particularly long for association with Walpole as a link with the great, busy, conventional world, a blotter to the melancholy introspection and truths of West's world. The nearer West draws, the more West may be tempted to escape to Walpole. This may explain in some ways the inevitable growth of the bonds between Gray and West as the inevitable truths clear, but could also explain Gray's apparently obdurate heart as he runs from full acceptance. Most probably, of course, between the fluctuations of the feelings of the three, there is something of all these emotions mixed through.

Line 29, "if only the beloved face were present, I would never rail at the great gods with querulous accent," holds too much the sense of a known, personal acquaintance, and links too closely to the "durus" lines, to leave much doubt that this poem, itself a direct response to Gray's, is a fine evocation of the poet's profound feelings for Gray. That West simply corrects Gray's high notions of immanent Reality and keeps to the actual desire for a pretty girl is possible still. It would be strongly supported by a later letter, number 84. Here West replies to Gray's admiration of Italian statues by commending real women, beautiful and living all over Britain. Again there is West's call to real life and a rebuke of Gray's safely distance aesthetics. Yet in the protestations, conscious or otherwise, there is too much of the early elegies of Milton in which he too declares his love for the beauty of women. Nor are the two readings, finally, exclusive of each other: West may not realize fully that his exhortations are a transferred articulation of his own passion. The flow of his poetry, however, the insistent interjections of love's rule, and particularly the closing lines, speak too forcefully of an immediate and felt warmth. They return us to his love of Gray: "With no regard for the blessings of fortune, or the gifts of kings, I would choose to die in those dear arms." West recalls the close to the Horatian ode employed by Gray: what Gray turns into a paean to the muse, what Horace used as a gentle way of saying "no" to Septimius, West makes a genuine and memorable declaration of, I believe, a personal love as well as the triumph of such love over all else.

In the deliberate and skillful refutation of Gray's Horatian ode, and in his careful opposition between the probity of individual affection and worldly wealth, there is the notable framework of so much of the great *Elegy*. Gray in retrospective mourning over West, treasured and immortalized perhaps the truths that his ailing friend's constant heart had exposed to him but which he could not see or accept at the time. The resonances of Gray's literary tribute and the awareness of West's early death surround this *Elegia* of West's with a rare and unforgettable tenderness of spirit.

Gray's next letter (58*) is in his witty strain. What grants such humorous pieces more and more the quality of fine humor is the sense of his deliberate efforts to disguise the pain of living. The comic surface is perceptibly tense here with the awareness of a writer who has quietly bid farewell to "risus" and is a little "subtristior." Between the excess and intensity of the show-off wit of his first letters to Walpole and this to West, a detectable sadness has interfused. Gray imagines the books in his study speaking to each other; Aristotle, Boileau and Swift all jostle for position. Were one selecting letters of Gray's for general readership, or even letters from the century as a whole, this one would have a fair chance of selection despite Lytton Sells's low opinion of Gray's epistolary skills. The humor is finely balanced and the timing exact. Gray is using the humor, however, to keep the darker humors away.

In letter 58**, from West to Gray, there is an imitation first of Horace and then of Pope. Both are cleverly designed mines to blow up the clumsier aspects of Miltonic teaching or Popean instruction. Again, the elision is most significant. If West is imploding the worst of Milton's drone "To trust in God & to obey God's Laws" or the most hackneyed of Pope's in "For know, the Man is grafted on the Boy," he is suggesting the danger of systems and organizations of thought. His appeal is that of pure Romanticism. If critics find early Romanticism in the *Elegy*, much of it can be attributed to the elements of West in it. He eschews systems and trusts entirely to the heart — to its memory, to its remembered union with others, to its promptings. The constant pain he endures, his sense of life's bitterness and brevity both intensify such sentiments and bind him yet closer to the work of later Romanticists such as Keats. His satire of Miltonic wit or Augustan control, "Sore shall he smart & most severely pay, / who lets his Passion o'er his Reason sway,'" invites a silent celebration of the spontaneity of the heart registered in earlier poems. This well-executed inversion also points to the roles of public English and private Latin, as well as the relation between the two.

In April 1739 we find the first of Gray's letters from the Continent where he accompanied Walpole on his grand tour. This is a watershed in Gray's life. It is a concerted, even desperate, attempt to make himself a part of that wished-for life of worldly activity, of bright urbanity. The bulk of the letters he sends to Ashton, West or his mother are deliberately or observably travel pieces, no more than, at times, showy or high-spirited (when under the Walpolean glare) accounts of places seen, and sights to criticize or yawn over. The persona of bored English gentleman is carefully constructed and usually well sealed off against any penetrating personal discovery. Yet the very constructedness tells of a need to glaze over, to keep away. It is this that cannot be disguised. The cracks are discernible at this level. The old Gray that we know, "subtristior" in the private admission of a dear friend, tries hard to take up the carefree guise of a public spirit, to follow the delights and airy reprieves of a society man like Walpole, but the noisy admissions are not supported by a close scrutiny of the text. Even the first lines of the first letter from Paris, to West, expose the discrepancy between the longed-for release of society's *nugae*, the pleasantly dulling opiates of receptions and balls, and the worried, islanded soul at heart: "Mr Walpole is gone out to supper at Lord Conway's, and here I remain alone, though invited too." Being left alone, pensive and out of company is so much the emergent truth of the man: it is the memorable sketch of the persona left in the fading half-light of the country church-yard. "Walpole is gone out" is just as much an apothegm of the other half of nature, of Walpole's irrepressibly gregarious soul.

Much later (letter 65), after several lengthy and bored descriptions of scenes, we discover again the distinction between the two travelers in a joint letter from Walpole and Gray to West: "the exceeding Slowness and Sterility of me, & this Place & the vast abundance & volubility of Mr Walpole & his Pen will sufficiently excuse to you the shortness of this little matter."[36] The "sterility" acceded to stands out in relation to Gray as a sort of repeated critique, even, as here, when let slip too glibly from his own mouth.

In letter 70 West speaks of his seclusion from the hubbub of London life. He contrasts his quiet studies with the whirl of Gray and Walpole "fluttering from city to city, and enjoying all the pleasures a gay climate can afford." He, on the other hand, "never go[es] into the gay or high world, and consequently receives nothing from thence to brighten my imagination. The busy world I leave to the busy; and am resolved never to talk politics till I can act at the same time."[37] The *beatus ille* tradition, the Horatian teaching of retirement, and its seventeenth-century beneficiaries, are well formulated in West's distrust of busy-ness — the mad carousel of ambitious contest. But West has a clear grasp of the distinction between what is and what might be. Possibly his precarious health allowed him to appreciate the fleeting joys of life for what they are. He contrasts the world of law, the "barbaras aedes," with the ideal of the green realm: "If wishes could turn to realities, I would fling down my law books, and sup with you to-night. But, alas, here I am doomed to fix."[38] The old dichotomy of business/adult world and Arcadia is present as ever. He longs for his quondam schoolfriend but not merely as a dream of the past: West doggedly believes in the realization of that ideal. Precisely this conviction in the reality of their love experienced might be what causes the timid Gray to evade its fulfillment.

West writes some short lines recalling the Arcadian world of their retirement identity — the blissful existence of an Eton:

> O meae iucunda comes quietis!
> Quae fere aegrotum solita es levare
> Pectus, et sensim ah! nimis ingruentes
>   Fallere curas:
> Quid canes? quanto Lyra dic furore
> Gesties, quando hâc reducem sodalem
> Glauciam gaudere simul videbis
>   Meque sub umbrâ?[39]

Oh delightful companion of my rest! Who used to alleviate almost entirely the pains of my heart, and gradually beguile the cares that increase too much. What will you sing? With what passion will you exult in the lyre, and when will you see Gray my companion returned and rejoicing with me, under the shade? (my trans.)

Gray used to relieve his companion's troubled breast: "aegrotum solita es levare / Pectus." Their togetherness could "nimis ingruentes / Fallere curas." The words "beguile/fallere" by now have acquired a whole context of meaning between West and Gray. 'Fallere' speaks of a desire to escape from time, particularly the time measured out in an alienating world. In this sense it harks back to the terrible image of the blind horse at the mill. "Fallere" recalls another reality, another country in space and time, once glimpsed in youth, happily spent beneath the spreading beech. As in so much of the poetry studied, this private anxiety at the root of the imagery attaches to areas of general experience such as innocence versus experience, Elsinore versus Wittenberg worlds, so that otherwise closed border posts are bypassed successfully. The poetry invades and claims readership in several zones.

The irruption of time upon the safe world of these young men, the incursion of this harsh consciousness of the endless cares of life and, at that, a bewilderingly alien one, render their previous state a memory sufficiently distant to be observed and irretrievable. The fact that he recalls a time when care was lost tells us that the state of innocence is past. The second stanza suitably ends in a series of questions. The inquiry is a search for that state lost — in this Wordsworth is a little prefigured in West's intensified awareness of a precious innocence and protectedness lost to the exposure of a violent and (to West) violating world. The particular anguish of the male love predicament has a large role in foregrounding this sense of loss and may be significant in the Romantic development of memorable innocence. The repetition in the interrogatives of "quid," "quanto" and "quando" achieves a searching and heavily nostalgic quality: "when again will we rest together beneath the beech?" The sad emptiness in the inquiry "What will you sing?" is echoed through the poem as a whole.

The final words, "sub umbra," portraying the protective and protected environment of youth, recall an entire tradition of pastoral poetry and end the lines as much with this general recollection and wistfulness as the particular knowledge of two schoolboys once lost in their own small, immeasurably contented place in the shade. West is ever in mind of his "quondam school-fellow, in behalf of one who has walked hand in hand with you, like the two children in the wood." Life *sub umbra*, in all its implications for Gray and West, is one half, the introspective and reflective, of that polarity in the *Elegy* and within Gray's own embattled consciousness. West's verses, like a persistent shadow, appear between the blaze of the Walpole travel pages. There is a resilient reality to his remembrances that consistently sets at odds the ostentation and, for Gray, easy escapism of visiting places in which, very often, he admits to an oblivion which encloses whole months lost to social chat and glamorous receptions. The next words, of letter 71, tell of this: "It is now almost five weeks since I left Dijon, one of the gayest and most agreeable little cities of France, for

Lyons, its reverse in all these particulars."[40] This is merely a travelogue which could have been written by either Gray or Walpole. Its lack of distinction in all respects is what lulls Gray. Possibly Gray even desires such hazy indistinction. But his mind and identity, maturing ahead of Walpole's, must assert itself. The clash must come.

In 1740 "West wrote a letter to Gray, which Mason thought 'too bizarre for the Public.'"[41] It is, of course, impossible to say in what respect it could have been so bizarre but, given the evolution of West's letters generally, that extravagance could not well have taken the direction of overexuberant, fantastical humor or loquacious murmurings; rather, going by previous letters, I suspect that the expression of affection was too plain in English for Mason to allow in a chronicle of greatness such as he proposed to construct for a famous poet's private writings. This censorship is telling of the same polarity between public edifice, the storied urn, and the pulse of true feeling that raced in West's heart. Such censorship is itself significant of attempts to square the public English voice with the private one often heard only in Latin. The majority establishment wants a great poet of its own design and it finds a ready agent in Mason who is prepared to tailor and snip at the domestic details to make him the model of a national genius.

In a similarly conformist vein, there is Gray's own continued attempt to appear part of worldliness, quick wit and sophistication. In letter 79, to Wharton, Gray writes in excellent Swiftian imitation:

> The Author arrives at Dover; his conversation with the Mayor of that Corporation; sets out in the Pacquet-Boat, grows very sick; the author spews, a very minute account of all the circumstances thereof; his arrival at Calais; how the inhabitants of that country speak French, & are said to be all Papishes; the Author's reflexions thereon.

or:

> a Cut of the Inside of a Nunnery; it's Structure, wonderfully adapted to the use of the animals that inhabit it: a short account of them, how they propagate without the help of a Male, & how they eat up their own young ones, like Cats, and Rabbets. supposed to have both Sexes in themselves, like a Snail. Dissection of a Dutchess with Copper-Plates, very curious.[42]

Again, were one selecting letters for general readership, or representation of the humor of the age executed to perfection, these paragraphs would rate with Swift's best, as indeed the whole letter would. But this high wit is far from the clamorous ostentation of the early letters to Walpole. There is a sense now of a deliberately constructed humor, the work of a professional writer. Beneath the surface there is the lonely Gray who feels the ebb of association with the world about him. The pangs of "subtristior" remain despite, or perhaps because of, the effort to attain the verve and joie de vivre of a Walpole. A certain hardness and urbane indifference has crept into the writing where there was before a bright confidence and ingenuousness in earlier pieces.

In April 1740 West wrote a short elegy to Gray.[43] The flow and pleasurable ease of his verse is quite different from Gray's rather more rigid and epigrammatic style. West advises Gray that he will not revere Roman statues in marble as long as he can admire the living beauty of English girls about him. As already noted, there is a significant clash between the removed aesthete and the more Keatsian voice of West who longs to imbibe life's pleasures. As with Keats, it is the proximity of pain and the experience of suffering that draw West to cherish the pleasures of life and to wish to clutch them. In the final couplet of the elegy, West juxtaposes the joy of travel and beauty to hand for Gray and Walpole with his own knowledge of pain: "let every day be full of joy for you, and may you never know what it is to suffer bitter times." His own unhappy family and his constant ill health render him particularly aware of the precious quality of life's immediate offerings. There is an unspoken censure of the often bored and listless tone affected by the two European travelers unfamiliar with bodily discomfort, monetary difficulty or bitterness at home. West's call to enjoy the whole of Italy as far as it lies ("et tota Italia, qua patet usque frui") takes on some sad strains against the effete selectiveness of the two young travelers.

Inevitably, Gray cannot keep up the charade — either to Walpole, to himself and least of all to West. The subtle duel of selfhood that can be traced in the letters has to reach a concluding contest. In the event, West's gentle insistence triumphs. Gray no longer attempts to deflect into the realm of pure aesthetics his feelings for, or commitment to, West. The emotional challenge thrown down boldly by West in his *Elegia* is finally taken up in Gray's superb poetic response, "Mater rosarum," written after seeing the thundering waters and torrents of the gushing waterfalls at Tivoli. Gray's facade of controlled and regulating indifference is suddenly charged with real wonderment. The sight of the cascading waters, splashing from rock to rock from great heights, moves him and in its beauty he sees this time not merely the shadow of a sublimating nature, Apollo immanent, but is in mind of West. The sweetness and strength of their friendship springs to mind with the same energy and pleasure as the falling waters that leap from one shelf of rock to the next. As in few other of Gray's poems, the Latin reveals a personal intensity and dedication that answers the unswerving love West has borne him from school and after, despite silences and patronizing rebuttals. For the first time, too, the verses are charged with an underlying emotional conviction that is hardly ever detectable previously. The soft phrasing of the opening line is a blandishment that takes up and sustains the metaphor of West and West wind. What was a schoolboy pun is now invested with a personal depth and significance of association which is held throughout the poem's central metaphor. West is the breath of Gray's being. There is a maturity and intimacy here which is immediately signaled by the tenderness of sentiment, and by the sheer beauty of the Latin. This is probably one of the finest examples of Gray's Latin poetry, or of his work as a whole, and it certainly could represent one of the highest points of English Neo-Latin in the century. It demonstrates fully that intensely lyric poetry was far from absent in the eighteenth century but often existed in the undercurrent of Latin, thus connecting the Horatian lyric, the odes of Casimire and the Romantic poets in a creative and recreative continuum.

> Ad C: Favonium Zephyrinum
>
> Mater rosarum, cui tenerae vigent
> Aurae Favoni, cui Venus it comes
>   Lasciva, Nympharum choreis
>   Et volucrum celebrata cantu!
> Dic, non inertem fallere qua diem
> Amat sub umbra, seu sinit aureum
>   Dormire plectrum, seu retentat
>   Pierio Zephyrinus antro,
> Furore dulci plenus, et immemor
> Reptentis inter frigora Tusculi
>   Umbrosa, vel colles amici
>   Palladiae superantis Albae.
> Dilecta Fauno, et capripedum choris
> Pineta, testor vos, Anio minax
>   Quaecunque per clivos volutus
>   Praecipiti tremefecit amne,
> Illius altum Tibur, et Aesulae
> Audisse sylvas nomen amabiles,
>   Illius et gratas Latinis
>   Naiasin ingeminasse rupes.
> Nam me Latinae Naiades uvida
> Videre ripa, qua niveas levi
>   Tam saepe lavit rore plumas

Dulce canens Venusinus ales:
Mirum! canenti conticuit nemus,
Sacrique fontes, et retinent adhuc
(Sic Musa jussit) saxa molles
Docta modos, veteresque lauri.
Mirare nec tu me citharae rudem
Claudis laborantem numeris: loca
Amoena, jucundumque ver in-
Compositum docuere carmen.
Haerent sub omni nam folio nigri
Phoebea luci (credite) somnia;
Argutiusque et lympha, et aurae
Nescio quid solito loquuntur.

To Gaius Favonius Zephyrinus

Mother of roses, for whom the gentle breezes of the West Wind swell, to whom sportive Venus leads her company, attended by choruses of nymphs and the song of birds!

Tell me, beneath what shade does Zephyrinus love to while away the busy day?

Perhaps he permits the golden lyre to sleep; perhaps, full of sweet rage, he wakes it again to sing in the Pierian grotto, forgetful of his friend strolling amid the cool shades of Tusculum or among the hills of lofty Alba, sacred to Pallas.

O Pine forests beloved by Faunus and the goat-footed chorus, I call you to witness, which of you soever the brawling Anio, rolling down the cliffs, causes to tremble with his headlong stream that lofty Tibur has heard the name of Favonius, as have also the enchanting groves of Aesula, and that the cliffs dear to the Latin Naiads have re-echoed it: for the Latin Naiads have seen me on the moist bank where the sweet-singing bird of Venusia so often bathed his snowy plumes in limpid dew. Then a miracle! To hear him as he sang, the grove became silent, and the sacred springs; and to this very day (for so the Muses commanded), the rocks, taught to sing, and the ancient laurels, keep repeating the soft strains.

Do not, then, be astonished that I, a novice of the lyre, struggle with limping numbers: lovely places and joyful spring have taught the song, badly composed though it be; for (be sure) under every leaf in the dark grove cling dreams inspired by Phoebus, and stream and breezes speak more melodiously than any virtuouso.[44]

In the first stanza the soft breezes of the West wind, Favonius, are described in words taken from Lucretius I.2. Thus Gray's opening lines, "Mater rosarum, cui tenerae vigent / Aurae Favoni," have behind them "Et reserata viget genitalis aura Favoni:" "mother of roses for whom the tender breezes of the west breathe life" depends on the Lucretian, "and the fresh generative gusts of the West wind enliven." Lascivious Venus is the companion of these fructifying breezes. The West wind, West himself, is thus the life spirit of Gray and Gray's poetic self. Gradually, as the dross of high living and its eventual alienation have closed over Gray's conscious mind, the true, enlivening principle, the one constant source of meaning in himself is recognized as the steady kindness and fidelity of West as well as that answering inner self within Gray. This poem marks the end of the escapist hope of a Walpolean urbanity and social identity — it is the rapturous acceptance of, and profound gratitude for, the founding reality of West's devoted love and faith in Gray.

The beauty of the water, its wild and unconstrained plenitude, awakens the romantic sensibility of Gray and opens immediately the recesses of his heart. No longer can West charge him with being harder than rocks or oak. Nature full and dynamic finally breaks through to Gray and awakens a part of his being that West so insistently called for in his *Elegia*. Where West rebuked him for trying to worship or recover a truth in nature and aestheticism, appealed to him to bare that part of his being made for love and tenderness, Gray now writes freely of the landscape of a humanized heart, in which feeling is allowed to bound spectacularly from place to place. The landscape of Tivoli triggers Gray's unconscious: the way Tivoli is described, full of easy plenty, displays the transforming power of perception charged with love's ease.

West is seen as the languid spirit who loves to beguile the day under some shade, or lets the golden lyre sleep. The quiet and tender intimacy of the opening line is reminiscent of the expunged stanza from the *Elegy* in which Gray describes the little footprints of the robin in the snow. Hardly anywhere else in his work does he allow himself this degree of candid tenderness of expression. He finds his voice perfectly in the delicate tonality of the Latin opening, in the whispering vocalic increase that suggests the wind's growth, to the final exclamation of song, "cantu," that ends the first stanza. (Significantly, the answering English passage in the *Elegy* is taken out.) Only in *In Memoriam* will the English form be sufficiently developed, and veiled, in funereal dignity and speculative convention, to suffer the same male love intimacy to be openly admitted. There is a somnolent completeness in the following stanza as Gray remembers West. The drowsiness of the images suggests the emotional sufficiency that West provides.

Gray contrasts his passing happy recollection of West with his own stultifying role of highliving sightseer. He half pouts at West's imagined forgetfulness of himself being dragged, now unwillingly, through the cold shades of Tusculum. The word Gray uses for himself on his travels, grown meaningless and listless, is "reptantis", creeping. The verb bears a death-like frigidity akin exactly to the proximate imagery of the "cold shades." Even if one takes "reptare" in the transferred sense of "listless wandering about" (Plaut. Frag.ap.Gell. 3.3.5), there is no more positive view of this last, disenchanted period of travel with Walpole. The high spirits of the grand tour have disappeared, the desire for that coruscating life of society has vanished; Gray knows now the ineluctable nature of his own self and, for the first time, gazes at the sheer abundance of nature with an answering voice within. He adjures the pine forests, the steep Mount Anio and even the deep Tibur to hear the name of Favonius. What makes the scene of beauty powerful and real is the remembrance of West's love. The perceiver is no longer a blank camera but must view scenes of torrential force with an inner resonance of spirit. Gray, momentarily overcome with the power of the Tivoli cascades, loses his guard and writes on impulse of the name of West, that soft spirit and gentle heart, who has supported him for so long, unquestioningly and spontaneously. The rocks are glad of his name and echo and re-echo it to the naiads of the land: "illius [nomen] et gratas Latinis / Naiasin ingeminasse rupes." In this joyous celebration of private soul and answering landscape there are significant intimations of Wordsworth.

Behind the surface lyric, however, the imprint of even more significant texts that were, rather than those to come, signals a message to the initiated, the learned members of the group: Propertius almost pre- dictably appears through the lines. Behind the lines that tell of the clam- orous echoes of the rocks and the persistent calls of the heart, there is the line: "ah! dolor ibat Hylas, ibat Hamadryasin" (Prop. I.xx.32). The imper- fect bears an aspect of continuity which is sustained perfectly in the lament by its mournful repetition. The fall of Hylas, down into the well and the hands of the waiting nymphs, is not only a familiar signal of the male love tradition but a deeply affecting emblem of the ring of sadness that edges that passion which Gray has so far cast aside but at last must embrace, even if briefly, in the passion of delight at Tivoli's tumultuous waters. In I.xx, Propertius warns his friend Gallus, who has a handsome slave boy, to be careful and protective of this valued prize. Propertius cites the exam- ple of Hercules as a warning against carelessness. Theocritus's original has undergone a massive change in the Latin version. Propertius makes the poem witty, and his own, but it does not have to do with mourning and actual death. West, receiving Gray's poem, would recognize at once the Propertian subtext and know the associations of love poetry inscribed. In the Roman poem there is a warning against women's love. This is similar to Milton's eschewing of female attentions in his early elegies. It tells us much about a particularly characteristic attitude of maleness: the male is seen as virtuous and alone, constantly threatened by seductive females. Propertius goes far beyond the Greek in emphasizing this particular aspect of hungry, hot womankind:

> cuius ut accensae Dryades candore puellae
> miratae solitos destituere choros,
> prolapsum leviter facili traxere liquore:
> tum sonitum rapto corpore fecit Hylas.
>
> (LXX.45–7)[45]

This view of women, when shared with other men, is a careful signal of homoerotic bonding; a common fear of the well articulates a desire for escape from consuming female desire. Milton's Eve, disobedient wife of virtuous Adam, and Delilah, seductress of noble Samson, both reveal a similar portrayal of woman as heated and unruly agent of chaos and suffering.

After the loud and reverberant sound of Favonius's name hollowed through the rocks and forests, there is the quiet of lyric resolution. "Nam" explains the means by which West's name is spread throughout the scene: "for the Latin nymphs have seen me on the damp shore." Gray identifies himself with the Hylas myth, in which the naiads clutch at the resisting Hylas, in which male love is an outrage to the drowning passion, the suffocating love of women. Gray's love has been seen; he has been spotted and is known. The mark of his passion is now immanent through the cascades, as if he had thrown a small stone into a placid stream and marked the recording ripples. As in Hardy's "Castle Boterel," the landscape is impregnated, seared with the moment of identifying love. So in this ode to Favonius, Gray shows the process and complication of landscape and inner love, the reflecting turmoil of cascading water and the more restricted, closely held turmoil within.

The naiads have seen the poet "where so often the bird of Venus washes its snowy plumage in the light dew, singing sweetly." The phallic shape of the curving swan's neck and its distinct identity as the bird of Venus combine to tell of the restive passion underlying a picture of sudden calm and exact stillness. The entire forest is silent at its song: "canenti conticuit nemus." The muse commands the stones and ancient laurels to silence. The swan's graceful and romantic song is a moment of perfect being — the graceful bird is the figuring of the inner calm and stillness of the bond between West and Gray. Their romantic friendship is the validating principle of their lives and Gray's full realization of this is epiphanic. The fact that the swan has only one partner for life seals the imagery of an identifying union.

In the final stanza Gray moves to a contemplation of Phoebus's strains. But this inspiring poetic force is quite different from the rarefied devotion spoken of in "Barbaras aedes." Here Gray articulates a poetic resolution of the contest of the will observable in earlier poetic correspondence. The impetus behind this true ode, of unmistakable urgency and beauty, is nature and the muse glimpsed through its perfection, a momentary sighting of that greater, controlling Reality but, particularly, the redeeming identification of both art and nature within the claims of another individual's love. The strength of this devotedness, and its final recognition, is what substantiates this verse beyond the elegantly descriptive, yet relatively pale enthusiasm of his earlier ode "Barbaras aedes." The hope of a jolly *L'Allegro* world is past for Gray and he now consciously embraces the shadowy walk of *Il Penseroso*. As much as the *Elegy* itself may be read as a striving between these two spirits, of heedless indulgence in life and the retired observance of its littleness, so here Gray is brought to a crucial moment in his struggle between the attractions of the Walpole sphere and that longfeared aloneness with the spirit of West — contemplating, rather than taking part in, the bustle and happy, if deceptive, engagements of mainstream life.

R. Martin, who remains one of the finest commentators on Gray, writes of the ode:

> C'est dans la lettre emportant ce cadeau que Gray disait: < Notre
> mémoire voit plus que nos yeux dans ce pays.> Il foulait la patrie
> d'Horace. Pouvait-on mêler avec plus de délicatesse — admettons
> l'ornementation toujours conventionnelle — au souvenir de l'ami
> absent, au souvenir du chantre admiré qui les patronne, la fable gra-
> cieuse qui flotte alentour? Gray porte partout sa conspiration avec
> West. Impalpable, celle-ci visite l'imagination dans le parfum du vent,
> et sa sonorité module les échos des torrents et des bois. Vénus passe,
> cette fois, en un cortège qu'ils aimeront regarder. Mais cette Vénus
> n'est plus que le mythe de la nature, l'âme des bruits et des effluves. Sa
> magie, cachée sous les feuilles, les transport divinement, et la sensibil-
> ité, galvinisée en un lieu consacré, se découvre héritière mystique
> d'Apollon. Gray se reconnaît de la race en captant la voix du monde
> qui s'épanouit. Cet orgueil deviendra son triomphe.[46]

The Tivoli ode could be taken as the point at which West's belief in Gray fuses with the passage of Gray's own troubled inner journey. In the force and conviction of the work, in the lyric intensity of its searching complaint, is the proof of a poet. The lyric, and the introspective examination it allows, the fluctuating "I" qualified and modulated in complex ways—all belong to the English poetry of the great Romantics. Here in Latin, preserved as in some precious amber, is a gem of Neo-Latin, sustaining through the cascading passage of its tensely held stanzas the tradition of Casimire and beyond.

Just as in the Tivoli ode, the sight of rugged and uncontrolled nature thrilled the poet, so that he is incited to recognize and speak out with a moving urgency, so in Gray's ode written at the Grande Chartreuse, he perceives the godhead more nearly through his view of the untrodden rocks and wild fields. (This ode is oddly not in Toynbee but does appear in Mason's 1778 edition of the letters.[47])

ALCAIC ODE

In the Book at the Grande Chartreuse
among the Mountains of Dauphine.

O Tu, severi religio loci,
Quocunque gaudes nomine (non leve
    Nativa nam certé fluenta
        Numen habet, veteresque sylvas;
Praesentiorem et conspicimus Deum
Per invias rupes, fera per juga,
    Clivosque praeruptos, sonantes
        Inter aquas, nemorumque noctem;
Quam si repôstus sub trabe citreâ
Fulgeret auro, et Phidiacâ manu)
    Salve vocanti rité, fesso et
        Da placidam juveni quietem.
Quod si invidendis sedibus, et frui
Fortuna sacrâ legi silentii
    Vetat volentem, me resorbens
        In medios violenta fluctus:
Saltem remoto des, Pater, angulo
Horas senectae ducere liberas;
    Tutumque vulgari tumultu
        Surripias, hominumque curis.

ALCAIC ODE

O thou, Holy Spirit of this stern place, what name soever pleases Thee (for surely it is no insignificant divinity that holds sway over untamed

> streams and ancient forests; and surely, too, we behold God nearer to
> us, a living presence, amid pathless steeps, wild mountain ridges and
> precipitous cliffs, and among roaring torrents and the nocturnal
> gloom of sacred groves than if He were confined under beams of cit-
> ron and gleaming with gold wrought by the hand of Phidias)—hail to
> Thee! And I invoke Thy name aright, grant to a youth already weary
> calm and peaceful rest. But if Fortune now forbids me to enjoy this
> enviable dwelling and the sacred rule of silence, despite my wish,
> sucking me back with violence into the midst of the waves, at least,
> Father, grant that I may spend the hours of my old age free of care in
> some secluded corner; carry me off in safety from the tumult of the
> mob and the anxieties of men.[48]

The godhead is nearer than in the finished and carved beam decorated with gold in a formal church. Gray creates a sense of an empathetic
relation, of nature granting an identity to characteristics of himself–dor-
mant and stunted until struck into life by the answering gleam of nature.
Gray becomes a poet, he becomes "*de la race.*" The majesty and gravity of
this ode are quite distinct from the Tivoli love song but also show the final
break with Walpole, what he stands for and what Gray himself has been
trying to resist—what West has quietly insisted on. Here more than anywhere is the voice of somber Wordsworth. He puts on the mantle of poetry,
accepting with it his identity as creative artist, *Virgilianus vates.* At the
same time he fully realizes the implications of this introspective and lonely
life of the soul. The bardic tradition is one with him from here on. So
much of his later work springs from this intersection of personal life and
profound identification with the mysterious spirit without and within, a
correspondence of vital energies. But the *Il Penseroso* life he knew would
be a sacrifice of the *L'Allegro* joy—there is a weighty dedication of the self
exactly reflected in the dedicatory sonnet to Mitford's edition of the poems:

> A lonely man he was, from whom these lays
> Flow'd in his cloister'd musings: He in scorn
> Held them, the unfeeling multitude, who born
> For deeds of nobler purpose, their ripe days
> Waste amidst fraudful industry, to raise
> In glorious wealth—But He, life's studious morn
> Gave to the Muse, so best might he adorn
> His thoughtful brow, with never-dying bays.
> And well the Muse repay'd him. She hath given
> An unsubstantial world of richer fee;
> High thoughts, unchanging visions, that the leaven
> Of earth partake not; Rich then must he be,

Who of this cloudless world, this mortal heaven,
Possesseth in his right the Sovereignty.[49]

His ending care, exactly as in the *Elegy,* and "Barbaras Aedes," is to be
"tutumque vulgari tumultu," safe from the madding crowd. In the sub-
lime peace of the Grande Chartreuse, Gray finds an echo of his own desire
for complete stillness. His poetic nature is discovered and molded through
the revelation of tranquillity all about him amid the great mountains. His
prayer to the immanent power of the terrifying landscape is "Da placidam
juveni quietem" "grant serene rest to this youth." This is a total disjunction from the whirligig, the opium of the social Walpole. Gray no longer
struggles to avoid or lose himself in a sphere that must finally be alien to
him. This is a different Gray from the man we met at the start of the tour
with Walpole, and certainly far from the insouciance of his first letters.
The forgetfulness afforded by luxury and wealth is erased. Claiming his
poetic consciousness, however, demands a sacrifice of much of his past.
The dark, brooding nature of the godhead here is well expressed in the
opening line, "O Tu, severi religio loci," "Oh you spirit of this severe
place." The clamatory joy of the Tivoli lines is here a profound searching
and almost gloomy assimilation of his fate. If "Fortuna" will not allow
him to be absorbed into the very material of this landscape, its foaming
streams and woods, then he appeals for no more than to end his days in
a remote corner, sheltered from the cares of human beings, "hominum
curis." Unlike Wordsworth, who finds a fulfilling bond with other human
beings in the strong links of raw nature and his own soul, Gray realizes,
in his confrontation of the self, his otherness, his penalty to be apart from
"the madding crowd." His genius, here too brightly scored on the inner
psyche by the revealing blast of nature to be denied any longer, cannot
rise to full Wordsworthian ecstasy for it is bound by the knowledge of
difference and isolation. Here is not the redemptive ring of broad humanity glowing from the liberation of the self, but the condemned soul, fated
to lonely introspection and dedicated art. Thus "a lonely man he was."
Far from criticizing Gray for the sterility of his life, we need to perceive
the extraordinary depth and understanding of his poetic identity, the
penalty inscribed within acceptance of the gift.

From now on Gray speaks with a spontaneity and immediacy of his
affection for West that almost goes beyond Favonius's own expressions of
love. It is as if, once the moment of acceptance has taken place, the break
with Walpole has occurred and all that it implies is past, Gray is able to exceed
West in the fullness of his dedication. Thus, writing from Florence in 1740,[50]
Gray speaks of his love and concern for West's fidelity and constancy:

P. Bougeant, in his Langage des Bêtes, fancies that your birds, who continually repeat the same note, say only in plain terms, "Je vous aime, ma chere; ma chere, je vous aime"; and that those of greater genius indeed with various trills, run divisions upon the subject; but that the *fond*, from whence it all proceeds, is "toujours je vous aime." Now you may, as you find yourself dull or in humor, either take me for a chaffinch or nightingale; sing your plain song, or show your skill in music, but in the bottom let there be, toujours, toujours de l'Amitié.

Later, after his return to England, Gray can no longer disguise nor does he wish to disguise his dependence on West and his identity with him. The break with Walpole is the loss of all hope of escape into an easy and unreflective social round (not that this implies Walpole himself or his circle *were* unreflective — it is what Gray wished for from them that rendered such a world facile and escapist). But Gray is forced to know himself and his role as poet. So he writes:

This, I feel, that you are the principal pleasure I have to hope for in my own country. Try at least to make me imagine myself not indifferent to you; for I must own I have the vanity of desiring to be esteemed by somebody, and would choose that somebody should be one whom I esteem as much as I do you. As I am recommending myself to your love, methinks I ought to send you my picture (for I am no more what I was, some circumstances excepted, which I hope I need not particularize to you); you must add then, to your former idea, two years of age, reasonable quantity of dullness, a great deal of silence, and something that rather resembles, than is, thinking; a confused notion of many strange and fine things that have swum before my eyes for some time, a want of love for general society, indeed an inability to it.[51]

The final sentence concludes the inner struggle for an identity with a gregarious self, a socially easy and popular self that Gray had hoped would do something to palliate the tendency toward introspection and minute scrutiny. But, after all, the West in him has won through and his acceptance that he will never be a Walpole is decisive. It takes up and finishes the intimations of this character that we saw in the first letter of the tour to Europe with Walpole: "Mr Walpole is gone out to supper at Lord Conway's, and here I am alone, though invited too."[52] Gray refers perhaps to his break with Walpole at the end of the tour in the following few lines from letter 97:

These are all the alterations I know of, you perhaps may find more. Think not that I have been obliged for this reformation of manners to reason or reflection, but to a severer schoolmistress, Experience. One has little merit in learning her lessons, for one cannot well help it; but they are more useful than others, and imprint themselves in the very heart.[53]

From now on the correspondence between Gray and West is intensely literary. It turns on translations and comments and one friend sustaining in the other the love of Apollo who has become the signifying god of their lives. But at this very moment of commitment we read of West's increasing ill health:

> I have been tormented within this week with a most violent cough; for when once it sets up its note, it will go on, cough after cough, shaking and tearing me for half an hour together; and then it leaves me in a great sweat, as much fatigued as if I had been labouring at the plough.[54]

He writes of this wracking sickness in a terrifying Latin poem. The anguish of the disease and the fear of death that is just perceptible through the tortured phrasing combine to create a spectral vision of the young, innocuous West thrashing about in exhausting agony. Nights of sleeplessness are exacerbated by days of restless troublesomeness. In a twist of mutual devastation, the coughing exhausts him further, as lack of rest weakens him. His physical weakness is made worse, of course, by an unhappy home so that his love of Gray is a single ray of light through a rapidly failing scene. In the intensity of the phrasing, the continuity of laboring phrases, one upon the other, we sense West's pale helplessness:

> Ante omnes morbos importunissima tussis,
> Qua durare datur, traxitque sub ilia vires:
> Dura etenim versans imo sub pectore regna,
> Perpetuo exercet teneras luctamine costas,
> Oraque distorquet, vocemque immutat anhelam:
> Nec cessare locus: sed saevo concita motu
> Molle domat latus, & corpus labor omne fatigat:
> Unde molesta dies, noctemque insomnia turbant.
> Nec Tua, si mecum Comes hic iucundus adesses,
> Verba juvare queant, aut hunc lenire dolorem
> Sufficiant tua vox dulcis, nec vultus amatus.[55]

A cough causes more distress than any other illnesses because it sets in

and continues sapping the strength from the very abdomen. For it
wields its harsh rule to the bottom of the chest, so exhausting the
weak ribs with a constant struggle. It distorts the face and changes
your voice with breathlessness. Nor does it stop there. But rapidly,
with a cruel speed, it subjects the soft sides of your body too and wearies at last your whole frame with the effort. As a result, every day is
troublesome and sleeplessness ruins every night. Not, even if you, my
delightful companion, were with me, could your words help. Nor
would your sweet voice or beloved face be sufficient to ease my misery. (my trans.)

There is more than the illness; there is a grating sense of life ebbing away,
and the will to live. His only lifeline is Gray yet in his tender final lines in
which he records again his enduring love of Gray and his single wish to
see his face and hear his voice, there is an emptiness and despair. He, for
the first time, doubts that even Gray's presence, his words and good company, could weigh against the rising force of this malaise. If there were
any doubt that Gray was the beloved addressed in West's earlier, and far
more passionate, forceful Latin *Elegia*,[56] the recurrence here of the phrase
"vultus amatus" tells of the link to that early poem in line 29: "si vultus
modo amatus." This confirms much of the reading and interpretation so
far.

    Gray increasingly realizes that the price of his becoming a poet is
high indeed and accepting his identity means that, like Tennessee
Williams, books and the world of the mind must become his one place of
freedom and open citizenship: "You see, by what I sent you, that I con-
verse, as usual, with none but the dead: They are my old friends, and
almost make me long to be with them."[57] Gray is bound here to a great
tradition of other writers and thinkers, the ghostly assemblage that peo-
pled Milton's private world and gave credence and dignity to him. The
soirées and receptions, the great entertainments of the European tour have
vanished. In their place is a far more sober group: the uncompromising
intellects of history, whispering and demanding. The cloak of the bard is
donned at great personal expense. Gray can look to no comfortable community of supporting and helpful society — he has truly tried. The fact is
as plain as that spelled out by Rowse at the start of this work: Gray is
alone; youth is over. Painfully isolated by the condition of his genius, separated from the *pecus* by his nature and emotional experience, he com-
munes with, and even longs at times to join, those pale faces from the
past, a substantial source of security, selfhood and consolation.

    West is alive to the dark implications of these intimations from his
beloved Gray. He responds with characteristic verve, and possibly a degree

of necessary ingenuousness, concerning the half-light world that Gray has had to embrace in the end. West replies:

> But why are you melancholy? I am so sorry for it, that you see I cannot forbear writing again the very first opportunity; though I have little to say, except to expostulate with you about it. I find you converse much with the dead, and I do not blame you for that; I converse with them too, though not indeed with the Greek. But I must condemn you for longing to be with them. What, are there no joys among the living?[58]

This letter is dated May 11, 1742. By June 2 Gray read of West's death in a newspaper. His last question to Gray now hangs in the air as a cruel irony: "What, are there no joys among the living?" The lines that West once translated from the Greek anthology, that tell of the small boy drowned and drawn to his mother's breast, of the tenuous line that divides a moment in life's play from the icy stream, seem at once to bear the substance of selfprophecy. Similarly, the poetic vision of his own fate in *Ad Amicos* is suddenly fulfilled:

> 'Tis like the stream, beside whose wat'ry bed
> Some blooming plant exalts his flowry head,
> Nurs'd by the wave the spreading branches rise
> Shade all the ground and flourish to the skies;
> The waves the while beneath in secret flow,
> And undermine the hollow bank below;
> Wide and more wide the waters urge their way,
> Bare all their roots and on their fibres prey.
> Too late the plant bewails his foolish pride
> And sinks, untimely, in the whelming tide.

Cadences from Milton's *Lycidas* and the fate of Hylas of the braided locks echo through these lines to sound a chill, unspoken reply to West's own last question: "What, are there no joys among the living?" West's inquiry is not entirely rhetorical. It does not have to assume an affirmative response, that is, "Of course there are many joys among the living." There is too much ambivalence in his wish, albeit well-meant, simply to raise Gray's spirits. The question, however, because it is a question, may betray a slight remonstrance if we accentuate "What" and "no." "*What!*" he asks, "are there *no* joys at all for me among the living?" In his own brief life there had been few enough. "Among the living," if they are men such as Gray and countless others, the health granted to them yet denied to West may be a blessing or it could be complained of, for it serves to lengthen their sentence to exist in a twilight world of alienation in which, for Gray, as for many others, there was little joy or fulfillment. Taken retrospectively, that is, knowing how close West was to death when he wrote this question, his call for the joys of the living only endorses his bravery of spirit and punctuates the cruelty of his fate.

As if in partial recognition of the uncertainty and injustice of things, Gray starts his letter to Chute, in which he tells of his shock at the news, with the words "this melancholy day." It is a memorable phrase which circles out in various rings of meaning. The words express not only the effect on Gray himself of a particular loss on that day but also suggest much of West's own melancholy existence. Gray's knowledge of this doubles and intensifies the sadness surrounding him. Such intensity of grief causes the phrase to resonate with a sense of the pity of life in general. These mournful words tell of one day but also describe the many days of suffering, both physical and metaphysical, that made up West's embattled life. Gray is filled with the intensity of this duplicated anguish. The sudden death reminds him of the bleakness of West's life. The fact that he died without the comfort of Gray's presence, that Gray himself had to read of it in a common newspaper, forces him to ponder the final loneliness of us all. "This melancholy day" also speaks for much of Gray's own life past and still to come — measured out, by his own metaphor, like the sightless rounds of the blind horse at the mill. The half-light, the dullness of a melancholy day, is the opening key of the *Elegy*. Finally, the phrase becomes an apothegm for the lives of so many others who endure their illness or otherness quietly and resolutely as West did. In the face of his harsh lot, West was tenderhearted and cared deeply for those he loved. Close to death, his concern was for Gray to enjoy life. He was young and his talents were great. He was in pain yet constant and perennially hopeful. Small wonder that such a loss, the significance of such a life and of such love in his life, drew Gray to contemplate loss, the significance of life, and love in life, and to construct for his beloved Favonius one of the finest existential meditations and literary monuments in English:

THE EPITAPH

HERE rests his head upon the lap of Earth
A Youth to Fortune and to Fame unknown,
Fair Science frown'd not on his humble birth,
And Melancholy mark'd him for her own.
Large was his bounty, and his soul sincere,
Heav'n did a recompence as largely send:
He gave to Mis'ry all he had, a tear,

He gain'd from Heav'n ('twas all he wish'd) a friend.
No further seek his merits to disclose,
Or draw his frailties from their dread abode,
(There they alike in trembling hope repose)
The bosom of his Father and his God.

A Deeper Voice

Arthur Hallam and Alfred Tennyson

Ah! Certe extremum licuisset tangere dextram,
Et bene compositos placide morientis ocellos,
Et dixisse 'Vale! nostri memor ibis ad astra.
Epitaphium Damonis

Respice et has lacrimas, memori quas ictus amore
Fundo; quod possum, juxtá lugere sepulchrum
Dum juvat, et mutae vana haec jactare favillae.
Ad Favonium

O, therefore from thy sightless range
With gods in unconjectured bliss,
O, from the distance of the abyss,
Of tenfold-complicated change
Descend, and touch, and enter; hear
The wish too strong for words to name;
That in this blindness of the frame
My ghost may feel that thine is near.
In Memoriam

One of the most pleasing connections between Gray's *Elegy* and Tennyson's *In Memoriam* is the current of allusion to Latin love elegy that runs below the surface of both poems. In Gray's work this allusion is a beautiful and articulate completion of the poem's larger impulse. Classical reference is used with the precision of Eliot's enriching allusions and affords the lines a powerful resonance. There is in a sense a double text, the actual descriptive text and the allusive text behind it. Latin, of course, provides a perfect opportunity for this duality. The reader's learning is tested therefore and his ability to read the text is gauged by erudition; many may follow the descriptive text but only a few are licensed by learning to appreciate the encoded intertext. So learning holds back the "vulgus profanum" from desecrating the fragile and delicately crafted temple of this rare love and otherness. Shatto and Shaw have identified the Propertian references in the vernacular text of *In Memoriam*.[1] Because the exact words from the Latin cannot be replicated in the English text, the allusive subtext is removed one stage further to isolate even more the number of uninitiated readers able to appropriate the larger sense of the mourning of Arthur as in fact a heartfelt love elegy to him. The poet consecrates his art to the memory of his beloved.

Robert Martin, in his biography of Tennyson, coyly discusses the difficulty of finding words to describe the first encounter of Hallam and Tennyson. It is, of course, Martin's difficulty and it tells a great deal about the margins of social control that are drawn alongside the life of a national poet, a poet laureate:

> It is difficult to write of the meeting of Tennyson and Hallam because of the inadequacy of our language to deal with deep friendship. There should be a phrase analagous to "falling in love" to describe the celerity of emotion that brings two persons together almost at first meeting; "falling in friendship" is what happened to Tennyson and Hallam.[2]

I do not believe this is true. They fell in love.

What Martin writes later, once he is over the uncomfortable circumlocution, assures us that not only did they fall in love but that this was a rare and wonderful marriage of true minds:

> Tennyson's reaction to Hallam was simple: "He was as near perfection as a mortal man can be," he said long after Hallam's death, when his memory was as green as if all the intervening years had dropped away. It would be hard to exaggerate the impact Hallam made on Tennyson; their friendship was to be the most emotionally intense period he ever knew, four years probably equal in psychic importance to the other seventy-nine of his life.[3]

Arthur was truly Tennyson's ideal and is in many ways his king, the idealized King Arthur of much of his later thought and poetic expression. The court of King Arthur is the once-perfect world of male completeness just as the Arcadian scenes of book 4 from *Paradise Lost* represent that briefly enjoyed wholeness in the security of Diodati's friendship. Guinevere or Eve are figures of an unruly, concupiscent woman who destroys the male kingdoms of order and virtue. They are the Hamadryads clutching at Hylas, dragging down the innocent youth dutifully in search of the purest water for his master. Camelot is Eden in another form, yet another extraordinary parallel in the writing lives of these poets. The bond of guardian and ward that is sacred in the erotic relations of Hercules and Hylas stands for male service and fidelity. Not dissimilar in its ordination and gravity is the chivalric code revered by the knights of the round table. Adam's words to Eve after her fall ring through the descendant male love texts: "How art thou lost, how on a sudden lost" (IV.900). Delilah is yet another characterization of this lost woman, the destroyer. The Hylas of Fureni's painting exactly captures the sense of dutiful male drawn away from the rule of his chivalric order, his soldierly service to Hercules, by lustful and irrepressible nymphs. He is fully clothed and resistant, the women are naked and drift about, lost in a tide of morbid sensuality.

We know that *In Memoriam* occupies the central position in Tennyson's *oeuvre*: it is both his best work and also chronologically at the heart of his development as poet. In Milton's case the construction of his *Epitaphium Damonis* marks the crucial point in his growth as a poet; so *In Memoriam* is to Tennyson and the *Elegy* to Gray. In each case the widowed poet suffers a desolation as acute as that felt by a woman losing a husband. Charles Diodati, Richard West and Arthur Hallam constitute the one perfect human bond to each poet; that one person who understands fully the mind and heart of the otherwise rather awkward and different artist. To make matter worse, when his friend dies, the poet is left with none of the customary societal consolation granted to an ordinary female widow. This male love is so outlawed that the poet resorts to ingenious literary strategies to assimilate the love and significance of the lost youth as well as to gain a literary and social acceptance that consoles the pangs of otherness. In Milton, Latin forms a large part of this strategy of excluding profane (that is potentially sneering) readers. In Gray less so, the vernacular precedent of *Lycidas* serves to ground the *Elegy* in a contemplative distance which is only resolved as a love elegy by its coordinate relation to the short Latin *Ad Favonium.* In Tennyson's case the strategies of deflection are complex and brilliant as the poet is determined not only to map the attainment of his artistic self in the love for Hallam but also to record as explicitly as possible his tender love for this man. Thus the poet plays with the social boundaries of a proscribed love and develops his art significantly by testing the power of the *vates* to move within the very citadel of social "normality" while at the same time not merely speaking but singing of a love not to be named in Victorian society.

Tennyson primarily takes over the tradition of elegiac male love poetry by adopting and adapting a mode of vernacular mourning in *Lycidas* and the *Elegy* that allows him both to say and not to say what the poem is really about. The safe seclusion of the meditative sequence is his first device, just as the distanced referential subtext of literary allusion is the second. Erotic love is apparently sublimated to love in general and in the abstract, just as the particular death of Hallam is screened by death in all. Of course this is not to deny that Tennyson really is moved by Hallam's love to consider Love; just as his death does make him grapple with the Hamletlike questions of existence and action that spring from a consideration of death. The acute pain of exclusion felt from an other passion particularly drives the poet to contemplate the purpose of his life, in a society that denies such feelings. This anguish of enforced silence inevitably charges the poet to envision a better existential landscape that can accommodate all. The social penalty thus becomes a creative stimulus. In each case the poet, Milton, Gray or Tennyson searches for a resolution of his predicament. Although the poetic formulation is differently colored by the tone and thought of his time, each poet discovers that this one centering love is the single truth of existence, the one sure absolute of experience upon which he is able to found any larger structure of meaningful work in a personal epistemology. The way in which this later construct is crafted and designed, however, differs considerably according to the peculiar temper and times of the poet.

Exactly as Gray had woven in phrases and remembrances of West into his *Elegy*, so Ricks explains Tennyson's identical construction of a commemorative poem which was carefully crafted to include memories of Hallam:

> Unobtrusively but persistently, Tennyson incorporated details of Hallam's life and writings; the wording of the poem incorporates reminiscences which then modify a reader's response.

> > 'Tis well; 'tis something; we may stand
> > Where he in English earth is laid,
> > And from his ashes may be made
> > The violet of his native land.
> >   (XVIII)

> With quiet grace and with a deeper timbre (this is no affectionate hyperbole), Tennyson is returning the compliment which Hallam had paid him: in his essay on Tennyson's poems, Hallam had quoted Persius, "*Nunc non e tumulo fortunataque favilla / nascentur violae,*" remarking, "When this Poet dies, will not the Graces and the Loves mourn over him?"[4]

This patient and tender interweaving is one means of saying yet not saying about his love of Hallam. The strategic arrangement of verses, and the music of Tennyson's opiate rhythms, are similarly effective in disguising yet revealing.

In the first line of *In Memoriam* can be seen both the technique of meditative distancing and the record of this intense personal love. Jesus is addressed as "immortal Love," a term reminiscent of the daring admixture of profane and sacred language in metaphysical poets such as Donne or Herbert. This duality of course sustains the undercurrent of real, experienced mortal love that runs through the poem (25, 45, 125). At 123 this is stated clearly as the grounding emotion, the "centerd passion" that creates meaning; opposing the seductive voice of atheism is the knowledge of love for Hallam. Belief in this experience of an emotion that elevates and refines the self confirms for Tennyson the existence of a greater love superintending life and giving it integrity and purpose: "And out of darkness came the hands" (124,23). For this reason the poet sings in triumphant resolution of the Darwinian doubt that plagued his age and the even more private doubt about his place as poet, the worth of his individual talent in the scheme of things. He sings of "Love" as the sovereign of his soul, the one sure touchstone of his life, just as Hallam's love was that one sure relationship that guaranteed the poet's purpose (doubly so as Hallam really did encourage Tennyson and substantiate his faith in his talent). Hallam's earthly love underwrites Tennyson's faith in Jesus as the embodiment of heavenly Love. Nature and Christianity both attain a credence for Tennyson in the identifying love of Hallam. The pastoral is as much a redemptive signature in the composition as the crowning life of Christ. In this way male love is finely secured as a means of assuring other meaning. Tennyson deftly builds it as the basis of his faith in life, nature and God. So, "Love is and was my Lord and King" (126,1) is sung out with a peal of joy at the close of the poem. Intimations of his beloved friend's nature so closely wedded to his own tie the poet to the King of Love himself: "And in his presence I attend."

As much as Diodati's love centers Milton's sense of election and secures his purpose as a poet, so Tennyson, cast into the well of uncertainty by Hallam's death, builds on the certainty of the love they shared to recover a coherent epistemological defense and purpose for his life as a writer. He adopts a martial metaphor, akin to so much of Milton's work, to suggest the guarded preservation of faithful love in God's kingdom on earth. The godly kingdom of love envisioned by Milton is founded on an intricately intellectualized and highly idiosyncratic model, quite different from that of Tennyson. In each poet, however, the rarity of their love is in accordance with their otherness, so that it could be expected that both poets not only feel acutely the pangs of exclusion, but also seek to imagine a better world ruled by the larger spirit of Love. They are required to negotiate meaning from a tangle of inimical proscriptions yet their ingenuity and probity triumph in their achievement as national poets. This negotiation is itself a fascinating testimony of the socialization to an identity, both intellectual and sexual. In Gray, too, the conception of a better world, another country, has a political analogue attached, a criticism of the imperfect society ruled by selfish conceit, pride and avarice. So in all three poets the search for a kinder community derives from a sensitivity to the ungenerous one about them, unkind because, among many things, it offers so little consolation for otherness. But the sight and experience of unlove does not succeed in deadening their spirits to the vision and hope of a society predicated on larger sympathies. In this way poetic generosity and breadth of feeling triumph over narrowminded prescription of sameness and parochial suspicion of difference. The light of personal love brightens a greater view of society ever increasing in tolerance and kindness. Tennyson's vision of political concord is ruled within the margins of Hallam's superintending benevolence. The rule of Love on earth perpetually indicts the destructive polarities of wealth and poverty, installing instead a middle way of amenable equity. Love for Hallam inspires a general faith in social love and harmony just as it secures Tennyson's belief in God's love. Such are the philosophical stepping-stones from love to Love. There may be an obvious breach between social order and religious dogma, between what is and what is hoped for in faith, but this will not shake the heart that is grounded in the experience of love. Tennyson's love for Hallam is again that centering passion: in all spheres its light radiates outwards to the rings of social order or religious belief. Stanza 127 memorably explicates Hallam's love for Tennyson as the bright creed of his being. It casts a full serenity over Tennyson's perceptions:

> And all is well, tho' faith and form
>   Be sunder'd in the night of fear;
>   Well roars the storm to those that hear
> A deeper voice across the storm,
>
> Proclaiming social truth shall spread,
>   And justice, even tho' thrice again
>   The red fool-fury of the Seine
> Should pile her barricades with dead.
>
> But ill for him that wears a crown,
>   And him, the lazar, in his rags!

> They tremble, the sustaining crags;
> The spires of ice are toppled down,
>
> And molten up, and roar in flood;
> The fortress crashes from on high,
> The brute earth lightens to the sky,
> And the great Aeon sinks in blood,
>
> And compass'd by the fires of hell,
> While thou, dear spirit, happy star,
> O'erlook'st the tumult from afar,
> And smilest, knowing all is well.[5]

The integrating force of love ensures harmony in the face of chaos, a belief in the coherent structure of a well-ordered society. Knowledge of the love that makes him alive to his own humanity bonds him to the potential for that same redeeming love in other human beings.

The real, lived experience of the fulfilling happiness brought by love is particularly vital in the life of a person who senses his alienation from the bonds struck between his peers. Robert Martin's belief that Tennyson's "four years [with Hallam] were equal in psychic importance to the other seventy-nine of his life" could be writ large for the emotional lives of Milton with Diodati or Gray with West. Their knowledge of the healing potential of such love actuates these three poets to found their thinking on the annealing strength of love, not only to heal the besieged inner self but to liberate their society into a more generous matrix of tolerant mores. So it comes about that the acuity of bewilderment and pain caused by otherness in turn causes the poet so intensely to question the fundamental assumptions of the establishment that he envisions a better world and puts the vision so well into words that the original society admires and seeks to imitate the beautiful and enlarged sympathies portrayed. This is Sidney's "right poet" or Shelley's ideal poet who legislates according to that ordering love which architects a harmonious and caring society. Otherness comes full circle. The excluded poet thus gains a purchase on his society through the admirable and imitable mediation of art. How to delight the reader and draw him to consider this better without offense requires great skill of the singer and determines the artful strategies that enforce the greatness of *Lycidas*, the *Elegy* or *In Memoriam*. It is fully understandable that these longer poems have become canonized by society. The writers of them strove to enshrine the memory of beloved friends in the public mind — to win for them the decency of burial in hallowed ground, that is the blessing of the community on their unhallowed love. Desire, and desire for acceptance, has been rewarded, however, by such

clamorous approval that it threatens to obfuscate the pulse of "centerd passion" within the subtext of each poem. The shift from private passion to
meditation upon eternal Love may cause the conformist reader of convenient sameness to screen the emotions, so that the work is revered as the
perfect statement of the age, rather than as a superbly ambivalent work
spoken in two voices.

Read one way, the first four lines of the poem capture exactly the hesitant conviction of religious faith in the face of irrefutable scientific dis-
coveries that so typifies the vacillating and troubled consciences of the
Victorian period. Yet there is a declarative faith by assertion here, a
protesting too loudly in these first lines, that gives away the inner anxiety, the unquiet heart, of the speaker. The statement of faith may be sincere and correct, after all the poet is determined to be taken seriously.
Taken over to other poems of the age one could quickly see how the surface protestation of the text might become venerated as the central and
serious poetic expression of the work, a manifesto of the age. But *In Memoriam* is shot through with the language of passion.

Read another way, the first lines are not so much powerfully assertive
but an extrapolation, a religious idealization, of the poet's earthly love for
Hallam. This experience of short but complete happiness is the focal
warmth of his being. This love is too real and enduring in Tennyson's
heart for there not to be that strong Son of God, who is the perfect incorporation of love, is Love itself and must therefore exist. The faith in
immortality that Tennyson embraces is built on the conviction of the mortal heart, the knowledge that "I have felt":

> I found Him not in world or sun,
>   Or eagle's wing, or insect's eye,
>   Nor thro' the questions men may try,
> The petty cobwebs we have spun.
>
> If e'er when faith had fallen asleep,
>   I heard a voice, "believe no more,"
>   And heard an ever-breaking shore
> That tumbled in the Godless deep,
>
> A warmth within the breast would melt
>   The freezing reason's colder part,
>   And like a man in wrath the heart
> Stood up and answer'd, "I have felt."[6]

The introductory stanzas to the poem as a whole are integral with this
assertion together with the confidence of "Love is and was my lord and

king," so reminiscent of Herbert. The first stanzas of the poem are a carefully molded inversion of the process by which the opening assertion of faith is made. They seem to start with a statement of faith in God and then reach a profession of love for Hallam: "Strong Son of God, immortal Love" (1) to "Forgive my grief for one removed / Thy creature, whom I found so fair" (37–8). In fact his slow climb up the ladder of existential faith from the pit of despair began with his certainty of Hallam's love as the one moment of absolute reality in his life and ended with a trust in Jesus, "strong Son of God," whom he immediately characterizes as "immortal Love." Tennyson reverses the genesis of the climb he made by meeting the reader at the most socially secure bridging point and then leading back to his love for another man. This deft inversion is a key to the wily structuring of the whole course of the poem's argument. The poet and the main part of *In Memoriam* begin at stanza 11, in the appeal to God, significantly, to "forgive these wild and wandering cries" (l. 41). Here is the voice of Hercules once again in inconsolable grief, the hero searching hopelessly for Hylas, and, later in the poem, the bereaved Tennyson at section 85:

> But I remain'd, whose hopes were dim,
>   Whose life, whose thoughts were little worth,
>   To wander on a darken'd earth,
> Where all things round me breathed of him.
>
> (29–32)

It is the dark tone of the initial stanzas of *Epitaphium Damonis* and the funerary lines to *Ad Favonium* by Gray. The sense of guilt for this excess of passion for another man's love is emphasized by the double "forgive" of stanza eleven, section 1. This is reduced in stanzas 9 and 10 above to the opening "forgive" placed alone. So the next stanzas *backwards*, that is lines 36 to 1, gradually wean the bereaved of his grief and take him through that process of reflection and reconciliation observable in the forward argument of *Epitaphium Damonis* or *In Memoriam* as a whole — the move towards an eventual and joyful reappropriation of life through the shades of sorrow that echo so often the structure of Dante's divine comedy. So the conclusion of a creed of religious faith appears first when it adheres most appropriately to the establishment auditor's sensibilities. To start with an appeal for forgiveness for loving another man too much would alienate such a hegemonic readership. The starting point, therefore, and real main clause of the opening is thus hidden by an ingenious, and typically Tennysonian, reversal.

How differently would a new reader approach the poem if, instead of the powerful and manly stop of the invocatory "Strong Son of God" there was instead the worried appeal of "forgive these wild and wandering cries"? In one there is the founded assurance and gravity of the patriarchal Victorian poet with Emily at his side; in the other is the voice of that shyly boyish admirer of Hallam. It is quite extraordinary that Tennyson succeeds in bringing these two voices, kept in tension between the Latin and English of Milton and Gray, into one vernacular structure here. Tennyson has significantly advanced the form of the male love elegy and assimilated it completely into English. He masterfully deploys the contemplative concerns that flow out from the anxiety of otherness by setting them first to greet the establishment reader, so bridging the gap in the safe territory of life reflection, then leading him back to the centering passion of his love. What an achievement lies just in these first stanzas that can tactfully include the line "thou seemest human and divine" within the same structural canopy as "thy creature whom I found so fair." The Theocritean style of idyll is bound to the immaculately intellectual: here certainly Milton's wish in the epitaph to bring Sicily to the Thames, to make the soft quivering blues of the Mediterranean part of the watercolor sphere of London comes true: "Dicite Sicelicum Thamesina per oppida carmen" (l. 3).

The means by which the reader is taken from general to personal may be described as a strategy of deflection. The poet's control of language and his shrewd awareness of its power to both conceal and disclose may too quickly be disregarded by the reader or critic who fails to read *In Memoriam* in the context of *Epitaphium Damonis*, *Lycidas* and Gray's *Elegy*. Unless the need for ambivalence is recognized, Tennyson's *In Memoriam* may as well be buried as a "perfect statement of the age." The poem is far more vital to us than this and as soon as it is read as the love elegy that it is at root, then the poet's extraordinary skill is observable. He is wonderfully alive to the ludic elements of socializing the unsociable, playing in his verse across the bounds of social conventions, awakening his auditors and challenging them at the same time. That Tennyson knows the power of language to say and unsay and that he employs this power to the full is, of course, phrased beautifully in the poem itself: "For words, like Nature, half reveal / And half conceal the Soul within" (5.3–4).

This section may be read as a continuation of the plea in the introduction for God to forgive his grief. Read this way, it is uncertain whether the poet holds it half a sin to put in words grief he feels because language fails to reveal enough of his grief or because it does not conceal enough. Does the poet wish at the outset to display his "large grief" or is he content to give us it "in outline and no more." If he uses language to wrap himself against the cold, there is the sense that words are used to dress the wounds, to conceal, to contain the agony of bereavement (especially male love bereavement). There is also the sense that Tennyson himself feels guilt for male-love: this is resolved in the poem by incorporating it into the identifying landscape and religious faith. This is a great movement forward from the indifference of the Theocritean countryside to Hercules's wandering anguish. Tennyson determines and writes of that love so beautifully that he makes it clear that this natural passion is beautiful too and thus a passion that is part of nature. This is close to the experience Gray has at Tivoli but Tennyson definitely advances the argument far further. Similarly Tennyson uses his defined love for Hallam as metaphor for Christian Love, thus detaching male love from its proscriptive associations and attaching it to a sphere of generative gladness and fulfillment. His love for Hallam is made part of that flourishing nature and part of the luminous divine. It is Tennyson's language that achieves this extraordinary trajectory.

Language, when measured, numbs the pain in a sad mechanical exercise "like dull narcotics" (5.8). Words, then, and the poetic employment of them, have a spell-like power for the true *vates*. Taking up the lyre is both an assertion of this immortal force of art and also a restitution of the artistic bonds that held the two living friends so closely together. Does Tennyson really apologize for the inadequacy of language or does he as poet turn its eloquent silences to his advantage, so exercising a sacred art? How much does he want to show of the "wild and wandering cries?" *In Memoriam* read as love elegy separates out to a meditative text of elegy and an allusive, subtly shifting love song in the subtext woven in behind the "outline" of the formally verbal elegiac structure. In unifying the double voice of Latin and English, of *Lycidas* and *Epitaphium Damonis*, he adopts new strategies to sustain the richness of his poetic tapestry. The ritual of mourning, the gradual assimilation of grief in *Epitaphium Damonis*, is marked by the eventual lessening of the sad mechanical exercise of the refrain "Ite domum impasti" which works exactly for Milton as "dull narcotics" of the word. Tennyson's own form of gradual "mechanic ease" in the verse may be quite complex as a strategy of deflection too: it numbs not only the poet's pain but lulls, we suspect, the prurient inquiry of the too-prescriptive reader.

The overall pattern of *Epitaphium Damonis*, from wild and haunting lamentation of the Hylas idyll to regenerate vision, is precisely the progress observable in *In Memoriam*. There is a closer similarity between *In Memoriam* and *Epitaphium Damonis* than between any other two of the elegies considered here: the pattern of graduated mourning that leads from dislocation through artistic identity to a renewed vision is particularly similar.

The burden of Tennyson's lament is that half-concealed love poem cast into the learned language by Milton. Tennyson finds "a use in measured language lies" not only as a therapeutic means of reconstructing a poetic self in the power of his art and the tender memorial of his beloved Arthur, but also in warding off the "pecus ignavum." In typically Tennysonian manner the apparent ease and smoothness of the verse belies a hardheaded poetic craftiness. The narcotic force of language, operating quite differently but with equal efficacy upon writer and reader, derives from the genre of half-concealed, half-revealed love elegy, from the apparently excessive use of heavily repeated Miltonic refrain in *Epitaphium Damonis*. This device is, however, at the epicenter of the male love elegy's genesis. It both proclaims grief and equally disclaims any hysterical pageant of an outlawed affection. The forceful dignity of this hypnotic repetition insistently demands a funereal somberness. It precludes any trivialization of the emotion. The narcotic refrain of "Ite domum" contains, however, within it the very seeds of the "questionable" intimacy. The famously slow rhythm of Gray's *Elegy* does precisely the same, as does Gray's use of the quatrain, in itself something of a closed unit sealing off one part after another, rather like a refrain structure again. In Tennyson the fourline form is taken over as a means of dulling private pain and lulling awkward inquiry. The closure of the quatrain and the fragmented composition of the stanzas cunningly prevent any continuous cumulative argument. The tearful poets here do not wish to expose their grief to clearheaded, proselike responses; they are drawing on emotional appeal and using all the techniques of poetic sorcery to do so. The strategy of concealment and disclosure is vital to the perfection in the vernacular of the ambivalent expression of a grief that can only be shown to be the warp of a verbal outline with the main statement left in the woof of allusion and suggestion. The sonnet sequence which alludes at all times to the sexually ambivalent Shakespearean vernacular model works too as a means of concealing and revealing; the "sonnets" of *In Memoriam* are not exactly integrated but plainly give the impression of fragments pieced together, much like Eliot's, against vacuity. Thus the poet disallows coherence not necessarily only because of the history of the composition, but by some degree of convenient and clever design as well. It is perhaps dangerous to take Tennyson too lightly and follow the easy flow of his verse too smoothly. It is wise not to underrate the extraordinary attention devoted to the artistic reconstruction of his love in art over so long a period. These fragments reflect the break-up of the sort of coherent world view, the confident intellectual system achieved by Milton, into what is in *In Memoriam* a precursor of the modernist incompleteness of the *Wasteland*.

This fragmentary form also reflects the poet's concern to wrap himself in sealing and concealing words; his grief is to be described and dignified in art, but not paraded and cheapened. Tennyson knew exactly what he was about and no better statement exists of the function of the vernacular or learned language in the poems by him, Milton or Gray than appears in section 5 of *In Memoriam*. Tennyson fully understands the inadequacy of the sign, the empty hieroglyph, but uses this very incompleteness to say that behind the bare sign of his elegy the real sum of his love could too easily be misread. The outworks of the metaphysical uncertainty, political implications, or aesthetic concerns that flow from the death of his partner, that rare male, are fully recorded in the stark and insufficient signs of language, scarecrow emblems set up for all to see. But below these safely general meditative concerns lies the plenitude of an emotional harvest of great rarity and depth. Neither Gray, Milton nor Tennyson will allow this love to be marginalized by a barbaric readership. Nor will they allow their love to pass unnoticed. Why should such sincere passion be sneered at or kept tamely invisible? Milton's initial genius in *Lycidas* in plotting a generic middle course between the Scylla and Charybdis of spiteful and reductive readership is taken up with equal ingenuity by his successors in the construction of the male love elegy which is one of the great treasures of intellectual and verbal virtuosity.

Sinfield, arguing from without the Milton/Gray intertext, observes the quality of "incantatory repetition" in *In Memoriam* but accounts for it, without reference to 5, in terms of "poetic music" which "seems to fill up the sign and remedy the defect of language — guaranteeing, as it seems, the metaphysical reality towards which it points."[7] Sinfield takes the line "Rapt from the fickle and the frail" (30) to show how the last two stanzas "give the rest of their song, and a concluding hymn of the poet which is both more personal and more general."[8] Sinfield's work on Tennyson is some of the most daring and challenging in recent scholarship. In pointing to the eloquence of the poetic music audible beyond the immediate elegiac text itself, Sinfield perceives the duality of what he also realizes is diction that is "relatively (perhaps surprisingly) conversational, but the syntax corresponds increasingly with the stanza shape and there is increasing use of incantatory repetition."[9] He concludes: "Thus it is the family's singing [section 30] which gives them confidence in something which transcends mortality: in the silences they experience emotions beyond language, but the singing both represents and goes beyond these emotions."[10]

Of course this duality of deceptively bland diction and highly crafted arrangement is the reflection of the parallel structure of coherently stated general meditation and halfconcealed personal lament. Sinfield is not quite alert to Tennyson's deliberate location of the emotional turning point, the axis of grief to incorporated self, within the bosom of the Victorian family. Sinfield's examination of Tennyson's linguistic skill here, the deft deployment of sign and articulate silence or linguistic gap, endorses the poet's own statement as well as the need for such duality within the tradition of the male love elegy. Eagleton, the editor of Sinfield's book, is quoted by Sinfield: "[Arthur is] nothing less than the empty space congregated by a whole set of ideological anxieties concerned with the 'revolutionary' decentring of 'man' from his 'imaginary' relation of unity with his world."[11] Yes and no. There is little sense here of Hallam as a real person of extraordinary intellect and attraction, whom Tennyson loved greatly, or the bitter pain of suffering real loss. It is Eagleton's use of a particular perspective, a particular pair of critical spectacles, that allows him to observe this space for Hallam, but one feels the empty space in Eagleton's own reading, a certain lack of human warmth and sympathy. Eagleton's statements would need, in terms of the Milton/Gray argument, to be reversed somewhat: the loss of the single meaningful relation in the poet's experience of otherness radically truncates and decenters the poet from the normative matrix of hegemonic consolation, so that the love elegies of Milton, Gray and Tennyson are no less than the poetic reclamation of, first, autonomy as an artist within the tutelary love of the deceased beloved and, lastly, an identity within an envisioned new society. The poet is not decentered from an imaginary relation of class struggle with his world by the revolutionary, nor is Arthur an empty space. Tennyson moves not from dislocation from an imaginary unity but from severe dislocation within a real society that is alien to his "different" nature towards the achievement of a resplendent and fully imagined world defined in accord with the refining love for Hallam. His ideological anxieties spring from the acuity of otherness; Arthur excites reexamination of all things that do not accord with the fleeting but unforgettable harmony of that brief companionship; he is not the hierophant of ideological anxiety; rather he directly prompts it. It is a bit scary to be so cheeky to Eagleton but there it is—I think he misses the point.

Unless it is accepted that the relationships between Diodati and Milton, West and Gray, Hallam and Tennyson were fundamental to the restitution of a consistent poetic self, the resolution to the elegies discussed necessarily becomes problematic and even questionable. Sinfield finds that the transfigured "Arthur" affords only an apparent resolution. Of course this objection is familiar from readings of the Miltonic elegy too. Sinfield and others need to see the extraordinary pattern that forms quite clearly when the glow of male love experienced in each life is granted its proper significance. In the case of these poets it is the central emotional experience of their lives and recovery and perpetuation of this love in their writing lives, is the imaginative impetus which projects them forward into artistic autonomy and accepted greatness. Milton before and after Diodati, Gray before and after West, Tennyson before and after Hallam are poets without the centered passion or absolute commitment to their art: but later they are "poets," who have been thrown into abysmal loneliness and regained a paradise of the private imagination.

Look at Milton's Latin before Diodati's death — impressively crafted, erudite, clever, but with nothing of the integrating pathos that draws on the strength of art to fill and console its emptiness. The art of his early Latin is therefore unattached and purposeless; it answers no need in the heart. But *Epitaphium Damonis* speaks in its highly wrought conventions of a deep hurt that makes the antique vocabulary and pastoral forms quiver with a real, felt suffering. This appropriation of his art as a dressing for his wounds speaks of the poetic supremacy lying ahead. In his epitaph for Diodati, Milton finds his poetic purpose. Gray's Latin poems before the shattering loss of West only approximate the integrated passion of the lyric ode when Gray hears the soft west wind whisper his great friend's name, when the landscape of Tivoli is that of his own heart. In Milton's early verse there are the blithe murmurings of unconcerned and incautious youth, in the other is the resonant record of a human being; it is poetry tested on the pulse. Tennyson's poetry before and after Hallam's death testifies to the same formative blow. Gray is a poet after the *Elegy* of West's death and Tennyson emerges as a poet after his bitter self-encounter in *In Memoriam*. In every sense he is then the worthy successor to Wordsworth; through suffering he has found himself as an artist and founded his art. The way in which the poet is catapulted forward artistically is first testimony to the degree to which the love of another man, the experience of otherness, is the crucible which takes the immature poet to dedicated maturity. The evidence of the massive advance in the poetry of each writer when faced with the problem of cruel, youthful extinction testifies most strongly to the resolution achieved by each poet. It is primarily an artistic integration, a determination to inscribe and describe the memory of an inspiring love. Reimagining the world according to the high principles of Diodati spurs on Milton to dedicate an epic vision of election to his beloved; reimagining the world according to the tender love of West causes Gray to formulate his enduring appeal for community; reimagining the world according to the powerful love of Hallam charges Tennyson to envisage a human progress ever upward to the crowned race of those like his hero. The transfigured Hallam or the apotheosis of Diodati do not merely afford "an apparent resolution." They are immortalized in the maturity and poetic record of the discovery of artistic autonomy. The formulation of an individual purpose, be it within the notion of election, community or progress, is determined by the crucial experience of a rare, identifying love. Otherness creates the need for, and fundamentally forges the poetic vision of each poet, searching by dint of otherness, to recover a brief but absolute love in the deathless realm of the imagination.

It is hard to agree then with Sinfield when he states that "by projecting his love onto eternity he [Tennyson] foregoes the human contact which was its motive force."[12] Hallam is alive in Tennyson's poetry because the experience of Hallam's love is, and is made, so much a part of Tennyson and his art, of Tennyson's reimagined world in which the hegemony is revised according to the radical reorganization of social love. Love of Hallam challenges the admiring Tennyson to make a worthy monument and thereby make himself a worthy poet. The certain knowledge of love informs the best work of each of these three poets. The "human contact" that prompts this urgency to "write paradise," or as Sinfield would have it, to project love onto eternity, is not forgone at all. The human contact is ever at the heart of each poet. No one ever meant more to Tennyson than Hallam, or to Milton than Diodati, or to Gray than West. Sinfield states that Arthur is absorbed by the end and quotes Tennyson's dislike of this absorption.[13] But Hallam is not "absorbed" in any negative sense: he is not wrung out and extinguished. Again, by the proof of Tennyson's work before and after *In Memoriam*, it can be seen that Hallam is the sustaining force behind the practice of excellence. Hallam's identity is not lost; rather it is the observable fulcrum in the exercise of Tennyson's art. He is the pivotal point in Tennyson's now felt articulation of loss, an element that would remain always with Tennyson the outsider, the other.

Sinfield argues that Tennyson's poem achieves closure or resolution through the political presence of Hallam superintending from a heavenly vantage.[14] Clearly Sinfield's own ideological bias takes him to this explanation. Hallam's immortality to a Marxist reader would be the enduring force of his political engagement. He succinctly points to several critics who feel that there is some shortcoming in the intellectual endowment of *In Memoriam*. As proof of Tennyson's struggle to resolve the lament, Sinfield himself cites section 95. Sinfield's response to the so-called problem of the beloved having to be both Arthur and the deity is similar to that of other critics most markedly in his and their complete omission of the tradition of bucolic elegy. In Theocritus's first idyll the ecphrasis about the two-handled cup is an image of the immortality of art. The verbal image of the idyll claims perpetuity for itself in the exquisite pains taken to craft the whole. The poet has power as a craftsman. In idyll 16 this is elaborated superbly: who would remember Ilion were it not for the singer-poet, the rhapsodist? In Milton's *Epitaphium Damonis,* the two-handled cup of Manso is an immediate signal to the reader of the Theocritean allusion and similar demonstration of the poet's potent creativity. So too Gray's *Elegy* is the immortalization of his beloved West. The poetry confers a timelessness upon the grieved-for subject. In each case this immortality is doubly enforced by the remarkable maturing and self-discovery won by the mourning poet from the emptiness of sorrow. In Tennyson's case, Hallam is also doubly immortalized; in the *memorial* of the crafted artifact, *In Memoriam,* as well as in the living genius of the poet matured through the constant memory of a completing love.

Furthermore the precepts that follow the experience of such love, different as they are in each of the three poets, also immortalize the beloved. Even beyond this, of course, Diodati, West and Hallam are assumed into the higher realm of heaven as superintendent forces over their faithfully admiring companions on earth. But this final heavenly immortalization is linked through the appeal for superintendence of the art of the poet. Here lies the resolution to the so-called problem of earthly and heavenly, ephemeral and eternal. Here is no facile *deus ex machina* for these elegies. Tennyson really does battle with devastating grief and wrings from this soul combat his poetic selfhood. Since the struggle is to recover meaning from abysmal nothingness, he builds on the memorial of the one certainty in this gulf, his definite knowledge of the love he felt for Hallam. "I have felt" is the foundational certainty which he uses to shore up the metaphysical emptiness overwhelming him. *In Memoriam* is like its antecedent intertexts, an ontology of love, a defense of love as the single essence of our being, proof of our humanity. In every sense then, as recovered person, as retrieved artist, as faithful friend, Tennyson does retain Hallam in his life. Hallam is in fact the reason for being in the life of someone who finds little or no hegemonic meaning or consolation à priori. In every sense Tennyson does rise on the stepping-stones of his dead self to higher things.

The fact that Milton, Gray and Tennyson endure as poets read and admired, immortalized then by so many, is greatly owing to the substantive force of their intimate friendships with Diodati, West and Hallam. Radically isolated by otherness, robbed of their rare and brief loves, they extracted at last a coherent meaning through suffering and claimed immortality for their love in their crafted verse, and for themselves in grasping the *vates*'s thyrsus. Not only does the desolation of grief move them to seek identity in art and in being artists, but the estrangement of being different radicalizes both their awareness of metaphysical isolation and their need to find a solution to it. It is not that, as Sinfield suggests, Tennyson has no resolution. It may be difficult for some readers, dare we say hegemonic or canonical readers, to locate a resolution in *In Memoriam*. But then the poem exists within a specific tradition of literary otherness which is enclosed again within a long tradition of pastoral elegy. Surely then the resolution is to be sought there and not primarily from a Marxist, archetypal or Romantic naturalist point of view. The poem is not an unattached artifact washed up like flotsam and examined under the lens of whatever is at hand or in fashion. The poem was written quite consciously in a powerful tradition and much of its subtextual speech, behind the bare outline of the immediate text, is to be heard in the echoes from this tradition. The resolution to *In Memoriam*, drawn largely from the anterior texts of Theocritus down, depends on the aesthetic force of art to enchant its readers and raise its subject into a crafted eternity. The Yeatsian perfection of this craft is what guarantees claims against temporal oblivion. But *In Memoriam*'s "resolution" does not depend alone upon the aesthetic achievement of the finished poem itself. There is no mathematical Q.E.D. to mourning or love or vacuity. The cunning deflection of Tennyson's verse structure, his own assimilation of Hallam's love as meaning, the appropriation of the text as mourning song for thousands of grieving mothers after the Great War or by Queen Victoria in her terrible loss, or by many others today — these are all aspects of that "problem of resolution," which is not a male puzzle to be solved by logocentric conclusion. It is a winding and deeply emotional course, the pattern of which we learn from and love in turn in Milton, Gray and Tennyson.

The poetry must reach the point of verbal enchantment. Here Tennyson is unassailable. For the treasured casket of his memorial poem which really does bear the life of his dear Hallam has found endless praise. Exquisite care, the care of love, shapes every verse. The poet's proper monument is the building of a worthy epitaph — the final funerary rite necessary to the liberation of the deceased and his beloved. In a way Diodati, West and Hallam are held back from their celestial liberation and ascent by the earthly grieving; writing out this grief allows the poet to offer the conciliatory poetic monument. The immortality of the subject so sadly grieved is in relation to the immortality of the poetic epitaph; so the resolution to *In Memoriam* is in relation to the aesthetic achievement of the poem itself. This relation between art and subject is woven into the liturgy of lamentation reaching back into ancient times. Hope Nicolson, one of the finest Milton philologists and teachers, explains this lucidly in terms of *Lycidas*, an essential part of the context of *In Memoriam*:

> The belief of our ancestors [was] that the spirits of the dead would not rest in peace unless some reverence was paid to the body, a belief deeply embedded in primitive and sophisticated alike, lying behind customs like funerals, or memorial services. If you have read the *Antigone* of Sophocles, you will remember that the custom of paying reverence to a dead body lay behind the tragedy of Antigone, torn between the law of the state which had forbidden any kind of burial rites to Polynices and the filial piety of a sister who must do something — even scatter earth or ashes upon the corpse — so that her brother's soul may rest.[15]

Milton, Gray and Tennyson are torn similarly by the need to remember, to publicly call attention to a death and especially the death of a bond of love as true and natural as that of a sister, and yet to fall into the silence prescribed for a proscribed love. Between laws of the state and laws of the heart poets have to negotiate funeral songs which will lay to rest the spirits of their beloveds while also persuading, appealing to their community. If one is deaf to this tragedy of division, the anxiety to speak beside the compulsion to be silent, then the tragedy of Antigone, the constant conditioning of society and the individual, must go unfelt too. The distress of each poet, I believe, flamed into some of the most triumphant poetry ever written. In this achievement there is the phoenixlike triumph of poetry not only but of the human spirit and, with it, the constant hope of a more humane and understanding society which will perhaps have a better and a kinder answer for West's question to otherness: "What, are there no joys among the living?"

Notes

Introduction

1. Tennyson, *In Memoriam*, 50, 9–16.
2. A. L. Rowse. *Milton the Puritan*. London: Macmillan, 1977.
3. *Ibid.*, p. 13.
4. *Ibid.*, pp. 37–8.
5. C. Hill. *Milton and the English Revolution*. London: Faber, 1977, pp. 31–2.

Chapter One — The Phoenix

1. *Theocritus, Select Poems*. Ed. K. Dover. Bristol: Macmillan, 1971, pp. 40–1.
2. *Theocritus, Bion and Moschus*. Ed. A. Lang. London: Macmillan, 1889, p. 70.
3. Milton. *Poetical Works*. Ed. H. Darbishire. Oxford: Oxford University Press, 1958, p. 560.
4. *Ibid.*, p. 615.
5. *Ibid.*, p. 594.
6. *Ibid.*, pp. 594–5.
7. Lang. *op. cit.*, p. 70
8. Spenser. *The Faerie Queen*. Ed. Smith and Selincourt. London: Oxford University Press; 1924, p. 263.
9. Lang. *op. cit.*, p. 70.
10. Rowse, *op .cit.*, p. 228.
11. F. J .Nichols. "'Lycidas,' 'Epitaphium Damonis,' the Empty Dream, and the Failed Song," in *Acta Conventus Neo-Latini Lovaniensi*. Leuven: Leuven University Press, 1973, p. 449.
12. R. W. Condee. "The Structure of Milton's 'Epitaphium Damonis,'" in *Studies in Philology*, Vol. 62, 1965, p. 586.
13. *Ibid.*, p. 580.
14. *Ibid.*, p. 582.
15. *The Cambridge History of English Literature*. Cambridge: Cambridge University Press; 1932, p. 97.
16. D. Dorian. *The English Diodatis*. New Brunswick: 1950, pp. 177–8.
17. Condee, *op .cit.*, p. 588.
18. *Ibid.*, p. 582.
19. *Ibid.*, pp. 577–94.
20. *Ibid.*, p. 582.

21. Nichols, *op .cit.*, p. 446.
22. *Ibid.*, p. 447.
23. Lang, *op. cit.*, Idyll 3 of Moschus.
24. G. Lee (trans.). *Ovid's Amores.* London: John Murray, 1966, pp. 76–7.
25. J. Camerarius, *Symbola et Emblemata*, Teil 1, Graz: Akademische Druk, 1986, emblem C.
26. Sir Philip Sidney, *An Apologie for Poetrie.* Oxford: Clarendon Press, 1907, p. 9.
27. J. T. Shawcross. "Milton and Diodati: An Essay in Psychodynamic Meaning," in *Milton Studies*, Vol.VII, 1975, pp. 127–8.
28. *Ibid.*, p. 157.
29. A. Sinfield. *Alfred Tennyson.* Oxford: Basil Blackwell, 1986, pp. 129–30.

Chapter Two—A Secret Sympathy

1. *Poems.* Ed. Philip Robinson. London: Longmans, 1988, p.73.
2. Roger Lonsdale. "Gray's *Elegy*: A Poem of Moral Choice and Resolution," in *Modern Critical Interpretations: Elegy Written in a Country Churchyard.* Ed. Harold Bloom. New York: Chelsea House, 1987, p. 37.
3. *Ibid.*, p. 36.
4. *Ibid.*, p. 37.
5. *Ibid.*
6. *Thomas Gray, Selected Poems.* Ed. J. Heath-Stubbs. Manchester: Carcanet, 1981, pp. 8–9.
7. *Ibid.*
8. *Ibid.*
9. Tennessee Williams. *Sweet Bird of Youth, A Streetcar Named Desire and the Glass Menagerie.* Harmondsworth: Penguin, 1979, pp. 9–10.
10. Lonsdale, *op. cit.*, p. 37.
11. *Ibid.*
12. Williams, *op .cit.*, pp. 10–11.
13. *The Complete Poems of Thomas Gray.* Ed. H. W. Starr and J. R. Hendrickson. Oxford: Clarendon Press, 1966, pp. 38–9.
14. *Sidney, Shelley.* Ed. H. A. Needham. London: Ginn, 1931, p. 79.
15. A. L. Lytton Sells. *Thomas Gray: His Life and Works.* London: Allen and Unwin, 1980.
16. *Ibid.*, p. 171.
17. *Ibid.*, p. 175.
18. *Correspondence of Thomas Gray.* Ed. Paget Toynbee and Leonard Whibley. Oxford: Clarendon Press, 1935, Vol. I, pp. 33–4.
19. Starr and Hendrickson, *op. cit.*, p. 7.
20. *Ibid.*, p. 8.
21. Toynbee, *op .cit.*, p. 210.
22. *Ibid.*, pp. 34–5.
23. Starr and Hendrickson, *op .cit.*, p. 92.
24. Lytton Sells, *op. cit.*, p. 170.
25. Starr and Hendrickson, *op. cit.*, pp. 168–70.

26. *The Poems of Thomas Gray.* Ed. John Mitford. London: White, Cochrane, 1814, p. 142.

27. Eric Smith. "'Gray: Elegy Written in a Country Churchyard,'" in Bloom, *op. cit.*, p. 53.

28. Starr and Hendrickson, *op. cit.*, p. 98.

29. Toynbee, *op. cit.*, p. 64.

30. *Ibid.*, pp. 213–4.

31. *Ibid.*, p. 62.

32. R. Bentman. "Thomas Gray and the Poetry of 'Hopeless Love,'" in *Journal of Sexuality*, Vol. 3, No. 2, 1992.

33. R. Martin. *Essai sur Thomas Gray.* Toulouse: Impremerie Regionale, 1934.

34. G. S. Rousseau. *Perilous Enlightenment: Pre- and Post-modern Discourses: Sexual, Historical.* Manchester, 1991.

35. Bentman, *op. cit.*, p. 204.

36. Martin, *op. cit.*, p. 153.

37. Starr and Hendrickson, *op. cit.*, p. 106.

38. Bentman, *op. cit.*, p. 213.

39. *In Memoriam.* Ed. S. Shatto and M. Shaw. Oxford: Clarendon, 1982, pp. 27–8.

40. Shatto and Shaw, *op. cit.*, pp. 141–2.

41. R. F. Gleckner. *Gray Agonistes.* London: Johns Hopkins University Press, 1997.

42. *Ibid.*, p. 106.

43. H. Weinfield. *The Poet without a Name: Gray's Elegy and the Problem of History.* Illinois: Southern Illinois University Press, 1991.

44. Gleckner, *op. cit.*, pp. 130–2.

Chapter Three — Points of Resistance

1. Toynbee, *op. cit.*, pp. 1–2.

2. *Ibid.*, p. 1.

3. *Ibid.*, pp. 5–6.

4. *Ibid.*, p. 9.

5. *Ibid.*

6. *Ibid.*, p. 10.

7. Lytton Sells, *op. cit.*, p. 247.

8. *Ibid.*, pp. 247–8.

9. *Ibid.*, p .249.

10. Toynbee, *op. cit.*, p. 10.

11. *Ibid.*, pp. 12–13.

12. *Ibid.*, p. 14–15.

13. *Ibid.*, p. 17.

14. *Ibid.*, p. 20.

15. *Ibid.*, p .21.

16. *Ibid.*, p. 25.

17. *Ibid.*, pp. 28–9.

18. *Ibid.*, p. 34.

19. *Ibid.*, pp. 34–5.
20. *Ibid.*, p. 35.
21. *Ibid.*, p. 39.
22. *Ibid.*, pp. 42–3.
23. *Ibid.*, pp. 45–6.
24. *Ibid.*, p. 49.
25. *Ibid.*, p. 56.
26. *Ibid.*, p. 56.
27. *Ibid.*, p. 57.
28. *Ibid.*, p. 59.
29. *Ibid.*, p. 63.
30. *Ibid.*, p. 66.
31. *Ibid.*, p. 70.
32. *Ibid.*, p. 73.
33. Starr and Hendrickson, *op. cit.*, pp. 138–40.
34. Toynbee, *op. cit.*, pp. 91–2.
35. Michel Foucault. *The History of Sexuality. Volume I: An Introduction.* Trans. R. Hurley. New York: Pantheon, 1978, pp. 95–6.
36. Toynbee, *op. cit.*, p. 114.
37. *Ibid.*, p. 121.
38. *Ibid.*, p. 120.
39. *Ibid.*, p. 121.
40. *Ibid.*, p. 121.
41. *Ibid.*, p. 137.
42. *Ibid.*, p. 138.
43. *Ibid.*, p. 151.
44. Starr and Hendrickson, *op. cit.*, pp. 144–5.
45. *Sexti Properti Carmina.* Ed. E. A. Barber. Oxford: Oxford University Press, 1964, p. 28.
46. R. Martin. *Essai sur Thomas Gray.* Toulouse: Impremerie Regionale, 1934, p .311.
47. *The Poems of Mr. Gray.* Ed. W. Mason. York: Dodsley, 1778, pp. 160–1.
48. Starr and Hendrickson, *op. cit.*, pp. 151–2.
49. Mitford, *op. cit.*, frontispiece.
50. Toynbee, op. cit., p. 178
51. Ibid., p.181.
52. *Ibid.*, p. 101.
53. *Ibid.*, p. 182.
54. *Ibid.*, p. 190.
55. *Ibid.*, p. 190.
56. *Ibid.*, p. 92.
57. *Ibid.*, p. 202.
58. *Ibid.*, p. 203.

Conclusion

1. *In Memoriam.* Ed. S. Shatto and M. Shaw. Oxford: Clarendon, 1982, pp. 26–9.

2. R. B. Martin. *Tennyson: The Unquiet Heart.* Oxford: Clarendon Press, 1980, p. 72.

3. *Ibid.,* p. 73.

4. C. Ricks. *Tennyson.* London: Macmillan, 1989, p. 209.

5. *Tennyson's Poetry.* Ed. Robert W. Hill. New York: Norton, 1971, p. 189.

6. *Ibid.,* p. 188.

7. A. Sinfield. *Alfred Tennyson.* Oxford: Blackwell, 1986, p. 115.

8. *Ibid.*

9. *Ibid.*

10. *Ibid.*

11. *Ibid.,* p. 117.

12. *Ibid.,* p. 118.

13. *Ibid.*

14. *Ibid.,* p.121.

15. M. Hope Nicolson. *A Reader's Guide to John Milton.* London: Thames and Hudson, 1964, p. 90.

Bibliography

Texts

The Complete Poems of Thomas Gray. Ed. H. W. Starr and J. R. Hendrickson. Oxford Clarendon Press, 1966.
Correspondence of Thomas Gray. Ed. Paget Toynbee and Leonard Whibley. Oxford: Clarendon Press, 1935, Vol. I.
In Memoriam. Ed. S. Shatto and M. Shaw. Oxford: Clardenon, 1982.
Milton: *Poetical Works.* Ed. H. Darbishire. Oxford: Oxford University Press, 1958
The Poems of Thomas Gray. Ed. John Mitford. London: White, Cochrane, 1814.
Theocritus: Select Poems. Ed. K. Dover. Bristol: Macmillan, 1971.
Thomas Gray, Selected Poems. Ed. J. Heath-Stubbs Manchester: Carcanet, 1981.

Criticism

R. Bentman. "Thomas Gray and the Poetry of 'Hopeless Love,'" in *Journal of Sexuality*, Vol. 3, No. 2, 1992.
J. Camerarius, *Symbola et Emblemata*, Teil 1, Graz: Akademische Druk, 1986.
R. W. Condee. "The Structure of Milton's 'Epitaphium Damonis,'" in *Studies in Philology*, Vol. 62, 1965
D. Dorian. *The English Diodatis.* New Brunswick: 1950.
R. F. Gleckner, *Gray Agonistes.* London: John Hopkins University Press, 1997.
Roger Lonsdale. "Gray's *Elegy*: A Poem of Moral Choice and Resolution," in *Modern Critical Interpretations: Elegy Written in a Country Churchyard.* Ed. H. Bloom. New York: Chelsea House, 1987.
A. L. Lytton Sells. *Thomas Gray: His Life and Works.* London: Allen and Unwin, 1980.
R. Martin. *Essai sur Thomas Gray.* Toulouse: Imprimerie Regionale, 1934.
R. B. Martin. *Tennyson: The Unquiet Heart.* Oxford: Clarendon Press, 1980.
F. J. Nichols. "'Lycidas,' 'Epitaphium Damonis,' the Empty Dream, and the Failed Song," in *Acta Conventus Neo-Latin Lovaniensi.* Leuven University Press, 1973.
M. Hope Nicolson. *A Reader's Guide to John Milton.* London: Thames and Hudson, 1964.
J. T. Shawcross. "Milton and Diodati: An Essay in Psychodynamic Meaning," in *Milton Studies*, Vol. VII, 1975.
A. Sinfield. *Alfred Tennyson.* Oxford: Basil Blackwell, 1986.
Eric Smith. "Gray: Elegy Written in a Country Churchyard," in *Modern Critical*

Interpretations: Elegy Written in a Country Churchyard. Ed. H. Bloom. New York: Chelsea House, 1987.

H. Weinfield. *The Poet Without a Name: Gray's Elegy and the Problem of History*. Illinois: Southern Illinois University Press, 1991.

Index